ABOUT THE AUTHOR

Cathal Guiomard was born in Galway in 1959. Despite an active involvement in student politics in UCG, he still found time to study a little economics there, and later squeezed in some more as a student in Northern Ireland and Britain. He worked for some years for the Central Bank of Ireland. Between 1990 and 1992 he was stationed with the European Union Central Bank Secretariat in Basle, Switzerland where he was involved in the work of planning for a single Euopean currency. Since 1992, he has been on the staff of the Economics Department at University College Dublin.

THE IRISH DISEASE
AND HOW TO CURE IT

COMMON-SENSE ECONOMICS
FOR A COMPETITIVE WORLD

Cathal Guiomard

Oak Tree Press
Dublin

Oak Tree Press
Merrion Building
Lower Merrion Street
Dublin 2, Ireland

© 1995 Cathal Guiomard

A catalogue record of this book is
available from the British Library

ISBN 1-86076-015-5

Printed in Ireland by Colour Books Ltd.

This book is dedicated to:

Pedro Aspe of Mexico
Leszek Balcerowitz of Poland
Domingo Cavallo of Argentina
Roger Douglas of New Zealand
Alejandro Foxley of Chile
Yegor Gaidar of Russia
Paul Keating of Australia
Václav Klaus of the Czech Republic

and all other current, former and future radical
Finance Ministers around the world.

It is also dedicated to the day when Ireland will
demand such reforms.

For Yann.

CONTENTS

ACKNOWLEDGEMENTS

Samuel Brittan's *Restatement of Economic Liberalism* (Macmillan, 1988) stimulated me to attempt something similar for an Irish audience. Alan Blinder's *Hard Heads, Soft Hearts: Tough-Minded Economics for a Just Society* (Addison-Wesley, 1987) showed how to make serious economic arguments accessible to a general reader. I found the economic strategy espoused by Dr T.K. Whitaker in his 1958 report *Economic Development*, even after 35 years, to be still perfectly relevant to economic policy work today. Finally, the influence of the ideas of Professor Joe Lee will be amply evident throughout the book.

Apart from these general intellectual debts, individual chapters of this book have been influenced by other books and writings. Some of the stories found in Chapter 1 are taken from Paddy O Gorman's *Queueing for a Living* (Poolbeg, 1994), others are from Joe O Connor's column in the *Sunday Tribune* and from articles in the *Irish Times*. Many of the ideas in Chapter 7 are drawn from David Osborne and Ted Gaebler's inspiring tract *Reinventing Government* (Addison-Wesley, 1992). Chapter 10 is an elaboration of themes found in Professor Mary Daly's *Industrial Development and Irish National Identity* (Gill and Macmillan, 1993). The concept of "victim Irishness" is adapted from ideas in Naomi Wolf's *Fire with Fire* (Chatto and Windus, 1993). Chapter 11 has drawn on my colleague, Dr Kevin O Rourke's paper on "Catholic Social Teaching and the Economist"(published in two mid-1995 issues of *Doctrine and Life*).

I am grateful to the *Sunday Tribune* for permission to quote from Joe O Connor's columns and to incorporate into this book passages from some opinion columns I wrote for that newspaper in 1994.

Barring possibly Einstein's, academic work is collective. It is discussed with numerous colleagues and often heavily revised on the basis of their comments and criticisms. What the reader sees is the revised work, not the inferior first draft.

But academics can also be paralysed by an unwillingness to write about any field except their own small area of specialism. "Very wide ranging" was one person's ambiguous reaction after reading a very early draft of this book. The comment was a warning that the book attempted to cover so much ground that some of it might not be adequately examined.

The book does cover a lot of ground, and not all of it evenly. However, in trying to ensure that none of it was examined in a grossly unsatisfactory way I was fortunate to have the advice of many other economists who read the book and made numerous suggestions that have improved it. None is liable for the contents of the book or for any remaining errors which are my responsibility alone.

In the UCD Economics Department, I would like particularly to thank Kevin Denny and Dave Madden, whose detailed comments on the entire text improved the book in hundreds of places. Other colleagues in the department, Frank Barry, Joe Durkan, Peter Neary, Cormac O Gráda, Kevin O Rourke, Aisling Reynolds-Feighan and Frank Walsh read parts of the book and made very helpful suggestions for its improvement.

Abroad, I would like to thank Canice Prendergast in Chicago, who contributed more to the book than anyone else and whose constant encouragement kept my spirits up until the job was eventually completed, Mark Wynne in Dallas, whose forthright reactions to an early draft steered me away from several sloppy statements, Olive Sweetman in Newcastle, who reviewed the book by e-mail, Nigel Jenkinson in London, famous in several countries for his drafting skills, who gave me his ever-precise observations, and Carlo Monticelli, in Rome, who kept phoning me up to ask if the book was finished yet and, when it was, sent me a detailed commentary.

I am also grateful to Tim Callan, Dermot Leahy, Alan Matthews, Paul Moore, Ronan O Brien, and Chris O Malley, who read the book and gave me their assessment of it.

I would like to record my particular gratitude to University College Dublin. I was able to write this book only because UCD gave me the time, the library facilities but especially the support of a large body of stimulating and vigorous colleagues. Without these, I doubt whether this book would have been written. It would certainly have been very inferior. At this stage, I am conscious of the book's remaining shortcomings but, as JRR Tolkien wrote of his *Lord of the Rings*, being fortunately under no obligation either to review the book or to write it again, I will pass over these in silence.

Of course, a book without a publisher is not much use. I am obliged to Oak Tree Press, and David Givens in particular, for giving the book their support and backing.

Over the years I have read thousands of statements in Acknowledgements like this about how the writing of a particular book disrupted the author's home life and placed an unreasonable burden on their partner. For the first time, I know the reality behind these bare words and I would like to thank Aileen for putting up with a distracted, stressed and obsessive husband for the past three years. I will try to normalise now.

PROLOGUE:
THE CHALLENGE

This book is an attempt to shine the blow-torch of economic modernisation up Ireland's collective posterior.

It is motivated by exasperation at our continued economic under-performance, which is partly related to our endless capacity to find ways of excusing that poor performance. And yet it need not be so. We are not a third-world country, though we've had plenty of third-rate leadership. If we want to, we can put our affairs on a sound footing and start the climb to continental living standards. Of course, it will not be easy and there will be a significant price to be paid, but if we genuinely want to be rid of the horrors of mass unemployment, shattering emigration and large pockets of deep poverty, it is the only way to go.

Similar opinions have, of course, been expressed before.

In the 1930s, Hubert Butler, the writer, noted the wide gap separating Ireland from the modern world. He decried "the terrifying intellectual isolation of Ireland, its power to breed ideas, ideals and emotions in rich abundance" but "its incapacity to nourish them or defend them" from the venomous dislike of their critics.

Thirty years later, in 1968, Charles McCarthy, the academic, observing what he called Ireland's "pleasant sloppy cosy way", felt that, despite the changes during that decade, Ireland had not really faced up to the challenges of the modern world.

And only six years ago, Professor Joe Lee of Cork published his celebrated history of Ireland, in which he castigated the second-rateness and mediocrity still prevailing in what he called this "small retarded country".

Again and again, this kind of critique breaks the surface of public discussion, leads to a fuss of one size or another, before the ripples fade away and mediocrity resumes its sullen course.

The challenge of modernisation still lies before us today and it simply will not go away.

This book tries to address that challenge. It is partly the result of the fact that, while working in Switzerland between 1990 and 1992, I was taken aback by the gap between living standards in the two countries and by the performance standards which lie behind Swiss prosperity. In Ireland, I had been ignorant of the real meaning of the income gap and this brought home to me our figurative as well as our physical isolation. If we merely compare ourselves with Britain, we grossly underestimate the magnitude of the catching-up that is necessary. Hubert Butler has described Ireland as being "dangerously tilted towards England . . . [a good place in itself] but best seen on the level". That was in 1957 but, partly for language reasons, it remains substantially true today. Yet, from the Swiss point of view, Britain looks almost as backward as Ireland; Heathrow and Zurich airports would not easily be confused.

This book discusses the economic and other reforms needed to begin the process of terminating Ireland's unnecessary backwardness by making it a modern, successful economy and society. Traditional policies are reviewed and their shortcomings exposed. Where it is necessary to do so, the blow-torch of modernity is wielded unflinchingly. Sadly, such an implement may well be needed to clear a path through the obstacles.

What are these obstacles? They go far beyond questions of economic policy and right to the heart of our culture; they include some of our old and cherished ways. To achieve economic and social modernisation, we must, for instance, throw off our ruinous defeatism and negativity, our anti-intellectualism, our tolerance of mediocrity, our inclination towards dependency, and our never-ending demand for subsidies (from London, from Dublin, from Brussels, from anywhere!).

However, this is not yet another "béal bocht" book! These objectives are achievable. Because previous generations failed to bring them about does not mean that the present generation will fail too. Thankfully, there is a generation of talented thirty-somethings that can be called on to assist today's sad and sorry sixty-nothings.

While there are extensive criticisms of many aspects of contemporary Ireland in this book, I have tried to match them with feasible proposals to begin to resolve our problems. Many readers will not find the solutions to their taste, and so be it. But unless the critics have workable alternatives to offer, they can expect only a continuation of our present malaise. Adults shouldn't expect a visit from Santa Claus, and those waiting for painless answers will end up spending their lives amidst the consequences of painful questions.

Because this book makes a conditional case for the market (a competitive and social market), its critics will inevitably portray its message as "harsh monetarism" or "an attack on the public sector" or whatever other shallow cliché first comes to hand. But insofar as I am attacking anything, I attack a system, not its servants. The problem lies in the kind of behaviour which Irish institutions reward, not with moral or other personal defects in our population. I ask the reader to stand back and look at the economic system in Ireland today. Is it one in which citizens — no matter how honourable or honest — could be expected to behave efficiently? If the answer is no, then it is pointless to blame the citizens but essential to change the system. To describe such a critique of the Irish status quo as "monetarism" would be laughable, an example of crass Irish anti-intellectualism.

In searching for better economic policies we must start with an open mind. There may be more scope for open-mindedness in the present decade than in the immediately preceding ones. The collapse of communism may encourage as much concentration on the choice between right and wrong as on that between right and left. In the past, ideological correctness was not always a good guide to economic policy, on either side of the divide. A person who was only concerned with the first five letters, would fail to see a difference between bullseye and bullshit. Maybe now there will be a greater opportunity to examine the full picture.

The solutions to Ireland's problems are not a great mystery. We just have to do what nearly every other state is doing to achieve economic advancement: converting to competitive capitalism. Capitalism, in this context, means a market economy, with profits for producers who satisfy consumer needs, where real competition between companies keeps prices down and where the state strives for equality of opportunity, so that all citizens entering adult life are able to make the very most of their abilities. I have christened this mixture of pro-market social democratic policies, the *Designer Economy*. It means a rejection of both the unthinking state interventionism and the anti-competitive business practices of recent decades.

It is especially important that we introduce more competition into the Irish economy. For this reason, we should welcome foreign competition via the single European market. At home, we need a still-stronger Competition Authority to oversee the domestic economy. Throughout the public and private sectors we must open up orders to wider tendering, we must make the maximum number of appointments open to outside competition, and we must bring to an end the monopolies, formal and informal, that dominate the domestic Irish economy. Agriculture — for so long a story of four green fields, five of them in disadvantaged areas — must learn to wean itself off subsidies; farmers in other countries have done it and ours must too.

The public sector needs a total revamp and redesign. If properly and carefully conducted, such a reform would raise both efficiency and job-satisfaction. Working in different parts of the Irish public sector over more than ten years, I have often found performance levels to be dismal and colleagues who are resigned to jobs that give them more pain than pleasure. The Irish state has become seriously overstretched and is unable properly to carry out those functions on which it should have concentrated. Under the umbrella of that state, a comfortable nexus of grant-givers and grant-takers (politicians, civil servants, businesspeople and executives of public companies) have established an economy — in the private just as much as the public sector — based on monopolies and near-monopolies. This has permitted them generously to forgive each other their many failings so that they could all continue to lead a quiet life. This is a certain recipe for mediocrity and corruption, and in Ireland we see both.

But just as state paternalism has major weaknesses, likewise there are dangers to be guarded against in a private market economy. In particular, competition must be safeguarded, the environment needs to be protected and equal opportunities need to be carefully fostered. There is no unconditional case for the market. But the Designer Economy version of the market, which balances economic efficiency with social equity, is to be strongly recommended. The way forward is to be clearer than Ireland has been in the past about the respective strengths of the public and private sectors and to reorganise their responsibilities accordingly.

The Irish welfare system must be reformed to offer a ladder as well as a safety net. The tax and subsidy system must be rebalanced to tempt more people into self-employment, where they should be allowed to keep much more of the rewards provided they don't expect taxpayers to bail out their failures. The time has come for us to stop wanting everything both ways.

The key issues are performance and the factors which promote it: motivation, accountability and flexibility, but especially the balance of rewards and penalties. It is not an issue of public versus private, worker versus employer, left versus right.

The bottleneck in the reform process in Ireland is in the political arena. We are up to our elbows in recipes: Culliton, Telesis, Commissions on This, That and the Other. But the Chefs hesitate at the breaking-of-the-eggs stage so there is rarely any omelette. The Chefs are unsure whether any recipe would please all customers. Unhappy customers are noisy so they, above all, must be kept satisfied; a silent majority goes unnoticed in the presence of a raucous rump. The Chefs, under pressure from the present electoral system, are keeping up a desperate — and hopeless — search for The Omelette That Will Satisfy Simply Everybody. Meanwhile, we get hungrier. Irish politics is one of the few cases where half a loaf today is scorned in favour of manna mañana. Personally I've had enough of it and I think we should change our political ways.

For a period which can be measured in centuries rather than decades, Ireland has largely looked on while various other parts of the world have embraced a system of dynamic economic change. We have pointed wide-eyed to the costs of that transformation, and then tried to negotiate to have part of the benefits handed over to us as economic aid. We have never been willing to bring a dynamic economy to our people and have instead watched, as though helplessly, while our people brought themselves to neighbouring dynamic economies.

By accepting the choice between stagnation or emigration, each new cohort of Irish people accommodates the status quo. Although at times I have wondered if I shouldn't feel grateful to be half-Breton and only half-Irish, mostly I am confident that today's twentysomethings and thirtysomethings will refuse to continue along the preordained path, and will reject stagnation and emigration in favour of modernisation.

This book is not an encyclopedia. Answers to all the country's economic problems cannot be set out in 250 pages. Instead, some key economic principles, which take account of the weaknesses both of the market and of the state, are proposed. Without principles, we merely accumulate separate and sometimes incompatible policies without having a coherent economic programme. Furthermore, each mini-policy will have a (usually uncosted) price tag and the total of all these price tags will be a completely impractical sum. This is a serious drawback to a "rainbow" approach to economics. It will be very colourful but, without a crock of gold at each end of the rainbow, no more than a fraction of the package can be implemented. The economic principles set out below are few and simple. Once they have been chosen, each particular issue can then be considered by reference to them. In this way a consistent policy package can be developed.

This book is most emphatically not the last word on any of the many topics it addresses. There can be no complete blueprint in a single short book by a single fallible author. There are others who would undoubtedly have made a better job of writing it. The debate it may provoke is certain to improve and sharpen the recommendations it contains. If the book had aimed at perfection, it would probably never have appeared, and it would certainly not have appeared this century. What it lacks in perfection and completeness, it may make up for in passion and possibly in timeliness. I can only offer a blunt and exasperated statement of some of the things about Ireland that seem to me self-evident and which we pay an enormous price by ignoring. This simply cannot go on; an abundance of terrible banality has already been born.

In the past we have chosen to pay the heavy price of underdevelopment. I think it's time we switched to paying for its solution, but I'm not pretending that there won't be a cost in each case. It is only when we demand a solution with no costs that there are no solutions. Ireland has spent the past twenty years twiddling its policy thumbs while it waited for a costless solution to our problems to come along. None arrived, none could arrive and 20 years have been lost.

*   *   *

While in Switzerland, I visited Geneva. In the middle of the city there is a large monument to the Reformation. It takes the form of a long cut-stone wall with statues of the Reformation leaders carved into it. Over the statues runs Calvin's motto. That motto is as relevant to Ireland today as it was to Geneva in the sixteenth century.

Post Tenebras Lux: After darkness, light!

Ireland can and must awake, arise and advance. We must start to live up to our magnificent potential and stop living down to our miserable record. It is time for Ireland to board the last train to economic modernity.

1

IN A SORRY STATE

Introduction
Ireland is doing just fine. Isn't it?

Growth is strong, or so the economists say. Or perhaps it's the politicians who say that. Well, anyway, the economy has seemed healthy enough for a few years now. And if the country is not organised as efficiently as it could be, well, a civilised pace of life is a valuable thing too, isn't it?

Does Ireland really need to change very much? Large-scale reforms would be disruptive and costly, at least at the start. Couldn't we just let things trundle along as they are? Maybe a rising tide would in time lift boats, and so on. We could wait and see. After all, most people are doing well enough.

Aren't they?

Poverty
In a recent Combat Poverty Agency book, *Telling it like it is*, women residents of an impoverished community in Dublin's Kilbarrack described their daily circumstances. Their neighbourhood was built in the early 1970s at a time when most households had work. Now, however, only 38 of the 80 families interviewed are headed by someone in employment. The other 42 families rely on social welfare. Most of the adults left school at 15 or younger and those at work are usually low-paid.

Their houses are small and poorly designed. Food is short; many mothers complained of having to constantly "police" the food supply to make it last all week. The expense of Christmas and First Holy Communion can be a financial nightmare, and most families need to borrow from the "loan man". For the unemployed, social life is nil. Illness is a serious problem and many of the women use tranquillisers, some of them heavily. Relatives are dispersed throughout Dublin, and bus fares to visit other family members cannot be afforded very often.

Much time is spent dealing with state agencies: the welfare office, the health clinic, Dublin Corporation and so on. The dependent position of welfare claimants means that their dignity is often trampled upon. Many residents complained that middle-class doctors and teachers showed little understanding and sometimes scant sympathy for their plight. One woman described how no fewer than four hospital appointments for a serious operation were cancelled, and how details of her case were passed on by her doctor to a university research department without her permission. A second explained that she was prescribed tranquillisers but not told that they were highly addictive. A third woman, whose husband had a drinking problem and whose family needed counselling, recounted an extraordinary tale. She was asked to bring her family to meet a psychologist. Only when she arrived did she discover that the psychologist proposed to sit in another room behind a two-way mirror and observe the family members talking among themselves. It later transpired that more than one psychologist was behind the mirror, but their exact number and identities were never revealed. Not surprisingly, the woman felt she was being treated like a criminal.

Kilbarrack also has two multi-storey blocks of flats, home to many single-parent families. The stairways and landings are dark and often filthy, slippery with water and urine. The lifts are usually broken. Rubbish spills out from the rubbish bins. The walkways and stairways in the flats complex are extremely unsafe, being a haven for gangs of youths who conduct noisy cider parties, use drugs and intimidate the mainly female residents.

Worst of all, these social conditions are likely to be reproduced in the next generation. Between them, the 80 families have 356 children. One hundred and fifty six of these have finished school, one-third (58) without any qualifications. Only 2 have proceeded to third-level education. Sixty nine of the 156 school-leavers still live at home. Of these, just 32 have found work, mostly low-paid and part-time.

Kilbarrack is not unique. In a March 1994 newspaper article, the living conditions in another Dublin community, Killinarden in Tallaght, were described by a school chaplain, Fr Liam O Brien. In this parish of 8,000 people, Fr O Brien noted that there is no Garda station, no telephone kiosk, no petrol station, no bank, no credit union, no building society, no clothes shop, no supermarket, no video shop, no florist, no barber, no dentist. He asked whether there is any medium-sized town in Ireland where the same is true? Overwhelmingly, his parishioners neither vote nor go to church. He described his parish's circumstances as one of social apartheid.

These general descriptions of Irish urban poverty are bad enough, but the personal tragedies lying behind them are far more harrowing. In his recent book *Queueing for a Living*, RTE producer Paddy O Gorman gives an account of interviews he conducted with the residents of what he calls the "welfare ghettos" of urban Ireland. O Gorman focuses on the strain poverty places on families, and the serious family violence that can ensue. In one case, he interviewed a woman who was being beaten by her husband. Late one night, she went to her bathroom and cut her wrists. Then she went to bed beside her husband, and left her arms dangling over the bedside with the blood flowing onto the floor. The reason she was able to tell this story to Paddy O Gorman was that as she lost blood her body grew very cold. To warm herself, she instinctively raised her arms up to her chest. But this blocked the wounds, the blood congealed, the bleeding stopped and her husband found her in the morning. Afterwards, domestic violence resumed and the woman later made another unsuccessful suicide attempt. The last time Paddy O Gorman visited the woman, he saw that "her face was blackened with bruises. One eye was nearly closed and there were finger marks on her throat." She was still being beaten.

A worse story unfolded over several interviews with a woman in Cork. This woman also had a very violent husband. They split up. Later, the daughter told her mother that the father had "hurted" her. It took a long time for the mother to accept that her daughter was saying that she had been sexually abused by her father. The mother promised that the daughter would never again be left on her own with the father. But a year after this interview, when Paddy O Gorman called back to the house, the woman looked at him in shock and refused to talk to him because "My husband is living with me again. We said we'd give it another try. Goodbye."

These stories, though distant from middle-class Ireland, are not about horrors taking place in some far-off country of which we know little and about which we can do little. They are stories about Irish citizens in the 1990s.

Anyone for reforms?

Drug Use and AIDS

In a grim special report written by journalist Maeve Sheehan for the *Sunday Tribune* in August 1993, she described the life led by a typical group of Dublin's drug addicts. Two pages of shocking photographs accompanied her report and showed young people with poor clothes, ravaged bodies, scarred, swollen and injured faces, as they queued to obtain a heroin substitute at the Baggot Street Hospital clinic.

The people the journalist spoke to were poor, unemployed, HIV-positive and drug-addicted. One woman's husband had died from using heroin mixed with rat poison. Another had lost two members of her family to drug use. At the time, it cost in the region of £80 a day to feed a heroin habit, about £30,000 a year. Addicts, when they are not in prison, spend their day robbing shops and houses, planning robberies and break-ins, and injecting themselves with drugs. In prison, there appears to be no difficulty in getting supplies of heroin. One of the three people who talked to the *Sunday Tribune* said that she took heroin for the first time while in Mountjoy Women's Prison. Many addicts are parents now, in some cases parents of HIV-positive children who have been placed in care.

They have absolutely nothing to live for and nothing to lose. Maeve Sheehan asked one of the addicts what his future was. She received a direct reply: "I'll get full-blown aids and then I die. What the f... do you think the future holds?"

One inner-city priest told the *Irish Times* in 1994 that the background of drug-users was so deprived that the addicts were treating themselves for "social pain": "Opiates are the best painkiller known to civilisation. This is self-medication to deal with social pain."

As everyone knows, the heroin problem first hit Dublin some ten years ago. Predictably, it hit Dublin's poorest inner-city areas the hardest. Some of today's drug addicts and Aids victims began to use heroin before the were old enough to smoke cigarettes. That these communities, already so deprived and marginalised, could have been left to the mercy of the drug barons and their henchmen is a sad commentary on the indifference — or, at any rate, the very inadequate response — of Irish society to "social pain".

In late 1993, a newspaper reported that the release from prison of many drug dealers jailed in the mid-1980s, and a halving of the price of heroin compared with 15 years earlier, were fuelling a renewed drug problem in Dublin and especially in the south inner city. A Fianna Fáil councillor claimed that on one single street, there were 40 drug pushers at work on any given day.

In late 1994, in a series of reports in the *Irish Times*, it was suggested that there could be 5,000-7,000 drug addicts in Dublin, of whom up to one-third could have the HIV virus. Only one in ten addicts was in treatment. The newspaper estimated that the level of drug addiction in Dublin would eventually kill about as many people as had died over the previous 25 years in Northern Ireland. The rehabilitation services are overwhelmed by the scale of the current problem. But even if their funding were increased tenfold, the drug problem could hardly be seriously tackled without addressing the multiple deprivations of the communities from which the addicts come.

Irish drug addicts are Irish citizens too. They're getting on just fine — no call for reform here.

Emigration
A recent National Economic and Social Council study estimated that in 1987 as many as 15 out of every 100 Irish emigrants to the UK faced serious social, economic and personal problems there.

Their circumstances can be grim indeed. The *Sunday Tribune* columnist Joe O Connor related an experience he had in the theatre district of London in mid-1993. A middle-aged woman came up to him with a baby in her arms. She handed him a note saying she was a refugee from Bosnia, had nowhere to sleep and that her child was hungry. The woman was in a dreadful state:

> She had that look that people who are really poor have. There's a desperation in the face, a darkness behind the eyes. It's a thing actors never get right. When people are utterly poor they look hopeless and frightened, the way this unfortunate woman looked.

O Connor had no money, but he explained to the woman where there was a nearby hostel, and he drew a map for her. And he walked on.

> The Bosnian woman began to walk alongside me, staring at me all the time. As I quickened my pace she broke into a trot. I began to get a little uptight. And she began to run alongside me then, panting and coughing, chattering away in what I presumed was the Bosnian language. Suddenly she thrust out her hand and grabbed my lapel. "Look," I said, "I'd love to help you but really I have no money. I'm sorry." And then a strange thing happened. She stepped back from me, this Bosnian lady, and put one hand on her hip. Her upper lip curled into a sneer. "Ah, would you fuck off with yourself," she exclaimed, "sure you're only a hoor's melt anyway." A telling moment. She was from Dublin, this poor woman. But she was pretending to be a Bosnian refugee, so that she could beg enough money to eat.

Just before Christmas 1992 O Connor told an even more moving story. He had been in a London railway station and saw a person whom he thought he recognised. But as he came close, he saw that the young man's clothes were shabby and his face grey; this was a homeless person. Suddenly, the man fell to the ground. O Connor helped him back to his feet.

> I gave him some money for a cup of tea. I wanted to get away from him, I'm ashamed to say. I wanted him to take the money and leave, but he looked up at me then. "Would you be able to come with me?" he said. He was Irish. He just wanted someone to go for a cup of tea with him.

They went to a late night coffee shop and the young stranger, who had not eaten for several days, told his story. He explained over tea — wincing in pain from a very bad cough — that he had had to leave his home in Athlone after being beaten up by his father. These rows happened after his mother had run off and his father's girlfriend had moved into the house. O Connor's account continued:

> I tried to ask him about his life in London. It was the loneliness that would get you, he said, rather than the cold or the hunger. It wasn't the begging, or the way that you had to shit into plastic bags, because they wouldn't even let you into the pubs to use the toilet. It was waking up in a doorway at six in the morning, freezing cold, and knowing that you wouldn't talk to a single person all day long. He said that it was a terrible thing to wake up by yourself, in your filthy clothes, and to know that you'd have to walk around all day, until it was time to go to sleep in a doorway again.
>
> I tried to give him more money, and he didn't want to take it. I insisted, and he started to cry then. He started to sob, the way a child would. I was very close to crying myself. He said that he didn't know what he was going to do. He kept looking around himself with a look of utter confusion and fear in his face. "I'm only hanging on by my laces" he kept saying. He was about the same age as me. He was absolutely despairing.

For one man, the laces eventually broke. In May 1993, the *Irish Times* printed a small report concerning an emigrant who had lost touch with his family in 1977. Later the same year, he inherited two small farms in Co. Leitrim. This news never reached him, because the man was homeless and couldn't be found. Sixteen years afterwards, on a morning in January 1993, a passing police patrol invited the man — still homeless — to sit in their patrol car to keep warm. Two hours later, the man lay in front of an express train and was cut in half.

Today, practically nothing is done to help these Irish citizens. Their agonies occur out of Irish sight, so out of Irish mind. No help is offered, no responsibility is accepted. Maybe we should consider subsidising our graduate emigrants a little less, so that we could help our starving emigrants a little more.

Our emigrants remain citizens of Ireland. But we shouldn't heed the demands they make for reform at home — everything's fine as it is.

The Nightmare Thing

It is customary for Europeans to look down on the US and say: American life if fine for the rich but, my God, what about the poverty? Yes indeed, what about the poverty. The Irish poverty.

Many Irish people are doing well from the status quo. Many more are not. There are heavy social costs associated with Ireland's present economic ways. These cannot be remedied without major reforms: a shift away from the messy mixture of state monopolies and private cartels that dominate the Irish economy today.

The above stories all relate to aspects of 1990s Ireland. It would be easy to tell more, about homelessness or travellers, for instance. But enough has been said to persuade a reasonable reader that ours is a status quo that does not deserve to be left undisturbed. Reform is essential and urgent. It is something from which we cannot flinch. Until it arrives, many of our citizens will continue to live in a sorry state.

So what is to be done?

One conclusion is relatively straightforward. In 1994, the Irish government spent some £13 billion. Of that, welfare transfers — pensions, child allowances, unemployment payments, free travel, disability allowances, medical cards, supplementary welfare, school transport, rent subsidies, special employment schemes, payments to lone parents — came to about £4.75 billion. These payments amounted to one-third of total government expenditure.

Despite the government's spending so much to finance the present welfare system, the amount obtained by each recipient, as these stories show, is too small to offer them a decent standard of living. If the circumstances of the poor matter, it follows that Ireland must do one of three things. Either redistribute still more of the available income towards those receiving benefits, or redistribute the present level of public spending more in favour of the least well off, or expand the size of the Irish economy so that it is possible to raise the incomes of those presently receiving transfers without the income of those in employment suffering a fall. Quite simply, we can rearrange the shares of a nearly-fixed cake, or set about expanding the size of the cake and thereby enlarge the shares.

The first course is hardly feasible, given taxpayers' existing disenchantment with the burden of tax. In 1994, government day to day spending corresponded to nearly £43 out of every £100 earned by Irish residents.

The second option would be an entirely logical step, and could make an important contribution. Social equity justifies transfers only from richer to poorer. But a lot of present-day Irish redistribution is of the opposite kind. The already better-off add to their advantages by obtaining cash from the state. Or privileged groups attempt to have the state intervene to rig the market in the group's favour, by excluding competitors or regulating high prices. Resisting these inequitable interventions would release resources for genuinely social programmes. But on its own this would be insufficient.

Only the third course — serious economic reform to create a dramatically more dynamic Irish economy — offers real hope of creating the jobs that would begin to pull deprived communities out of their present predicament. Only reform would begin to generate the private and public incomes that would allow social catastrophes like drug abuse, emigrant destitution and community decay to be tackled with public help by the communities themselves.

But how are we to stimulate Irish economic growth? This book proposes one way to achieve such an objective.

2

THE VISION THING

Introduction

Not only black American civil rights leaders have dreams. Irish citizens dream too. Mine is an economic dream. I call it the Designer Economy. It's a variant of what some people call the social market. In this book, I explain what that is. A Designer Economy would be a modern-day version of social democracy, built around two principles: productivity and equity. The first means arranging an economy's resources to give the highest level of production and income. The second means, where necessary, devoting part of that production to helping citizens begin their adult lives on a more equal footing, as well as offering some protection to those who subsequently fail to make it. In other words, an economy that would be prosperous and fair.

This combination of productivity and equity has been called a policy of "hard heads, soft hearts" — sensible but compassionate economic policies. Those who find such objectives attractive should also want to judge public policies on the same grounds: do they increase productivity? And do they increase equity? If possible, public policies should be designed to increase both but should at least improve one.

In this chapter, the meaning of productivity and equity are elaborated in a little more detail. Some readers may find these objectives to be very modest when set against greater ideals. So they are, in a way. But Ireland is so far from achieving even these goals that to attain them would be a vast and historic break with previous performance.

Productivity: Creating Income

At any given moment, an economy has a fixed stock of resources: human effort, whose quality can be boosted by education; physical capital, such as machines and buildings; and endowments like land and minerals. If such resources are used to produce many goods and services, that production is available to be distributed amongst the members of the community. If we fail to make the most productive use of our resources, less is produced so there is less to distribute. In other words, inefficiency makes a community poorer.

What is required in order for an economic activity to be productive? The answer to that question is surprisingly simple. There are two requirements.

First, the value of what is made must exceed the cost of the resources used up. In other words, productive activity turns something worth less into something worth more. That's all.

The productivity of an enterprise has nothing to do with the part of the economy in which it takes place. It has nothing to do with manufacturing versus services, nothing to do with exports versus home sales, nothing to do with the public versus the private sectors. A farm, a steel mill, a government department and a public hospital could all be productive. Or none might be. It would depend on whether the value of the good or service that comes out of the business exceeds the value of the resources that went in.

If less is turned into more, the business will make money because the revenue earned from selling its produce will exceed its costs. New income has been created. In contrast, in a loss-making business, costs are larger than revenues, so something worth more is being transformed into something worth less: income has been destroyed.

Note that while a productive business makes money, not all businesses that make money are productive. Drug-pushing is very lucrative but hugely destructive of the user's health. A little pile of powder is worth the price that drugs command only because of the consumers' addiction and the product's scarcity.

The second condition for productive economic activity is that there must be a net addition to the income of the community, not just the individual. One person's income must not just take away another's. That would only be to shift a given community income from one person to another.

Suppose that a farmer finds a way to achieve a higher yield from a particular field. They will have produced more and raised their income without anyone else's income changing. On the other hand, if the farmer receives a larger headage payment, their income will have grown only because the income of taxpayers has fallen, leaving total community income unchanged. Headage payments shift income, they do not enlarge it.

Let's look briefly at the productivity of a farm, a steel mill, a government department and a hospital.

A farmer is productively engaged when he or she produces food which sells for more than the cost of the land and the labour (the inputs). Less-valuable land and labour is being turned into more-valuable food. This transformation makes the community better off, because the value assigned to food by consumers in the marketplace is larger than the community's valuation of the land and the farmer's time. The more an economy encourages enterprises to be productive, the more that economy produces and the higher the community's income when that produce is sold.

Even if we believe that how the economy's goods are distributed amongst the population is as important as the amount of production itself, the size of a cake's shares still depends on the size of the cake, and the size of the cake depends on the productivity of its producers.

Back on the farm, if the business is losing money, this means valuable resources are being used to make food that sells for less than the resources did. Economically speaking, this must be a bad thing. Any activity which is unable over the longer term to cover its costs is economically wasteful, and any resources committed to such businesses are economically unproductive.

The good news is that, in a competitive market, such a business would soon go out of existence. The bad news is that there are two ways in which the collapse of the business may be prevented.

First, the public purse could be used to subsidise the activity. The farmer may decide it is time to park her tractor in a shed for a day, and go to her local TD's clinic to lobby for headage payments or some other income transfer. Note that, in this case, her day's work produces nothing for the community; in fact, a day's farming work is lost. Moreover, the headage payments, if obtained, merely transfer income from one part of the community (EU taxpayers) to another (Irish farmers). Although Ireland's income may rise, total EU income has not been increased, merely redistributed from Hans-Peter to Pauleen. Any efforts or money that farmers or their representatives devote to lobbying is, from an overall economic viewpoint, unproductive. The community is getting no increased production or income from such activity, merely a redistribution of a given cake.

The same, of course, applies to lobbying for other cash transfers whether industrial, educational, residential or other, as long as these merely redistribute the community's income without adding to it.

The second way for a loss-making project to avoid bankruptcy is to rig the market in order to push up prices. After all, a project is loss-making only at the prevailing prices. If the selling price could be raised enough, the project would appear "profitable". If the farming sector could manipulate farm prices upwards — by colluding to restrict output, or by getting a law adopted which fixes prices at a high level — the costs of the business could be more than covered, no matter how inefficiently high these may be. By rigging the selling price, any activity can be shown to make money.

Prolonging the life of a loss-making farm by means of a public subsidy from the taxpayer or by rigged prices are economically almost identical policies. Artificially-high prices are a hidden subsidy taken from consumers and given to producers with a result that is equivalent to a state subsidy taken from taxpayers and given to producers. Each redistributes income from others — whether taxpayers or consumers — to the farmer. But that still does not alter the underlying wastefulness of the farm.

Therefore, the test of the productivity of a business is not just that it makes money but that it does so on an open, competitive market, without state subsidies or artificially-set prices. The prices used to compare the value of a product with the cost of the resources should be prices determined under competitive market conditions. Competition will drive prices down to their lowest sustainable level and it is at these prices that a judgement should be made about whether an activity is converting less into more.

Exactly the same considerations apply to a steel mill. Just because this business can call itself a "manufacturing" facility does not guarantee that the plant will be productive. It will be so only if it converts inputs of a certain value into steel of a greater value. If the mill makes losses, its activities are economically wasteful. In the summer of 1994, one defence of the loss-making Irish Steel was to point to the number of people it employed, the taxes it paid to the state and so forth. But these are the business' *costs*. The important question is what is obtained in return for using up these costly resources. Otherwise, why not double the staff of Irish Steel and likewise the income taxes paid by its workers? In fact, why not recruit thousands of unemployed into Irish Steel if its wage bill is deemed to be a benefit without regard to the value of what can be produced (and sold) in return? That would be silly: employing people in a business that is a long-term loss-maker is, in fact, nothing other than disguising unemployment.

In a competitive market, a loss-making steel mill, like a loss-making farm, will soon close down. Only a public subsidy, or an artificial rise in steel prices, would keep the business in existence. But, of course, neither would make the business productive.

What of the case of a civil service department? In principle, the story is just the same. What does the department produce? Presumably information, policy analysis, administrative and other services. Are these services worth more than what they have cost to produce? A most interesting question. The costs can probably be measured without inordinate difficulty, even though in practice they rarely are. But what is the value of the services? This is a more difficult question. Since these services are not sold, it is not easy to say what value the consumer would place on them. No customer has had the opportunity to pay, or to decline to pay, for them. Nonetheless, a value could be placed on these services. It would be difficult, but not impossible, to do so. Many countries today have organised what they call "internal markets" within the public sector to establish what users are willing to pay for publicly-produced services.

In a traditional-style public sector, focusing on inputs (salaries, rent, heating) but hardly measuring outputs, the question "What are we getting in return?" is rarely posed. In such a system, there is likely to be much unproductive work going on. By bringing the relationship between costs and benefits to the fore, senior officials and ministers would at least be asking themselves sensible questions about the productivity of their operations. Productivity would be one guide as to which services should be supported and which discontinued, which expanded and which shrunk. If a market is considered unacceptable as a way of indicating the value of a service, some other measuring scheme must be chosen, otherwise it will never be known which public activities are worthwhile and which are wasteful.

In Ireland today the value of individual public services is generally unmeasured and so unknown. Worse, their productivity is just not the way that public services are thought about. We are usually totally in the dark when it comes to assessing the productivity of a government department. We are not in a position to say for sure whether many departments are productive or wasteful and, if so, in regard to which activities. Parts of the civil service may be very productive indeed; others may be hopelessly wasteful. What we may presume is that total ignorance is a poor signpost and we are unlikely to have stumbled across a perfect civil service on that basis.

Finally, what of the hospital? Is it productive? Once again we have to compare, service by service, the value of the health care provided with the costs of its provision. In a private hospital, the value of the services will be indicated by what customers are willing to pay for them. In a publicly-financed hospital (with free, or heavily-subsidised, services at the point of use), we are faced with the usual difficulty of valuing any unpriced activity. It is not much help that doctors are taught to assert that health care is priceless beyond measure. That would be fine in a world of infinite resources where any desired amount of priceless health care could be supplied. But within a finite health budget, more of one service ultimately means less of another and choices must be made. Rationally, the choice should favour the medical service with a higher value in the community's estimation. It will be difficult to determine such values. But it should be remembered that — behind the scenes — exactly these valuations are being made *implicitly* in decisions to allocate money to different parts of the medical system. Explicit valuations would have the advantage of clarity. But unless some measurement of value is attempted, we cannot know which are the productive services offered by the health system and which may not be.

There is one last and important wrinkle to judging an activity's productivity. The assessment should be made incrementally or, as it is sometimes put, at the margin. For example, the closure of some Irish Army barracks was proposed by a team of consultants in 1994. This was resisted on a number of grounds, including the high value of the Army's national defence services. There is little doubt that the Army does provide a valuable service. But it has many barracks. What does the least efficient one contribute to national defence? Even if the total value of Army activities did exceed the total cost, the same would not necessarily hold for every single barracks.

Productivity needs to be assessed for the marginal case. The productivity of farming must be judged at the level of the individual farm, the productivity of the civil service at the level of the individual service offered and the productivity of health care on the basis of individual medical procedures. Otherwise, individually valuable or individually wasteful elements may lie hidden in much larger totals.

A successful economy needs an institutional framework which promotes productivity, whether in farming, industry, the civil service or health care. Possible institutions for doing so include the private market, the public sector and the social market. The differences between each are discussed in detail below. I hope to persuade the reader that the social market combines the best features of the other two. Later chapters will discuss how these different institutional systems work and their effects on the economy. It will be argued that the present Irish economy embodies key shortcomings both of the private market (weak competition and unequal opportunities) and of crude state intervention (waste, unaccountable bureaucracy, political constraints), without managing to capture enough of either system's advantages.

Material living standards are not everything. But they are the foundation for economic prosperity, something that most people value highly. A successful economy must therefore put a large premium on productive activity. An economy structured so that productive activity is lucrative, while unproductive activity is not, must generate much higher living standards than one where the opposite is true.

Social Equity

The case for including equity as an objective of economic policy rests on ordinary humanity. Most people do not want to see fellow-citizens destitute, homeless or dying from affordably-treatable disease. They wish to minimise poverty and deprivation, to avoid gross inequalities in income and wealth, and to ensure that every person has sufficient health care, education and housing to help them to lead a dignified, productive and happy life. Indeed, the full development of every individual, regardless of birth or circumstance, and the full expression of their human spirit, would be many people's ultimate aim.

After all, the justification for the forward sweep of the economic machine is to provide people — citizens — with the material basis for life: food, shelter and clothing. In the developed world, it also provides the cascade of material goods that raises the standard of living and gives people the income to pursue non-material interests, artistic and spiritual or other.

But at the same time that they produce, economies also distribute the fruits of production amongst consumers. People earn an income, or receive a transfer of income from their family or from the state, which in turn gives them the ability to acquire a fraction of the economy's production.

Different economic systems give rise to very different patterns of distribution. Some countries' pattern leaves their streets filled with beggars by day and the homeless by night. In other states, these problems are barely present. Even for those with jobs, different countries have very different degrees of income inequality.

If a population were composed entirely of the high-skilled, with enough work to keep them all fully employed, then the income distribution would hardly be a matter of concern. Not many populations, however, meet this exacting requirement. More plausibly, some economic regimes would leave unskilled people impoverished or wholly dependant on charity. Even when deprivation is less extreme, self-respect still suffers. In the words of the US economist, Arthur Okun, starvation and dignity do not mix well. For this reason, many people will want to adjust the market's income distribution. A mechanism involving some mix of tax and welfare will be needed to do so. The principle is simple, though postwar experience has shown how the actual design of such systems is full of traps and difficulties.

Of course, social equity does not establish a carte blanche for public intervention. First, it needs to be shown, and not just assumed, that a particular measure will in fact advance its social goals. It is not enough to announce a public initiative in the name of tackling some social evil.

Second, the costs — direct and indirect — of public intervention need to be assessed. Public initiatives are not costless. If a new programme is launched, either another must be curtailed or additional tax revenue must be collected. Taxation involves some hidden costs. Costs must be compared with the benefits arising from the public programme before it will be possible to say whether the initiative will do harm or good. We cannot avoid taking cost into account. After all, crime could be eliminated by having a Garda every ten steps along every road and street. But what would we have to give up to pay for that?

The objective should be to find ways of pursuing social goals at the least cost.

Greater Income Equity

In many economies, a person without wealth or saleable labour will be dependent on support from relatives or from charity even to survive. As the US experience shows, under these circumstances many people live in appalling conditions. Anyone who values all society's members as full citizens must consider such an outcome to be intolerable. Therefore, some type of welfare and income redistribution system is needed (a) to provide a decent safety net for those who are unable at a particular time to provide

for themselves and (b) to raise the incomes of those who are in-
adequately able to look after themselves.

It is a matter for political decision as to what should be the
value of the transfers paid and the conditions of entitlement.
These are obviously matters of the greatest importance both to
those dependent on the transfers and to the society that pays the
bills.

But a welfare system to protect those affected by economic
changes and to achieve a minimum standard of living would not
deliver complete income equality. In fact, it should not even try to
do so. It would offer generous but selective benefits, sufficient to
give as good a standard of living as would be compatible with
maintaining a strong incentive for recipients to return to work as
soon as possible. The income redistribution system would make
transfers to the low-paid, as generously as the community is
willing to bear, taking account of the harmful impact of the necessary taxes in other parts of the economy. As will be explained
later, taxes have hidden economic costs. A balance must be struck
between these costs, which can include job losses for some, and
the social benefits of redistribution.

Greater Equality of Opportunity
Welfare and income redistribution systems are about making outcomes more equal after the event. However, there is also the matter of improving opportunities at the start of the economic contest.

That is an immense challenge. In a market economy, a person's
income depends on their talent, effort, acquired skills plus what
can be earned from any assets they own. The wealth (if any) our
parents bequeath to us is outside our control. But effort may be
varied according to a person's inclinations. And, most important
of all, talent may be fostered by education. Many educationalists
today argue that education in the earliest years, such as pre-
schooling, is crucial to a child's later development. For that reason, access to high-quality education must be the cornerstone of
policies to promote opportunity in society.

Playing fields are rarely level and, while it may not be feasible
to make them fully so, a true meritocracy would want to assist
those who face serious disadvantages in life so that they could

nonetheless enter adulthood able to make the most of their innate abilities and energies. The class handicaps and privileges which can so distort the starting point of the economic race need to be modified. At a minimum, all citizens must have sufficient health care and education to allow them to put their skills to use. Otherwise, an economy can make no claim to equality of opportunity.

Note that these latter arrangements are for the purpose of helping people to compete. They do not seek to suppress competition.

Aiming for equality of opportunity means attempting to help those facing the greatest disadvantage. This is not to deny that much of what happens in life is outside anybody's control. Chance factors will benefit some people and hinder others in a random way. In some cases, little can be done about that. Often, the levers available to a government, and the information available to it, are not sophisticated enough to allow "surgical" interventions.

Nor would more equal opportunities ensure equal results. A great deal would — and should — depend on people's own efforts. Equalising opportunities only means aiming for greater equality at the point where citizens enter adulthood. Thereafter outcomes would depend on performance.

But a Limit to Income-shifting
There is a strong case for some income redistribution and for more equal economic opportunities. But these measures have two defects. First, as we have seen, they shift some of the community's income from one set of citizens to another without adding to the total. Second, there is a danger that the recipients, if they are without an income of their own, may become dependent on the transfer.

If every household at an address with an even number gave £100 to a household at an odd-numbered address, much money would change hands but the overall community income would be the same as before. Income transfers cancel out: they are a zero-sum game. For that reason, there must be some limit to redistribution.

A society needs most of its members to spend most of their energies enlarging their income in ways which enlarge the community's income, rather than trying to redistribute the latter in their own favour. This especially holds for a community's already-advantaged members who have little or no claim on state or other cash transfers.

Furthermore, it is much better when community assistance to needy citizens is arranged in a form which puts those citizens in a position to help themselves, rather than to become dependent on permanent transfers. Redistribution is organised through the political world but, in a politics-driven economy, people may become passive. A community — national or local — that lives from transfers can never grow out of dependency because the need for the transfers never ends. Only when such a community starts to generate its own income will its dependency lessen. Transfers are only ever a partial solution to a community's problems. In the long term, it is not possible to neglect productivity.

Institutional Options: The Dream, Degenerate, Decree and Designer Economies
How should objectives like productivity and equity be pursued?

There are three, and only three, mechanisms with which to do so. Each differs fundamentally in terms of the principles on which it is based and the mix of productivity and social equity which it delivers. But some system must be chosen. Those who will have no truck with one must hitch a ride on another. There are no other ways and, in particular, no painless alternative that remains to be discovered.

The **Dream Economy** is the simplified world of a perfect market economy. Competition would drive prices down to the lowest level consistent with a business covering its costs. Prices would reflect all costs. An income-creating business would be rewarded with a profit and would continue in operation. A loss-making firm would have to improve productivity or close down. No subsidies would be available nor would there be any possibility of rigging markets.

But this kind of perfectly efficient economy is only found in textbooks. As an ideal of high productivity, it is a useful standard for judging alternative systems. For this reason, its workings are explained in Chapter 4. But it is not available as an actual institutional option. Besides, a perfectly efficient economy might still be a horrendously inequitable one.

A purely private economy, left to itself, is subject to regular breakdowns or "market failures". The result is the **Degenerate Economy**. Such an economy lacks a mechanism to safeguard competition and prevent the cosy arrangements that companies like to reach amongst themselves. It also cannot take account of costs for which there are no prices, such as pollution. Nor is it well-suited to providing goods which are consumed collectively, such as infrastructure. And it suffers from the same shortcomings in regard to income distribution as the Dream Economy. As a result, a "free" but uncompetitive economy will be a lot less efficient, and no less inequitable, than its Dream Economy equivalent. The Degenerate Economy and its weaknesses are described in Chapter 5.

As a response to the failings of purely-private markets, the state has taken a greater role in the economy. This is the **Decree Economy** option, centring on state leadership and directions. Traditionally, state services, nationalised industries and public administrations have been run on this basis. Competition and the market are generally absent. Such a structure generates its own inefficiencies, including bureaucracy, political conflicts of interest, and high costs. Governments of a Decree Economy, half-informed about market failures but generally quite blind to government failure, tend to intervene crudely, doing less good than they might and at times considerable harm.

This system also risks being commandeered by sectional interests, and thereafter driven by politics rather than productivity. Despite much rhetoric about social redistribution, the privileged and politically-favoured groups may capture much of the benefit of public spending. The shortcomings of traditional-style state management are discussed in Chapter 6.

The **Designer Economy** seeks to avoid the worst pitfalls of the Degenerate and Decree options. It tries to minimise market failures but only within the limits of a realistic assessment of governmental capacities. It is firmly founded on the market economy, so private firms are rewarded for productive economic activity. But, in recognition of the defects of an unregulated market, the state intervenes to police competition and to correct other serious market failures which a private economy cannot resolve on its own. However, such state interventions are designed with a clear awareness of the shortcomings of crude government intervention. The state will only intervene after ensuring that there is a net social benefit from its actions. The objective is one of level playing fields free of political footballs. In the social sphere, the state intervenes to promote equal opportunity.

This mixture of private and public elements is the social market economy option. It is the most likely to promote high living standards by offering strong incentives for productive economic activity but the minimum of reward for unproductive behaviour. This system and the way it seeks to avoid the shortcomings of both statism and cartelisation are set out in Chapters 7 and 8.

Before examining these various models, let us turn back to the Irish economy. We have seen how, as a sorry State, it falls short of the objective of social equity. But how good is the Irish economy at promoting productivity?

3

THE IRISH DISEASE

Introduction

There is so much that is good — even wonderful — about Ireland today. And then there are the other things.

On the good side, there are magnificent achievements in sport and in culture. Our soccer team's performance in the World Cup, Sonia O Sullivan and Michele Smith in athletics and swimming, Michael Carruth and Wayne McCullough in the 1992 Olympics. Earlier, Sean Kelly and Stephen Roche in cycling. In music, there are international successes like the Cranberries, U2, Sinead O Connor, Enya, and Clannad. Our record-breaking three wins in the Eurovision and, out of the blue, the Riverdance bombshell. Jim Sheridan's films have triumphed at the Hollywood Academy Awards as have Brian Friel's plays on Broadway. In literature, Ireland has produced four Nobel Prize-winners in Yeats, Shaw, Beckett and Heaney while present-day literary writing is already filling anthologies; Roddy Doyle's achievements are just one of many.

These are world-beating successes. All the lists could be extended, some of them considerably. You don't have to think a lot of the Eurovision, or know anything about soccer, or be a regular reader of the latest novels, to see that Irish citizens, by the various standards in all of these areas, have been able to triumph against all comers.

But then there is the other side of the coin. As our gaze moves away from sport, music and writing, the picture alters considerably. In the economic sphere, we seem to be laggards rather than leaders. Our living standards trail behind most other EU members. Our unemployment and emigration problems seem incapable of resolution. People are sceptical about whether further economic growth can solve Ireland's economic problems. Although economic conditions are steadily improving as we move into the second half of the 1990s, there remains an underlying disquiet in Ireland about our economy and society. The whiff of economic and civic bankruptcy characteristic of the 1980s is not so very distant a memory.

The Irish Disease: Creating and Shifting Income
The contrast between profuse Irish success in sports and culture but piffling success in our economy is important. Why are we very productive in some areas but much less so in others? You would have thought that the factors that produce success — including talent, hard work, and a determination to win — would be common to the two. Is there some disease in the economy, not present in some other areas, that disables talent, weakens resolve or misdirects effort? I believe there is.

A complete explanation for our contrasting performances, drawing in all the various threads, would be a tremendous challenge which I must leave to those capable of undertaking it. Here, I will try to describe the Irish Disease mostly in terms of failings of our economic structures.

From an economics viewpoint, the Irish Disease could be described as "institutional failure". The core of Ireland's economic problem is that we are lumbered with an institutional framework in which rewards are not based on merit. Since talent and effort are not sufficiently rewarded, our economy is quite unproductive.

Rather than raising its income by producing more and selling more, thereby expanding the size of the Irish economy, each significant social group is busy lobbying political representatives either (a) to have someone else's income transferred, via public spending, in its own favour, or (b) to have laws passed which rig the market in the lobby's favour. People evidently believe it is easier to raise their living standards through politicking than through producing. Hence we have a lot of politicking and not enough producing.

The grand scale of this redistributive and interventionist activity and the fact that it is at the expense both of productive activity and social equity, is at the heart of Irish economic underperformance.

By separating rewards from productive effort, initiative is discouraged, talent is wasted and mediocrity slinks into the breach. That is the Irish Disease. To beat off this disease means lowering the scope and the reward for rearranging a fixed pie while raising the reward for productive increases in the pie's size.

Well-designed institutions, public or private, encourage productive activity and discourage wasteful politicking. Otherwise, skills and energy will lie underused, unused, or even misused. Unfortunately, many important Irish institutions are not well designed. That institutional set-up has produced the economic performance described so trenchantly by UCC's Professor Joe Lee as "the least impressive in western Europe, perhaps in all Europe, in the twentieth century."

Of course, these institutions and structures didn't just drop, fully-formed, out of the sky one morning. There are reasons why they evolved as they did. If we had a good understanding of those reasons, a better programme of reform could then be devised. But with even a partial explanation, we can get started. We can begin to change the many things that are blatantly wrong in Ireland today, and to redesign structures which have visibly and grossly failed.

The Irish Disease is home-grown. Our institutional set-up is something we decide for ourselves. We can begin to change it if we are willing to make the effort. There is no external obstacle to doing so. There is, of course, an internal obstacle. The beneficiaries are pleased with Ireland as it is. They believe they are quite productive enough. They would prefer not to have to exert themselves more than at present. They certainly don't want to be pushed aside by more capable and suitable people, regardless of how much the community in general might benefit from a redesigned economic system. Insiders will always choose a plodder's pace in preference to what they would call a rat race.

The Importance of Institutions
The 1993 Nobel Prize winner in Economics, Douglass North, has attempted to explain why some countries have developed rapidly while others remain underdeveloped. Here is a summary of his ideas, which have considerable applicability to Ireland.

Human talents and efforts are invariably put to use within institutions. Some of these institutions are relatively small-scale and
obvious to the naked eye, like the company we work for. Others
are much more distant and abstract. For example, the boundary
between the state and the market leaves no physical mark but it
does have economic and political effects. Almost equally invisible
are the details of the laws governing company behaviour. But
these too are part of a country's institutional framework and have
economic consequences.

Douglass North argues that a country's institutions determine
whether it is more rewarding for citizens and companies to engage in productive or in unproductive tasks. It matters a lot
whether theft or thrift is more lucrative. If institutional arrangements reward economic behaviour which increases the community's income, the economy will expand. But purely redistributive
activity leaves the income of the economy no larger than before.
Equity considerations require some redistribution to take place.
But if the reward from redistribution becomes too large, it will
divert energy from productive activities and the economy will be
slow to grow.

The problem is that production and distribution occur jointly:
goods do not spontaneously present themselves for distribution.
The set of institutions by which an economy operates determines
both how much people decide to produce as well as to whom the
income accrues. A feudal principality, a Soviet dictatorship and a
modern industrial democracy, even with the same labour force
and stock of machinery, would produce utterly different quantities of goods and services, and would also allocate them in entirely different ways. Under feudalism and communism, producers have little incentive to work hard, because a disproportionate
share of output ends up with the Prince and the Politburo. As a
result, relatively little gets produced. In a competitive industrial
democracy, more of the rewards accrue to producers and there is a
much stronger incentive to be productive.

People will try to organise any society in their own interests. If
they are allowed to do so, well-connected interest groups will
seek to manipulate the rules to improve their own position. But
will the rules that generate a large income for the members of the

interest-group also be the kind that promote productivity and long-term economic growth?

Not necessarily. The norm for most human beings and most human history has been a set of institutions that have delivered economic stagnation. Likewise, Ireland's present institutions, while failing to deliver the kind of economic advancement that Irish people aspire to, are very agreeable to those who run them. To begin to change that, we need to understand what kind of institutional set-up would be needed to promote faster growth. Happily, this is not a mystery.

Four Channels to Boost Productivity

To explain growth or its absence, North focuses on four factors. Each influences the reward from productive economic activity and therefore the amount of such activity that takes place.

First, there are the **formal rules**, like constitutions and parliamentary laws. It makes a difference whether the law requires every business to obtain a licence from the state, or permits citizens simply to get on with their affairs. It matters whether there exists a competition agency to police private businesses and to intervene effectively against arrangements that are not in the public interest. Without such a regulatory regime, a small number of businesses will tend to create a cosy and profitable cartel, passing on high prices and inferior service to customers. In overregulated or cartel-ridden economies, the difficulty of doing business will stifle new competition.

Second, there are the **informal codes of conduct** that prevail in a society. The cost of doing business will be lower in an honest country than in a state where people believe that tax evasion or inflated insurance claims are legitimate behaviour. The dishonest society pays exorbitant insurance charges and bears the costs of legions of tax officials armed with draconian powers. The honest economy escapes both burdens and is a more attractive place to do business.

Third, there is the ease or difficulty of **enforcing the law**. When law enforcement is uncertain, incompetent, subject to political interference, or unaffordably costly, community members will be reluctant to establish an enterprise that depends on the commitment of others. Business is undoubtedly a more challenging prospect in Beirut or Belgrade than in a well-ordered society like Basle.

The fourth institutional element is the sum of the **attitudes and beliefs** through which the public makes sense of the world around it. Although invisible, these can still be tremendously powerful. It matters if people see economic success as a sign of the Lord's pleasure or, instead, believe that it is easier for a camel to get through the eye of a needle than for a rich man to get into heaven. Suppose people believe that business is mostly exploitation which should be subject to strong government controls. In these circumstances, workers, feeling exploited, are likely to be uncooperative and businesses, feeling under siege, will be defensive. Co-operation between the providers of labour and capital is made very difficult. Management will have to engage in costly monitoring of workers. And companies will not be willing to get involved in activities that depend on their staff acting responsibly on their own initiative. In contrast, the belief that economic arrangements are broadly fair and that people mostly get the results they deserve are the kind of ideas that enable modern business methods to be put into practice.

Ideas have power. A society infused with airy deValerian notions about frugality and spirituality will have a very different economy to one inspired by a muscular materialism that seeks, in the first instance, to close the income gap between home and abroad. In these ways, ideological and cultural factors enhance or diminish an economy's productivity.

North concludes that in countries where the political system has a record of arbitrary or confiscatory behaviour, where citizens believe that any kind of chicanery is justified and where law enforcement is lax, productive activity will be discouraged. Companies could find themselves at the mercy of thieves, commercial rivals, predatory politicians and even their own staff. To minimise these risks, businesses will be small-scale with little hardware and few long-term agreements. Large businesses will seek the shelter of government protection. While such firms may then obtain subsidies and monopoly privileges, they will on the other hand face risks of political payoffs and interference. In such economies, the result is likely to be both private and public inefficiency. The first because of small scale and the second because of the state's tolerance or promotion of anti-competitive market practices.

In contrast, countries where competition is strictly policed, where law enforcement is effective and impartial, where there are high standards of personal integrity and an honest and professional political system, offer a much more attractive site for business enterprise.

A Fixed or a Growing National Cake?
The test of an economic change is whether the net gain from the change is positive or negative.

Lester Thurow coined the phrase "zero-sum society" to describe the condition of a stagnant economy, in which an income gain for one person must mean an income reduction for someone else. From the fact that the gains and losses total up (or sum) to zero, comes the expression "zero-sum" society. Until very recently, a majority of countries lived under close to zero-sum conditions. Even today, in significant parts of Africa, economies are actually shrinking rather than growing.

Nonetheless, it is possible for economic change to produce gains that completely dwarf any losses and leave economies much larger than before the change. We do know something about avoiding economic stagnation. Many people, and not just in developed countries, today live in a positive-sum world. During the 1980s, the size of the economy of the industrial countries grew by no less than one-third. In the same period, the growth in the Japanese economy — on its own — equalled the total size of the French economy. East Asia, the most successful region for economic growth since the last war, more than tripled the size of its economy between 1965 and 1990. Living standards are higher today in Singapore than in Ireland ($11,200 per head in 1990 as against $9,500, according to World Bank figures), even though they were well below the Irish level thirty years ago. In 1960, Japanese living standards were half of Ireland's, but today ours are less than half of Japan's. Plainly, the way these countries were run led to economic gains that far outweighed whatever losses there may also have been.

How can positive-sum outcomes be promoted? By favouring economic changes which enhance productivity. When economic resources can be rearranged in a way which increases their productivity, the overall size of the economy grows. Growth depends on being able to move resources around as new opportunities or threats appear. In contrast, distributional rules are generally very inflexible. They make response to changes very sluggish.

Someone who can see a way of rearranging resources so as to produce more should not only be free to make the rearrangement but should be rewarded for doing so. But in a poorly designed economy, that may not be what happens.

For example, imagine that trees planted on a particular piece of farmland could generate a much higher income than farming could on its own. In this case, it would be inefficient to leave the land in its less-productive (agricultural) use. The forester could rent the land from the farmer for at least the same money that the farmer can earn from farming — so the farmer would be no worse off — while the forester could still make money from the project. Since the farmer's income would be no less than before whilst that of the forester would be greater, the community's overall income would be larger. The value of the total change is positive. Since one member of the community is better off, and no one is worse off, it seems reasonable to conclude that the community as a whole would have gained.

However, now assume that the farmer is also entitled to income transfers from the state. Suppose the total of the two incomes, deriving from farming proper and from the welfare payment, exceeds the rent the forester could afford to pay for the use of the land. The result would be to keep the land in its less productive use, to penalise the more productive forester, and to stop the economy from being as large as it could be.

Most economic changes involve both winners and losers. Imagine, for example, that a new financial company sets up in Ireland offering much lower insurance premia than those currently available. Clearly, this would be a gain, perhaps a sizeable one, to existing buyers of insurance. In addition, at the lower prices there would be more insurance bought. Some of the people who previously did not find insurance good value would now find it worthwhile to buy some. On the other hand, either profits or incomes or employment, or all three, would fall in the costlier companies. One important determinant of the size of the latter losses would be the extent to which those losing jobs with high-cost insurance firms could find employment elsewhere in the economy. What would be the net effect of all these changes?

Given the level of Irish insurance charges today, it is likely that the gains would comfortably exceed the losses. Competition, in the form of a new insurance seller, would then be a positive-sum game for the Irish economy. But a rule restricting competition, a derogation from EU single market laws, for instance, would prevent such gains being realised.

A growing economy, as North argues, goes hand-in-hand with formal and informal social arrangements and attitudes that support flexibility and dynamism. A dynamic spirit could hardly be further from the conservative ethos found under static economic conditions. Growth offers possibilities for self-advancement without anybody necessarily being displaced. But when someone else's gain could be your loss, envy and begrudgery are to be expected, also, deep suspicion of change, possibly sabotage of other people's efforts and a general mean-spiritedness. Individuals seek to protect what (little) they have in terms of hard-and-fast distributional rules, such as demarcation, "closed shops", promotion by seniority, last-in first-out, or market-sharing by suppliers. These rules control the allocation of the shares of a cake that is believed to be fixed.

North's ideas are consistent with what Professor Joe Lee of UCC has called the absence of an adequate "performance ethic" in Irish life. Lee argues that in Ireland we reward people for their possessions — land, jobs, education, wealth — rather than for their performance or enterprise. This goes a considerable way towards explaining Ireland's dearth of enterprise. There is no reason to be surprised that Ireland has failed to produce much of an entrepreneurial class when its economy offers bigger rewards for unproductive behaviour.

A Revealing Comparison

Part of the explanation, then, for the contrast between Irish sporting/cultural success and economic sluggishness is the difference in the way the contests are arranged. Sporting, musical and literary contests are organised, however imperfectly, on the principle of open competition. In terms of North's criteria, the rules, codes, adjudication systems and sense of fair play are designed to reward merit and to encourage high performance. But this is not how we run the Irish economy.

Take sport. It is not too idealistic to say that sport is organised on a competitive basis. There are no "closed shops" or "winning by seniority". No team receives an automatic share of the medals. The competition is refereed by a generally impartial adjudicator. In terms of attitudes, there is a widely-shared idea of what is fair play. Players broadly accept that sporting contests are fun fairly: on balance, a competitor gets the result that reflects his or her talents and efforts. Unlike the way it is sometimes portrayed in business, competition in sport is not seen as "the law of the jungle".

In practice, of course, sport is nonetheless an imperfect contest. Things do go wrong. No one would claim that an Irish boxer who trains in a prefab on a run-down housing estate is on a "level playing field" with a foreign boxer who is coached night and day. But at least the rules of the competition are "level". The other boxer cannot exclude the Irish contestant from the competition, cannot play according to a different set of rules, cannot choose his twin brother as referee. If the Irishman's talent is great enough, he cannot be denied his victory. If he fails to outpoint his opponent, he cannot avoid losing. His talent is not the only influence on the result of the contest — it must be enough to outweigh the other boxer's coaching advantage — but it is the single most decisive ground for success. This makes it worth the boxer's while to strain every sinew in his body to achieve his best possible performance. When rewards are based on merit, it pays to try one's hardest.

Much the same applies to musical and literary contests. These too are open to all comers and are organised on broadly competitive principles. Rules are transparent. Adjudications are made by independent panels. Participants are willing to accept the outcome as generally fair. Nonetheless, opportunities are not in any sense equal. Four youths strumming guitars in their front room have little hope of winning the Eurovision. But they are free to make the attempt, and their rivals cannot exclude them, cannot rewrite the rules in their own favour and cannot act as judges. This is precisely why the contests are regarded as relatively fair.

Ireland does well in these merit-based contests, and not just in sport and music. Since 1976, no fewer than 14 of the 20 winners of the Young Scientists Competition have gone on to scoop top awards at the European or US level of the competition.

But winning on merit is not the principle by which we run large parts of the Irish economy. It is not just that there are unequal opportunities. The rules themselves, by suppressing competition, make the playing field even more lop-sided. In a contest where the results are largely predetermined, why should anybody bother about effort? Merit doesn't matter.

In the Irish private sector, weak competition policy has allowed incumbent companies to become dominant in large parts of the Irish economy. In the state sector, companies have almost always been created as monopolies. Unlike sporting competitions, the rules of economic contests allow competitors to be excluded. Economic winners have even been allowed to rewrite the rules to protect their leading position. And, traditionally, Irish commercial law has offered no effective remedy.

If sports referees could be paid consultants to teams, if sporting teams could be excluded from matches, if sports rules could be redrafted to favour winners, there would be public outrage. But distorted economic contests pass almost without comment.

Few would be happy for foreign TV soap-operas, in competition with RTE's, to be banned. To force Irish football fans to watch only League of Ireland matches would probably lead to a revolution. Yet we accept the suppression of competition in industries like energy supply and in areas like bus transport with hardly a murmur.

Nor are rules the only kind of measure that fail to reward merit. Too often, income transfers — which should be about equalising opportunities — also act as a barrier to merit.

Farmers, for example, rather than earning a livelihood from producing and selling food that people want at prices they are willing to pay, have negotiated a range of subsidies and supports for farm-owners. Intending householders, instead of buying homes they can afford, have obtained mortgage subsides which

allow them to buy bigger houses. The employed have significantly added to their earnings in the course of recent pay agreements. The already-educated middle classes have obtained increased subsidies for their children in higher education. Current
wealth-holders benefit from Ireland's negligible property and
wealth taxes.

The result is that part of the income tax paid by people who
wash dishes and sweep floors for a living is used to finance state
transfers that raise farm-owners' incomes, subsidise home-owners
and increase the earnings of the employed. The cost of higher
education is reduced for the children of lawyers and doctors, so
that they may in turn become lawyers and doctors. What Professor Joe Lee calls the "possessors" — of the land, the safe jobs, the
education and the wealth — have established arrangements in
Ireland which further advantage their position at the price of
lower overall living standards and a slow-growing national economy.

One of Ireland's problems is its undeserving rich: those whose
prosperity rests, not on productivity, but on politically-inspired
income transfers and politically-engineered distortion of markets.
Deserved wealth derives from productive economic behaviour.

Rigged markets and poor-to-rich transfers are not new developments in Ireland, which is part of the reason why our sluggish
economic growth is an old problem. In his history of twentieth
century Ireland, Professor Lee paints a picture of a country where,
traditionally, each sector of the economy and society has managed
to set up barriers to protect its position and privileges. In industry,
before the free trade of the 1960s, he notes that indigenous industry "consisted overwhelmingly of small firms enjoying a captive
domestic market and enduring few competitive pressures. They
were not, in this respect, very different from government departments or university departments. They were small, sheltered and
rarely obliged to cope with the threat of competition. When the
threat materialised in the 1960s, their instinctive response was to
seek subsidisation and protection through the 'grants' economy,
rather than face the challenge of the market." These groups were
not concerned about performance or productivity. If their busi-

nesses were loss-making, they turned either to state subsidies or rigged markets, or both, to sustain their position.

The factors that have delivered Irish success in the cultural and sporting areas — talents, effort, determination — have been undermined in our economy. A continuation of this institutional framework would mean a continuation of economic mediocrity. We have allowed the possessors, those who set the rules in Ireland, to establish an economy which guarantees a quiet life for themselves at the price of undermining the prospects of a generalised rise in Irish living standards and employment. These barriers must be broken down. Inequitable interventions must be rolled back, releasing the resources to make genuinely equitable transfers. Rules that override merit must be ended. Competition must be given freer play. Incomes need to be better linked to performance, determination and productivity and detached from preferential rules, rigged markets and hidden subsidies.

Can Bad Institutions Be Reformed?

Douglass North emphasises how today's poor institutions can have effects which last far into the future. A country that wants to stay productive needs institutions that reward adaptability. There need to be incentives to acquire knowledge and learning, to innovate, to take risks and to be economically creative.

North contrasts the likely development over time of an economy based on unproductive piracy and productive business. The pirate economy would have an incentive to reward research into military and naval technology, reinforcing the unproductive character of that economy. The business economy would pay for investigations into science and management, accentuating its orientation towards productivity. The future evolution of these economies is likely to be very different.

It is the losers and potential losers who prevent or delay the switch to a more productive institutional framework. Their resistance is individually rational but socially damaging. Just because there would be large overall gains from economic change does not mean that there wouldn't be significant individual losers. If potential losers are powerful, they will seek to block the change.

This fate can be escaped if two requirements are met. First, the costliness and inefficiency of the status quo needs to be clearly explained along with the benefits from economic reform. That is what this book attempts for Ireland.

Second, potential winners must be able to negotiate change with potential losers. If some of the costs of adjusting to reform fall onto disadvantaged groups, there would be a case for assisting them with the adjustment, in a transitional and temporary way. People might have to learn new skills, to move into new activities, to make many other changes to their lives. Temporary, targeted public assistance could help them to do so and thereby lessen their resistance to reform. In effect, part of the expected gain from reform would be used to smooth the path of the reform.

On the other hand, there would be a much weaker case for compensating groups who were merely having undeserved privileges withdrawn from them.

A Tale of Two Americas

Douglass North makes much of the contrasting histories of North and South America as an example of the important role of institutions in economic development. Two hundred and fifty years ago, North America was an English colony and South America a Spanish colony. Both were colonies, both were poor and underdeveloped. But these two Americas diverged in the economic institutions they constructed. One opted for the market economy, the other for state planning. One rewarded productivity, the other rewarded politicking.

Latin America copied the political and economic structure of feudal Spain, where a large centralised bureaucracy administered decrees to further the interests of the Crown. The result proved to be national debt, economic decline and centuries-long stagnation. The form of the state's heavy involvement in the economy meant that a business's success or failure depended on political "pull" more than economic performance.

In contrast, North America adopted market institutions resting on individual initiative, private ownership and a decentralised economy. There was a presumption in favour of the market. But in cases where the market was found to fail a certain kind of state intervention — very different to the Latin model — was available. It did not involve national planning or regulation from the centre and it certainly did not involve state-owned commercial enterprise. Rather, the US authorities sought to identify the nature of the market failure and to take steps to correct it. For instance, during the nineteenth century, public land was sold to farmers and ownership rights were secured to promote rapid land settlement and increased food production. Farm productivity was raised by an Agriculture Department which supported a network of agricultural colleges and experimental stations. The eventual impact on productivity is instructive. In the late 1700s, almost the entire US labour force was made up of farmers. In the late 1900s, a total of just 3 million farmers, out of a total workforce of 120 million, fed a population of over 250 million people. In other words, it takes only about 2 to 3 US workers out of 100 to feed the US today. In Latin America, it still takes between 10 and 20 out of every 100. The productivity gap is even greater outside agriculture.

A Tale of Two Asias

A contrast has also been drawn between the experiences of Asia's tigers (such as South Korea) and its tortoises (such as India and the Philippines). In 1961 South Korea had a per-person income of $180, about two and a half times that of India ($73). Over the next 25 years, India's income rose four-fold in real terms to $300. South Korea's rose fifteen-fold to $2,690.

Difficult though it is to believe today, after the second world war the Philippines was seen as the country most likely to develop rapidly. In 1967, the Philippines had a per-person income of $210, in the same ball-park as South Korea's $240. Twenty years later, in 1987, real average income in the Philippines was just short of three times higher ($590) while South Korea's, as we have seen, had shot ahead by a factor of eleven to $2,690.

In these decades, India followed the path of a planned economy, the Philippines had an unregulated private economy dominated by corrupt cartels, while South Korea opted for a market-led economy in which the state distributed opportunities, especially education, widely. The results are a matter of record. It is no surprise that during the 1990s both tortoises have been trying to copy the tiger.

Curing the Irish Disease

We are proud of Irish sporting and cultural prowess. In comparison, our economic performance is puny.

But then, the two kinds of contest are arranged so differently in Ireland. Sporting and cultural competitions are open, they are run competitively, they have impartial rules and winning is on merit. A wise use of talent is rewarded.

But admission to economic contests is often restricted, their operation is biased and subject to improper influences, there is leaning rather than levelling of playing fields, and merit doesn't matter enough. Wasteful use of resources is not penalised.

These practices have dogged Irish economic performance for decades at least. But institutions can be reformed. Lessons can be learned. A more dynamic economy is there for the building.

4

THE DREAM ECONOMY

Introduction
It is useful to examine the workings of a simplified market which is devoid of complications, a Dream Economy. This offers an idealised picture against which the performance of actually-available options — the Degenerate, Decree and Designer Economies — can be judged.

A market turns out to be nothing more than a device — a particular institutional framework — to co-ordinate the millions of interdependent decisions of consumers and producers. To achieve that co-ordination, three key mechanisms are used: (a) prices, which reveal consumer tastes and producer costs; (b) profits, which reward suppliers who meet consumer demands cheaply; and (c) competition, which encourages efficiency by restraining costs and prices.

Such an economy, when functioning well, rewards participants for productive economic behaviour. It is flexible, innovative and decentralised, leaving decisions to the household and the firm. But the market performs much less well in terms of social equity. It is highly productive precisely because it gives large rewards to those who can and choose to be productive. If offers only meagre rewards to the disadvantaged who have little saleable labour or other productive resources.

How a Simple Competitive Market Works
Achieving an efficient economy is all about co-ordination. Discovering what consumers want to consume, allocating resources to the different parts of the economy to meet that demand, selecting the more productive techniques from among available methods, and reconciling the millions of individual producers' and

consumers' intentions, so that what suppliers want to supply broadly matches what consumers want to demand, and vice versa. Without a powerful co-ordinating mechanism, there would be gross wastage, with resources or products lying unused in some parts of the economy, unsatisfied demands in other parts, and many dissatisfied people in-between.

The tasks may seem abstract, but in fact they concern everyday decisions. Every night the people of Ireland go to bed confident that when they awake next morning, the shops will be full of food, clothes, petrol and the countless other items sent here from places thousands of miles away. But how can this be? How do Middle Eastern oil producers and Asian textile firms know what to produce for the Irish market? No one is responsible for planning on behalf of everyone else. Each supplier makes an independent decision. So why are shops not empty one morning and overflowing the next?

If Irish residents decide to start to eat more meat, how do the makers of animal feed know to increase production so that the extra animals can be fed? How do the farmers, the meat factories, the refrigeration plants, the lorry drivers, the butchers and all the others co-ordinate their businesses? How can they possibly do so, when most of them do not know each other?

How is it all achieved?

Some mechanism must be at work behind the scenes to ensure that tastes are discovered, resources allocated, techniques chosen and supply and demand brought into line with each other, with as little waste as possible. Competitive markets rely on three instruments to efficiently co-ordinate economic activity: prices, profits and competition.

However, the operation of a market first presupposes a legal framework, with clear-cut ownership rights and an effective way to enforce business agreements. There is no reason to produce if one can get away with simply stealing. Governments provide a legal and administrative framework for the market system. Before a government extends itself into other areas, it should get these fundamentals right. Some argue that honest and well-run public administration is the scarcest economic resource of all. As the example of Russia today shows, a government which is unable to maintain commercial law and order will soon find its economy run by criminals. But this is a failing of the state's responsibilities rather than a defect of the market.

The concept of private property, and its specific protection in the Irish constitution, is sometimes the subject of criticism in Ireland. This criticism is not always well-founded since secure private ownership of goods and other property facilitates their efficient use. Property that is not privately owned is often misused: two current Irish examples are over-fishing in the sea and allowing sheep to over-graze on mountain land. No rational person would overuse a resource they themselves owned. But as neither the sea nor the mountain is owned by anybody in particular, each farmer and fisherman works them as intensively as possible, since it is not their job to see that such resources are not overworked to the point of destruction.

When Prices are Fixed, Economies are Broken: The Role of Prices in a Market Economy

Prices are a subtle system for gathering information and for keeping supply and demand in approximate balance.

People reveal their preferences by their spending decisions. They are willing to pay more for things that they value more, and less for goods they like less. So, straightaway, merely by looking at prices in the market we can tell that the community values Porsches more highly than it values parsnips. If farmers tried to sell a parsnip for the price of a Porsche, no one would buy and the farmer would be left to draw his own conclusions about what the public considered a parsnip to be worth. Prices therefore act as a kind of information signal in an economy.

But the information flows are in both directions. Producers reveal their costs by their pricing decisions, transmitting cost information to consumers.

Supporters of Soviet-style economies failed to grasp the economic role played by market-determined prices. They believed that fixed prices were desirable. Some boasted that the price of bread, and the rent charged for a Moscow flat, had not changed from the 1920s to the 1980s. While at first this sounds delightful, it is a bit like selling Porsches for fifty pence. Problems quickly develop. An unofficial (or "black") market soon forms, and the underpriced good becomes unobtainable at the official price. To actually get bread or a flat, a price much nearer their true value must be paid. Also, bread in 1980 cannot be profitably produced at 1920 prices, so there is a huge hidden subsidy in the bread price which has to be collected from some other part of the economy. If the objective is to make bread affordable to the poor, it is not necessary or sensible to make it cheap for everyone.

Provided that they are free to adjust, prices will reflect both consumers' tastes and producers' costs, and they will settle at a point where buyers and sellers are willing to transact a certain level of business. If conditions change, prices adjust to the changes. For instance, as incomes rise, there is a change in the mix of products that consumers wish to purchase and the price that they are willing to pay for them. So sustained price movements contain information for existing and potential suppliers about consumers' evolving demands. By watching prices, suppliers can learn about consumer tastes. Likewise, by observing prices, consumers learn about the evolution of producers' costs.

If there were no prices, or if prices were fixed, some other way of collecting the information about tastes and costs embodied in market prices would need to be found. In the 1950s it was thought that computers could be used to process the necessary information. But the problem is more serious than that. Computers can only calculate, they cannot extract the truth. If you are not paying, there is a strong incentive not to tell the truth. The attraction of the market is that prices reflect information without it needing to be directly collected. Prices save the cumbersome, costly and, in the end, probably impossible task of collecting taste information from consumers and cost information from producers over the entire spectrum of existing and potential products.

That prices have an economic role to play in a well-functioning economy probably sounds very obvious and dull, but it is a lesson often ignored. Many prices are controlled. Professions try to set a floor for fees, and trade unions wish to maintain a "going rate" for the job. The EU sets the price of a large number of agricultural products, and the government decides what fees — if any — Irish third-level colleges can charge. The information in these controlled prices certainly tells you about the government's preferences, but nothing very reliable can be deduced about consumers' preferences or true production costs.

Third-level fees offer an instructive example. If set on the open market they would reveal which courses were popular with students and how much it actually costs to educate different types of graduate. Without fees, all this information is lost. (Clearly, the level of college fees raises many other issues besides the information they reveal but, since the latter is not obvious, that aspect is emphasised here.)

To control prices, it is necessary to control the operation of the market. To keep prices artificially high somebody must mop up the resulting excess supply, otherwise that surplus would drive prices back down to their old level. Likewise, if prices are kept artificially low, someone must make up the supply shortfall or the shortage will drive prices back up.

In Europe, the EU policy of high food prices would normally have brought a flood of cheaper imports from countries outside the Union, leaving European farmers unable to sell their expensive produce. To maintain fixed prices, the EU had to suppress competition from lower-cost suppliers by restricting imports. Likewise, the medical and legal professions could never maintain their high incomes (above those merited by skill differentials) without being able to keep out the large numbers of potential entrants who would be attracted by those very salaries. Similarly, the bank officials union has kept up the pay of bank clerks by its closed-shop power to prevent banks from employing someone for less. The result has been high prices paid by Irish consumers for food, for medical and legal services and by way of bank charges. An individual or group able to restrict competition in this way will of course do so, but it is not in the interest of ordinary consumers that they be allowed to.

If the information contained in prices is lost, it will be hard to know what consumers really want (would be willing to pay for) and what it is productive for society to supply.

A national planner, for instance, who lacks information about production costs and consumer demand, would not know what instructions to give to subordinates. In the USSR, the planning system took over an existing economy and carried on meeting existing demands. In a static environment, the match between production and consumer demand may initially have been quite good. But as tastes evolved and production costs altered, problems inevitably arose. Changes in tastes were not discovered and there was no incentive to find ways to reduce costs or to innovate.

Without market prices, activity can be privately profitable but socially loss-making. A dramatic example, and a true story, concerns the Soviet Union. In the last days of communism a European politician visited the USSR and reported that he met a woman at a street stall selling melons. He asked her where she had got them. The woman explained that she grew the melons in her garden in a town 200 miles away. Each week she picked some and flew by Aeroflot to the town where she sold them at her stall all day, and then flew home in the evening. This was a profitable transaction for her because, under communism, Aeroflot prices were kept absurdly low and bore no rational relationship to the real expense of transporting this woman. Naturally, for Soviet society, this woman's transactions were enormously loss-making when the true cost of air travel is taken into account. But the melon-seller couldn't know this because — in the Western sense of the term — there were no prices in the USSR. Without market prices, something may continue to be supplied for which there would be little or no demand if the full price were charged.

The profitability (productivity) or otherwise of an activity will be apparent when prices are free to fluctuate and are not restricted by legal or administrative controls. This may sound innocuous, but in fact it is not. The implications come to light as soon as the principle is applied to that most special price — wages and salaries. For just the same reasons that hold for other resources, it is generally unwise to regulate wages. If the price is set at a level where the labour costs more than its value to the employer, the labour will just not be used.

There is a better way to achieve income equity than wage controls. (This argument is set out more fully in Chapter 8 on productive jobs but it can be summarised here.) Leave the wage to settle at the market rate. Then improve the short-term position of those citizens who have only low-value labour to sell by a redistribution of some income through the tax-and-welfare system to top up their living standards. In the medium term, the value of their labour can be increased through training. In this way the workers and society retain their jobs without living standards falling towards or below impoverishment levels. In contrast, the wage-fixing alternative destroys jobs, dumps thousands into long-term dole-dependency, enlarges the burden of welfare on taxpayers, and, at best, leaves the living standards of the disadvantaged no higher.

In addition to information gathering, prices carry out a second important function. Consumers' and producers' decisions interact with one another: buyers cannot buy more than suppliers are willing to sell and producers cannot sell at a price consumers are unwilling to pay. Each side's behaviour affects the other side. What ensures that these decisions will all be compatible? Some co-ordinating device must bring markets into balance so that demand and supply are broadly matched. That mechanism is prices.

In a glut, price falls stimulate demand while discouraging supply until the glut is eliminated. In a shortage, price rises discourage demand while stimulating supply until the shortage is again eliminated. Of course, these adjustments generally need time to occur.

When artificial shortages drove up the price of oil in the 1970s, it was not possible to discover new sources of supply or to abandon energy-intensive production methods overnight. But it certainly was possible to do so over the medium term, and exactly this happened. In contrast, there was no self-correcting mechanism when the agricultural policy of the EU made food artificially expensive. Predictably, demand has declined while farmers have rushed to increase supply, leading to the CAP food mountains. But in this case, prices have not adjusted, the imbalances did not disappear, and there has been huge waste. The absurdity of the policy, the impatience of taxpayers, and the looming Uruguay GATT agreement eventually combined to force some modifications to the CAP.

Prices play two economic roles in the economy. They discreetly gather information and they adjust to clear a market. Both functions facilitate productivity and minimise waste.

Fat Cats, Fur Coats and Ferraris?: The Role of Profits in a Market Economy

Profits are not a gift to capitalists for which society gets nothing in return. They too are a device to promote productivity: they are an incentive to meet consumers' needs using the fewest inputs.

A person who wishes to make a profit must produce something which consumers actually want. It may be possible to sell thousands of tons of unwanted food into a non-market system like agricultural intervention, but in a market economy you must offer consumers something they are prepared to pay for. The profit motive therefore helps to point producers in the direction of consumers' needs. It is an economic form of democracy, although only a limited one.

In the absence of profits, consumers may be completely ignored. Jeffrey Sachs, a leading US economist who spoke in Dublin in late 1994, described the planned economies of eastern Europe (whose post-Communist governments he has advised) as follows. First, they built steel mills to make steel. Then, they built factories and turned steel into mining equipment. Then they dug coal mines with the mining machinery and brought coal to the surface. And the coal? Well, that got burned in the mill to make more steel, to make more machinery, to mine more coal, to make more steel. A lot of activity, a lot of resources used up, but to no avail whatever in terms of offering useful goods to citizens.

Aside from attending to consumers, a profit-seeking producer will be impelled to choose the cheapest method of producing a product, and to use inputs sparingly. In this way, there is an incentive to use more plentiful and so cheaper resources and to economise on the scarcer and dearer inputs.

Profits link payment to performance. Otherwise, staff and managers are neither punished for failings nor rewarded for success. A senior official of the (now disbanded) British Communist Party, who has switched his allegiance to capitalism, admitted frankly in 1990 that the problem with communist planning was that "there is something missing — motivation for the individual".

Profit stimulates the efficient use of resources. Without it, efficiency must slacken. With given resources, this means less is produced. And since we can only consume what we produce, ineffi-cient production must reduce consumption and lower average living standards in the community. It is in all our interests that resources be used efficiently, and this is exactly what the profit system rewards.

But surely the profit motive isn't the only rule for promoting productivity? Couldn't some other rule do even better? Well, much of the twentieth century has been spent looking for such a rule and none has been found. However, along the way many rules that are immensely inferior to the profit motive have been discovered, to the impoverishment of the populations used as economic guinea pigs.

If there were no profits, what alternative target could firms be asked to meet? Could farmers be paid by acreage? But payment by acreage would be wasteful. It would then make sense to sow seeds very far apart, covering a lot of acres but not producing much of a harvest. Would harvest tonnage be a better basis for payment? But in collectivised agriculture, where the farmer does not pay for the materials used, payment by weight would make it worthwhile for farmers to increase output by pouring all the seeds, fertilisers and labour they could get into their farms, with-out regard to the cost of those resources. That would also be wasteful. On the other hand, an instruction to farmers to maxi-mise output whilst economising on inputs would just be a redis-covery of the concept of profit.

The same problems would arise in manufacturing. If workers and managers in a thumbtack factory were paid according to the number of thumbtacks produced, the factory would make lots of small short thumbtacks. These would be of very little use to any-one. If the plant were instructed to produce thumbtacks of a cer-tain length, it would use low-quality materials. And so on. Only if the planners tell the factory that rewards depend on the factory's output being saleable on the open market, against the output of rivals, and at a cost no higher than that of rival factories, will it be worthwhile for the factory to produce good quality products as cheaply as possible. But, of course, this just amounts to telling the factory to maximise profit, so why not allow it to do so directly?

Marxists argued that production should reflect need not profit. They failed to realise that without profit to guide production and to stimulate efficiency, the amount of production available to meet needs might be much smaller than otherwise. The history of the USSR and its satellite states has demonstrated that a policy of "production for need" could barely generate enough food to feed the population, let alone to support western-style living standards.

Many people think of profits as a repugnant and dispensable boil on the face of society. This is a mistaken view. Profit is an encouragement for consumer needs to be met, and for costs to be contained. In its absence, there would certainly be fewer cigars and fur coats, but there would also be many unhappy consumers unable to obtain the products they wished to consume and paying excessive prices for those goods they could obtain.

The pursuit of profit promotes productivity. But profits, like any other payment, should not be larger than the minimum necessary to get the job done. A producer who is trying to maximise profits will have every reason to push down costs and push up prices as far as possible. This could mean taking advantage of suppliers and consumers. To prevent such a result, it is necessary for suppliers to be able to turn to other (better paying) buyers and for consumers to be able to switch to other (less costly) sellers. In other words, competition is needed to restrain the profit motive.

Profit is not a four-letter word. It is just a way of encouraging producers to meet consumers' needs while using the fewest resources to do so.

"Put 'em Under Pressure!": The Role of Competition in a Market Economy

There is a popular view that competition is chaotic, uncoordinated, wasteful duplication. Economists, ever perverse, think the opposite: competition reduces waste.

Competition means that an enterprise may be threatened by the lower cost and selling price of a competitor, adding an extra spur to efficiency. It is the degree of this competitive pressure, more than anything else, that distinguishes different market economies. The US, Ireland and Greece are all market-based economies. But some — the more competitive ones — demand far more of their firms and citizens than their less competitive rivals.

Like the rest of us, entrepreneurs prefer a quiet life. In business, low levels of competition produce a much quieter life than high levels, while also delivering larger profits to entrepreneurs. Naturally, therefore, if businesses are left to themselves they will seek to restrict competition and to keep out potential new entrants. For just this reason, the matter cannot be left to the businesses concerned and the public authorities must pursue a policy of competitive (rather than "free") markets.

This issue is not one of public versus private sectors. It is quite possible for public companies to perform well, provided they are operating in a competitive market and are given no political privileges. Indeed, it is necessary for them to perform well if they face competition and if they want to survive. In Ireland, however, public sector companies have typically been granted monopoly status, and they could rely on a bail-out from the public purse. So the market's pressure for high performance was absent. Irish state industries, like CIE, Aer Lingus, Telecom and An Post, have exacted a heavy price from Irish consumers down the years. When they charged high prices, there was nowhere else for the consumer to go. When they lost money, they just billed the taxpayer. As long as they had a captive market and a compliant exchequer, there was no reason for these companies to change their behaviour. In Ireland, "public enterprise" has often been a licence to lose money. Now that competition is looming or, in some cases, has arrived many of these former monopolies are in severe difficulties.

Competition drives prices down to the lowest level at which a business can cover its costs. In doing so, competition reveals the true minimum cost of producing something: the cost of the resources that went into its production. If prices reflect costs, consumers only buy a product if its value to them is greater than the cost of the resources used up in its production.

Unrestricted entry to and exit from industries allows firms to produce the most profitable products, namely those for which consumers have indicated the greatest priority by being willing to pay the highest prices. The increase in supply to which this very process leads then dampens down prices and chips away at "excess" profits. In this way competition prevents profits from being permanently excessive and, in the course of doing so, signals to other potential entrants that there is now less of a shortage in the industry in question.

Freedom of exit explains why over the past thirty years more and more Irish farmers have moved out of agriculture. The income farmers could expect to earn from working a farm with other members of their family was much less than their expected earnings in other parts of the Irish (or international) economy. So they left the agricultural sector and moved to another.

Freedom of entry explains why the prices of personal computers have fallen dramatically in the early 1990s. The biggest single reason for these reductions is that many new manufacturers have been free to enter that market and to undercut the price of the original suppliers. Could we expect the same to have happened if IBM had been able to restrict entry? Certainly not.

If cinema owners had directly or indirectly controlled the market for all film products, would videos have been able to take away so much of the cinemas' traditional business?

If we are better-off for being able to buy cheaper PCs and to rent videos, shouldn't there be a presumption in favour of competition in other parts of the economy too? It is possible to get a new phone in a day in the US; shouldn't someone willing to offer this service in Ireland be allowed to do so? If a bank wants to open on Saturday, or on any day, should its rivals or the IBOA be able to stop it?

Competition reduces waste. It obliges companies to produce at least as cheaply as their rivals. And it stimulates innovation. New entrants are free to enter the market and offer an improved or cheaper product. Competition keeps firms on their toes.

Equity

It is clear that a well-functioning market is very good at promoting productivity. But what about securing social equity? Can the market be relied on to spread economic opportunities and incomes widely throughout the community?

Only very unevenly, in fact. In its responsiveness to consumer demand, the market can be viewed as a form of economic democracy. But there is a critical difference between buying and voting. In a democratic election, each citizen has a single, equal vote. In the market, incomes differ dramatically and therefore so does a consumer's power to command a response from the market.

An economy composed exclusively of private markets distributes income in only two ways. First, on the basis of the market value of a person's labour. This depends on the person's skills as well as the demand for those skills. A brain surgeon can typically sell their services for considerably more than can a person loading boxes onto trucks. They can also sell their services for a lot more than most (highly skilled) mathematicians earn, because of the much larger demand for medical services. Secondly, income is earned by wealth-holders. This could be interest paid on bank deposits or dividends received on shares.

In an economy populated only by the diligent, the skilled and the rich, by people who start life already wealthy or who possess or can acquire valuable labour skills, social equity would not be a pressing problem. But no economy meets such a requirement. And in a system of purely private markets those of little productivity — the low-skilled, the no-skilled, the slow-coach, the old-aged, the sick — will earn correspondingly little. Sometimes this may be very little indeed.

In a market-only system, such people would have to depend on support from relatives or from charity to survive. A social democrat, who grants equal value to every citizen, regardless of their wealth or their productivity, would be unwilling to leave income distribution totally to the vagaries of the market.

To ensure even a modest degree of equity, social democrats would want to supplement the market with a safety net to protect the income of those unable to work and to boost the income of those unable to earn much of an income from work.

The response of the hard-hearted is to say that those who contribute little should expect to collect little. Arguably, this would be fair enough for people who deliberately refused to acquire skills that would give them a decent income. But are there really so many such people?

Those who think not will want to supplement the operation of the market to boost a disadvantaged person's chance to acquire skills, and to set an income floor for those who, even if through their own fault, remain unskilled.

Market mechanisms enhance efficiency. But those who are also concerned about equity need to adjust market outcomes in the areas of welfare, income redistribution and opportunity. Not even a Dream Economy can do so through the unaided market.

Conclusion

A well-functioning market has three attractive features: it promotes productivity, it is accountable to consumers and it is flexible and innovative.

Prices, profits and competition each act to make the economy productive. Prices *reveal*: they show what it has cost to produce something, and so whether or not a particular activity is productively transforming resources of lesser value into an item of greater worth. Without market prices, the true productivity of a particular activity is extremely difficult to assess. Profits *reward*: suppliers make money only when there have customers for their products at the prices being charged, and more money is made by those who economise on inputs and employ the best production techniques. Competition *restrains*: it prevents overcharging and exploitation of customers and suppliers, while the threat from actual and potential rivals encourages high performance and innovation. The more that each of these mechanisms is free to work, the more productive will be an economy's performance. Insofar as these mechanisms are restricted, lower productivity and greater waste can be expected.

The operation of these mechanisms is not obvious. Indeed, to many people they are completely hidden and the market appears to be a chaotic jungle without any order. By ignoring the economic roles of prices, profits and competition, those who advocate fixed prices, capped profits and restricted competition can be totally surprised at the harmful and quite unintended side-effects their proposals produce.

The market favours the survival of the productive. If a business is income-creating, it is rewarded with a profit and continues in operation. If it is loss-making (income-destroying), it must improve productivity or disappear. There is no escape from the need to be productive: no subsidies are available nor can markets be rigged.

The result is higher living standards than would be found in a non-market economy. But it is not Utopia. Like any human institution, a market regime has its defects and its costs. While the market offers prosperity, it certainly doesn't guarantee it. In many respects it is a hard taskmaster. Many people find the hustle-bustle of the modern economy quite alienating. But all the alternatives have costs too. For those willing to take command of their lives, the market offers a promising basis for a better way forward.

If that was all there was to be said, we would already have nearly come to the end of this book. There is, however, a practical problem with this kind of simple market economy. It is only found in textbooks. Only under the simple conditions of the Dream Economy will the interests of private individuals be aligned with the social goal of high productivity.

But, of course, the actual world is more complicated. A private market, left to itself (the Degenerate Economy), would diverge considerably from a Dream Economy. An actual private market would be less efficient than its Dream counterpart while suffering from the same or greater social inequity.

However, even though the Dream Economy is not on offer, it nonetheless suggests some conclusions about running an economy. Prices should be free to adjust; they should not be fixed by governments, business associations or unions. As long as markets are competitive, the profit motive should be allowed free rein. And healthy markets are competitive markets; a lack of competition seriously injures the public interest. Competition needs to be preserved where it exists and extended to where it does not. But those who care about equitable treatment of fellow-citizens will need to supplement the operation of the market in this area.

Having explained how a Dream market would operate, the next three chapters turn to consider the Degenerate, the Decree and the Designer Economies to see whether they would be able to match the private market's productivity and if they would be more successful in delivering social equity. In considering these options, other conclusions about economic policy are reached.

Then, in Chapter 9, these conclusions are compared with current Irish practice.

5

THE DEGENERATE ECONOMY

Introduction
The last chapter explained the workings of a simple Dream Economy which was found to be very successful at achieving high productivity but weak at promoting social equity.

But, of course, the actual world is more complicated. A private market under laissez faire (left to itself) would be subject to important breakdowns or "market failures". The result would be a Degenerate Economy: capitalism without competition. The characteristics of such a market would diverge considerably from those of a Dream Economy. It would be less efficient but no better, and probably worse, at promoting social equity.

In a Degenerate Economy, it would no longer be true that the unaided market would necessarily align private interests with the social goal of high productivity.

The Inefficiencies of a Degenerate Economy
Markets cannot do everything. They are not such perfectly self-regulating mechanisms that they can be turned over entirely to prices, profits and competition and thereafter left to their own devices.

A private market might not produce smooth economic growth, free of severe booms and busts. In which case, unutilised labour and capital would be wasted. It might not be able to safeguard competition from the kinds of cosy arrangements that companies like to reach amongst themselves. So consumers might not get the lowest possible prices. In a private market some costly activities, like pollution, would have no price and so socially-wasteful activities might be privately profitable. Furthermore, some kinds of goods and services are consumed collectively (public parks, street lighting, national defence, civil administration). In a private market, who would pay for these, when the non-payer would have the same access to them as the payer? The market is bad at providing "collective goods". In a private market, a lack of good information about the calibre of experts might mean that fraudsters, quacks and other poor-quality suppliers would fail to be weeded out. Finally, the private market might generate a highly unequal distribution of income and of access to basic healthcare and educational services. Whole classes of people could essentially be denied the opportunity to participate in the economy. Unlike the Dream Economy, in a Degenerate Economy there would be many deviations between the private interest and the community interest.

Because a Degenerate economy is a purely private market system, it cannot on its own address the kinds of market failures to which such systems are prone. These different types of market failure and their consequences are outlined below. Ways of resolving these problems — where they can be resolved — are discussed in the chapter on the Designer Economy.

Stabilising the Economic Cycle

Over time, economies swing from recovery to recession and back to recovery. These cycles are sometimes gentle and sometimes sharp. During recessions, labour and machinery lie unused and therefore wasted. These costs are magnified if workers who are too long out of work find it very difficult to re-enter employment. A citizen's potential to be productive may then be lost permanently to the economy, while the welfare payments to which they are entitled become a permanent imposition on other workers.

Nor is joblessness just wasteful. It damages social equity, since unemployment affects already-disadvantaged groups most severely. Even for privileged groups, a high-unemployment society is likely to be a much coarser place in which to live.

So there are good reasons to wish to see unemployment kept low. Unfortunately, unemployment cannot be pushed down to zero, or anywhere very close to it. There are two reasons why this is so. First, economies are constantly changing; firms close down and others set up. At any moment, a certain proportion of the labour force will be in-between jobs and searching for work. This unemployment is necessary if an economy is to adjust to changing consumer demand and changing technology. If this were the only kind of unemployment, it would mean that many people could expect to experience several spells of unemployment over their lifetime, interspersed between periods of work. The spells out of work would be relatively short. This kind of unemployment, which was typical of the 1960s, seems rather mild compared to European unemployment today.

A second reason why unemployment will be above a negligible level is because of the effect that rock-bottom unemployment would have on inflation. One factor influencing the growth of wages and other prices is the state of the economy. In a booming economy, suppliers, including workers, will push for higher prices. If this behaviour becomes generalised, inflation will accelerate. There are a number of economic reasons to resist inflation but one important reason is that the public dislikes it intensely, both for its own sake and because of the economic disruption associated with it. Those who lived through the early 1980s (when consumer inflation exceeded 20 per cent) will remember how opinion polls at the time showed inflation to be at the very top of the public's concerns. For this and other reasons, it is desirable to keep inflation in low single figures. Historically, that has been difficult to do as soon as real economic growth exceeded, in Ireland's case, say, 5-6 per cent. But economic growth at those rates would still leave some unemployment in the system. In the US, economists believe that today a rate of economic expansion which pushes unemployment below about 5 per cent causes inflation to accelerate. This sets a floor to how low unemployment can be driven by those who wish also to keep a lid on inflation.

It is therefore not possible for governments to decide that unemployment will be kept at some arbitrarily low level, if they are also concerned about objectives such a flexible economy and stable prices.

Suppose we accept that there is an unemployment floor. Will a private economy be able on its own to keep unemployment close to this level? This is the subject of decades-long disputes amongst economists. Some believe that an "active" economic policy could deliver lower average unemployment. An active policy means either a central bank adjusting interest rates, or a government adjusting its spending, towards a medium-term goal of as strong a rate of economic growth as will not stoke up inflationary fires. Other economists believe that since the public authorities are un-likely to be able to improve on the market-determined level of unemployment, and can certainly do worse than the market, it is best to leave well enough alone.

However, for Ireland, this disagreement is actually beside the point. First, interest rates and levels of public borrowing are in-creasingly being set at European rather than at national level. Second, the context in which these arguments arise concerns whether unemployment should, or should not, be pushed down from, say, 7 per cent to 6 per cent or from 6 per cent to 5 per cent. This is not the kind of unemployment problem facing Ireland to-day.

Over half of Irish unemployment is now long-term (lasting more than 12 months) and is essentially unrelated to the economic cycle. Nudging an interest rate here or some public spending there is not going to make any appreciable impact on the kind of unemployment from which Ireland suffers.

The causes of long-term joblessness, insofar as they are under-stood, have different, deeper and much more intractable roots. (They are also far from being exclusively attributable to the mar-ket). The issues involved will be discussed in Chapter 8 on pro-ductive job creation.

As far as the Degenerate Economy, and short-term unemploy-ment, are concerned, we can say that a purely private market system might at times suffer from overly-severe booms and busts and this would be both wasteful and inequitable. A prudent cen-tral bank with a clear mandate to dampen down recoveries while easing up in a recession could improve economic performance in a modest way. But here we are only talking about a couple of per-centage points one way or the other. Neither interest rates (i.e. monetary policy) nor public spending (i.e. fiscal policy) is a magic wand which can deliver whatever economic targets happen to be desired by policymakers.

Unfortunately for Ireland, government spending policy in the 1970s and 1980s managed to exacerbate, not dampen, the economic cycle in the economy. Although Irish state involvement in the economy has often been justified in terms of economic stabilisation, its effects in recent decades have been exactly the opposite.

Monopolies and Cartels

A cartel is a group of companies behaving as though it were a single firm. Cartels are therefore very similar to monopolies. But what is the harm of either?

In a competitive market, a supplier can earn a profit only by finding a way to convert resources into something for which consumers are willing to pay more than those resources cost. However, in the absence of competition, a market system permits firms and individuals to collect profits in another way: by rigging prices. The selling price can be driven up to excessive levels and kept there because potential rivals who would undercut these high prices are prevented from entering the industry. Prices no longer reflect minimum costs. This has two consequences: some consumers pay more and some have to do without altogether.

Compared to a competitive market, a monopolist can sell at a higher price. This redistributes income to the producer at the expense of those consumers who previously could purchase the good more cheaply. Since the producer's gain and the consumers' loss cancel out, arguably, overall welfare is unchanged.

But there is a second effect of a monopoly which is a pure loss. Higher prices cause some consumers to stop buying a product because they no longer consider it good value. The economy has been distorted. A monopolist's high prices cause the market to shrink. The loss to consumers (from being unable to purchase the good) has no offsetting gain to the monopolist.

Less business is always conducted at high prices. By pushing up prices, monopolies push down the amount of buying and selling that takes place. Under monopoly, the economy shrinks.

Telephone charges are an example. Outside business, people use the phone less when charges are high (at "peak" times of the day) than when they are low, in the evenings and at weekends. Why? Because the high charge discourages use of the phone. Calls that would be considered worthwhile at the lower price are not worth making at the higher price. Higher prices discourage consumption.

The same holds for legal services. The law is at present unaffordable to many people. The costs of a large legal action, requiring many days in the High Court, runs into tens of thousands of pounds. Fewer restrictive practices, and less expensive law, would make legal services more affordable and more used (although no doubt still relatively expensive).

In a competitive market, overpricing would not last. Somebody would enter the market and undercut the high price, driving it down towards the level of costs. All those who would benefit from consuming the product at its true cost could again afford to do so. But undercutting hinges on freedom to enter and leave an industry. If there is restricted entry, the supplier can overcharge without fear of losing business to a rival. Exactly the same thing occurs when a number of suppliers come together to form a cartel and behave as though they were a monopolist.

This is why society needs to minimise monopoly. In industries where competitive conditions can be sustained naturally and where freedom of entry alone is sufficient to maintain competition, the private market can be left to itself. But where there is evidence of anti-competitive conditions, other policies are needed. By definition, the private sector cannot provide these, and so tough competition laws are required.

In what kind of economy is the risk of monopolisation greatest? In a small economy. A large domestic market has room for many middling-sized suppliers. None will dominate and there will be too many firms to easily negotiate a cartel between them. A conspiracy of the many is harder to organise than a conspiracy of the few. However, in a small economy like Ireland's, there will often be room for only a few suppliers. If any one firm can become significantly larger than the others, it may then be able to force its rivals to the wall. Alternatively, it may force the other suppliers into a market-sharing arrangement.

A key issue in maintaining competition, especially in small economies, is liberalised international trade. The domestic dominance of a large firm will be much less harmful if it faces genuine foreign competition. Unfortunately, Mr de Valera's policy of import controls delivered the Irish economy into the hands of a cluster of domestic suppliers. We have not yet completely recovered from this blunder.

There is one possible exception to the general presumption in favour of competition. In some industries, there may be a what is called a "natural monopoly". This means that the costs *per unit produced* fall sharply as production is increased. In other words, the product or service can be provided more cheaply by one very large-scale producer than by several middling-sized ones. Arguably, the ESB and Telecom Éireann could be cases in point. Building a power station to heat a single house is not an economic proposition, whereas heating half the country from one is very cheap for each house. Likewise, laying a cable network to connect half-a-dozen phone-owners sprinkled around the country would be absurdly costly to each user; doing so for millions of users is comparatively cheap.

The "natural monopoly" justification cannot, however, be offered for most Irish semi-state monopolies. Air and surface transport are not natural monopolies, nor are broadcasting, insurance, banking or turf production. There is no "natural monopoly" basis for most Irish semi-state activity, and so no good economic case for their monopoly privileges.

Even for the ESB and Telecom, the aspects of these businesses to which the natural monopoly feature really applies are the distribution networks, rather than the production facilities. It is doubtful if duplication of the electricity power grid, or the telephone service's phone cabling network, would add to competition sufficiently to warrant the enormous extra cost. However, it can make sense to have many phone companies or electricity generators use the same distribution network. For this to be possible, it may be necessary to take the networks into collective ownership so that access to these facilities is available on an equal basis to all potential users. Otherwise, the monopolist will look for ways to drive away potential rivals. It will be remembered that in the early 1990s, the price RTE wanted to charge its commercial rival TV3 for the use of the national broadcasting network was one that TV3 said it could not afford to pay. In the end, no rival to RTE materialised.

Except for "natural monopolies", where keeping costs low justifies the existence of few or one producer, monopolies distort the economy by causing higher prices and a smaller market, at the consumer's and at society's expense. Firms and individuals should be free to compete since monopolies and cartels use resources less productively than they could be used.

Of course, monopolies and cartels are not solely a market failure. Indeed, the most secure cartel of all is one underwritten by the state. For instance, in Latin America and in Africa, economies have often drifted into a deal between the state and the business sector. The state guarantees the position of certain favoured firms and the firms bankroll or otherwise facilitate political leaders. Such countries are primarily interested in redistributing income rather than in generating it. The redistribution in question is not, of course, to the poor, but to a small business and political élite that depends on the state and on which the state élite depends.

A Degenerate Economy may not be able to safeguard competition, the foundation on which market productivity rests. Only carefully designed legislation and, where necessary, regulation can protect against such an outcome. In its absence, cartels may become dominant, especially in a small economy.

Unfortunately, the Irish authorities have a very poor record in policing competition in the private sector. The position is even worse in the public sector, where the state has actively created a large number of monopolies. Whatever the motives for Irish state involvement in the economy, evidently they can have had little to do with tackling cartelisation.

Spillovers
Some costs and benefits are not borne by the people who cause them but "spill over" onto third parties. The market has no incentive to minimise such costs (as it would have with others) since it doesn't pay for them.

Normally, if one person wishes to use resources belonging to another, such as their labour services or their land, a payment must be made. However, when resources are owned collectively, no prices attach to them. Clean air and peace and quiet are not anybody's personal property and so may be "used" without any payment being made. Pollution and smoking use up previously clean air but there is no charge to the user. Loud music from a neighbour's house in the early hours of the morning disturbs peace and quiet, again at no monetary cost to the noisy party.

Spillovers need not be negative. Positive examples include the pleasure obtained from a neighbour's beautiful garden, or the windfall rise in property values in parts of Dublin which found themselves adjacent to the DART railway. These benefits are obtained free of charge.

When a person does not bear the full cost of their actions, they will engage in more of such activities than if they had to shoulder all the expense themselves. A person who would be sparing in the use of costly resources may be extravagant in using "free" air, "free" water and any other "free" facilities. Conversely, if the benefit from a person's behaviour accrues to another party, there will be less such behaviour than when the reward is received by the person responsible for the deed.

Take the cost of running a car. This is greater than the cost to the owner. In addition to the owner's costs (purchase price, fuel, tax and insurance), there are also the costs of car pollution which fall onto third parties and of road building which is borne by the taxpayer. In the same way that higher car or fuel prices would discourage the use of private transport, likewise, a car owner who had to pay for pollution (or road building) costs would choose a lower level of car usage. But, in a Degenerate Economy, these costs are ignored and so a higher level of polluting activity takes place. A private market has no mechanism to resolve this problem.

The pollution that a factory belches out onto neighbouring areas is a cost of production. But depending on the prevailing laws, the factory may be able to entirely ignore it. If the company had to compensate its polluted neighbours it would have to include that expenditure in its production costs and charge the consumer a higher price. But it does not do so. Private costs therefore do not properly reflect social costs. An activity that is privately profitable could be socially less profitable or even loss-making.

The cost of spillovers should not be thought to be negligible. The European Commission has estimated that the cost of transport spillovers alone (pollution, accidents, traffic jams), today amount to between 3 per cent and 4 per cent of the Community GDP, or some £150 billion each year.

Social benefits from a highly-educated population, to the extent that these exist over and above the private benefits that a student obtains (and takes account of), would be a positive spillover. However, the claim that such benefits exist is controversial. Educational spillovers are more often assumed than demonstrated. But if they could be shown to exist, it would not then be desirable to leave education completely to a private market system in which the individual students would fail to take account of the total benefits of education (the private benefit plus the public spillover). The student cannot charge the community for the spillover benefit to help the student to pay for that education. Consequently, we would expect to see a less than optimal supply of education from a social point of view.

The market cannot deal with activities for which there are no prices. Strictly, this is not so much a failing of the market as the absence of a market for the effects in question. One possible solution would be to mimic the way in which a well-functioning market would operate. If the value of the spillovers could be measured then, in principle, the public authorities could levy *fees* on certain activities (to reflect the neglected spillover costs) or offer subsidies on others (to take account of positive spillovers). This would adjust the prices faced by decision-makers to their true social levels. Pollution might be charged for, and subsidies offered for education. This would be an example of how prices could be used, that is, modified, by the public authorities to achieve the goals of public policy.

An alternative response would be to make legal *rules* requiring that account be taken of the spillover. Over the last 100 years, industrial accidents have been converted from a spillover to a business expense. By passing laws on safety or by obliging companies to take out accident insurance based on the company's accident record, it becomes necessary for the company to take account of the costs of accidents and to minimise them.

In terms of the choice between *fees* and *rules*, decentralised incentives have three advantages over centralised controls. First, the adjustment is borne by those firms which can do so at the lowest cost. Firms which can cut pollution cheaply save themselves the fee. Production facilities which would be closed if they were forced to meet a blanket obligatory regulation, choose to pay the fee. The plants and their jobs survive while the overall level of pollution still falls. Secondly, once the mandatory pollution target has been met, firms have no further incentive to cut pollution; with fees — which levy a charge as long as any pollution lasts — companies have a reason to keep finding less-polluting forms of production. Thirdly, the administrative process for setting up mandatory regulations leaves lots of scope for large polluters to fights the rules in the political arena, inside the regulatory agencies and finally in the courts. Companies may invest more in lobbying than in pollution control. And if the penalties proposed by the law are too severe (plant closure or draconian fines) the authorities may simply be unwilling to invoke them.

Controls have proved to be a very high-cost response to pollution. Governments should think globally and act economically.

However, the existence of spillover effects is not enough on its own to justify public intervention. It would not be hard for any and every interventionist to dream up a supposed spillover to support their pet project. For this reason, it is important that the value of the spillover is first assessed, along with the exact role public intervention is expected to play, and the way in which the effectiveness of that intervention will be assessed. To take short cuts in this process would reveal that the motives for the spending plans had little or nothing to do with the economics of spillovers.

In some instances, the spillover effect may be judged to be too small or too uncertain to be worth bothering about, when allowance is made for the costs of the intervention itself, since plainly this will not be free. In other instances, the risk of the intervention suffering from a "government failure" (of the kinds to be discussed in the next chapter) may also make it best to accept an imperfect market outcome. For example, it is necessary to be confident that the public officials who would intervene in cases like these are motivated by the community interest and are not just acting as agents for some private interest. Only in cases where the market failures are costly enough, and where there is sufficient confidence in public measures to correct them, would market-correcting public interventions be justified.

Fish kills and "bungalow blitz" holiday homes are examples of Irish spillovers. One merits action, the second may not.

During the dry Irish summers of the late 1980s, the dumping of waste or chemical substances into rivers by farmers or industrialists caused a large number of major fish kills all over Ireland. This dumping imposed a large cost on other users of the rivers and a heavy clean-up charge on the taxpaying public. Such a (literal) spillover cannot be ignored and intervention is clearly called for here.

Unsightly holiday homes in scenic areas of Ireland undoubtedly distress other visitors to these areas. Although the distress caused is quite real, the house-owner is not required to offer any compensation. But in this case the spillover cost is rather small and it is not clear that, after allowing for the costs and the practical difficulties, public intervention would make the overall situation better. Spillovers of a small or uncertain size are best ignored.

For a market economy to function well, it is important not just to have prices but that the market's prices reflect all significant costs and benefits. In a Degenerate Economy this would not always happen. As a result, resources may be committed to activities that are privately profitable but socially wasteful. The market cannot itself take account of effects which are external to it and so, when these are large, a carefully-designed public policy is needed to correct the market failure.

However, it is in fact rare to hear Irish state economic intervention analysed in these terms.

Collective Goods
A further defect of a market economy arises because it is in the nature of some goods and services that they are consumed collectively. They are provided either for everybody or for nobody. Examples include national defence, policing and, in a given locality, public parks and street lighting. To add an additional user costs almost nothing extra and does not significantly reduce the amount available to existing users.

In contrast, to exclude an individual from enjoying the use of these goods or service is either impossible or prohibitively costly.

Consequently, a private company would be reluctant to provide collective goods since it would be very difficult to procure a payment for them. Nobody would want to be the one to pay since everybody would expect to be able to use the service whether or not they paid. The best strategy for the public to follow would be to pretend never to use such services while hoping that everyone else would pay up. The sneaky person would then get a "free ride". However, if too many people tried to be sneaky the revenue which could actually be collected would not cover costs and a private supplier would be unable to provide the good or service at all.

One solution to this problem is for the public authorities to finance the provision of the good or service from general taxation which, being general, will be collected from all the beneficiaries. Actual provision might be left to private suppliers, whose payment would now be secure. This is the basis of the increasingly common distinction between (often public) "purchasers" and (often private) "providers".

Although collective goods have a value to the consumer, a private supplier may not be able to cover its costs when the good is automatically available to everybody. So it will not be worthwhile for a private company to produce the good or service in question. A Degenerate Economy will therefore supply too few collective goods. This leaves a role for intervention. However, in Ireland, state programmes are rarely set up in these terms

Information Shortages
The case in favour of the market economy assumes that people have the information to judge costs and benefits. But this may not be true, so correct assessments may not be possible.

Take the problem of finding a reliable plumber. The plumber knows whether they are reliable or not. The householder does not. Unreliable plumbers have no reason to disclose to the householder the kind of worker they are. Quite the contrary: certain businesses may attract unscrupulous people precisely because their unscrupulousness will be hard to detect until it is too late.

Nor will the price charged help the householder to distinguish the craftsperson from the charlatan. If the householder only considers plumbers quoting a low price for the job, this will make the work particularly attractive to workers who propose to use inferior materials and workmanship. So consumers may have to pay too much in order to protect themselves against unreliable work in markets where the quality of work is hard to assess. The total amount of plumbing which takes place is likely to be less than well-informed consumers would demand.

Much the same problem can arise with insurance products. But now it is the seller (the company) rather than the buyer who is in the dark. The customer knows how prudent or irresponsible their behaviour is, while the insurance company lacks that information. Low-cost insurance policies will be very attractive to highly irresponsible customers, which could cause the insurance company to end up losing money. If an increase in the premium drives away responsible customers (who decide the insurance cover is not worth the price) whilst the irresponsible customers remain, the company's losses would only increase. As a result, the Degenerate Economy may simply not offer certain insurance products.

Informational problems are not limited to plumbing and insurance services. Anyone who needs to use an "expert" — a doctor, a lawyer, an economist — lacks the information to assess the expertise of the expert and might therefore be taken advantage of.

In the UK in the late 1980s, millions of people switched from state pension policies to private schemes on the advice of private financial advisers. Often, the private policies actually offered inferior benefits, but the customers did not understand that they were leaving a better pension scheme to join an inferior one. It is unclear what the "expert" advisers believed, although a number of the largest British insurance companies have since had to suspend their sales staff for "retraining". It remains to be seen what will happen to their customers. A million people may have lost out in the British pensions scandal, at a total cost which has been estimated to exceed £1 billion. Some estimates go a lot higher.

In medicine, too, the supplier (doctor) has an enormous informational advantage over the consumer — that's what makes the doctor a doctor — and the consumer could be taken advantage of. How is the consumer to know whether a highly expensive procedure which the physician has recommended (and which is highly remunerative to the doctor) is actually necessary? How are they to know whether a cheaper alternative is available?

Sometimes there is a market solution to these informational problems. It is called "reputation". If a business expects to have repeated dealings with a customer it will have little incentive to pull the wool over the customer's eyes. However, with some large purchases — buying a car or a house — the seller only expects to deal once with the customer, and the same restraint need not apply. It's not for nothing that second-hand car dealers and estate agents have their well-known image problem. Furthermore, there are services where low-quality provision would be so harmful to the consumer that it would not be enough to rely on reputation. In medicine, finance and air travel reputational considerations play a helpful role, but this would be little consolation to those who die, or lose their lifetime savings, at the hands of companies willing to risk their reputation.

Where reputation is an insufficient corrective for informational shortages, other measures are needed. For this reason, we see heavy regulation of finance, medicine and airlines as well as general "truth in advertising" legislation.

But, of course, regulations can also fail. Public agencies set up to regulate an industry in the public interest can lose their way and descend into mere servants of the industry's — not the public's interest. Do you usually think of the Department of Agriculture as regulating agriculture in the interests of affordable food for consumers? Or as a defender of high food prices for farmers? Do you notice the Central Bank bearing down on commercial bank fees and charges? Or did it for many years allow a cartel to openly operate in the interests of the banks? Has the Department of Transport freely awarded licences to all interested operators of the London-Dublin air route? Or did it for decades allow Air Lingus to operate a cartel to suit Aer Lingus? Little debate there.

The same difficulty arises with self-regulatory bodies covering professions. Are some of these glorified closed-shop agreements masquerading as organisations to maintain high professional standards? Is there any effective way to regulate these regulators?

There are no easy answers to these problems. Limited information plagues the market but also the public sector, and is therefore especially difficult to resolve. Public regulation is not itself free from failures, including failures caused by information shortages. Whatever regime, or mix of regimes, is adopted must be alert to all the dangers.

The Inequities of a Degenerate Economy

Market mechanisms enhance efficiency but, on their own, they are unlikely to achieve social equity. So a Degenerate Economy would suffer from all the inequities of a Dream Economy already discussed in the previous chapter. Indeed, matters would be worse since in a Degenerate Economy economic rewards would derive from the privilege of cartel membership rather than productive economic performance. A cartelised economy would cater first for cartel members, leaving few resources for social objectives.

Those who value social equity, who wish to see widely-distributed economic opportunities, to have a welfare safety-net and to avoid gross income inequalities, should not expect these to be provided by a Degenerate Economy.

Conclusion

Markets can achieve a lot but not everything. Under laissez faire, they may not keep the economy on a stable growth path. They may not prevent monopolies and cartels forming. They cannot take account of the hidden costs of spillovers. They will under-provide collective goods. And the lack of good information about buyers and sellers may cause some products and services not to be supplied or customers and firms to be exploited.

The Degenerate Economy — capitalism without competition — fails to promote productivity in the way a Dream Economy would. The principle of the survival of the productive disappears: loss-making businesses no longer have to improve productivity or close. Markets can be rigged to keep prices high and businesses profitable, so there is less pressure to be productive. The principle of the arrival of the productive is also lost: potentially highly-productive new arrivals are kept out, denying consumers the better or cheaper goods they would offer. If these market failures go unchecked, a wasteful Degenerate Economy will be the result.

Nor is the Degenerate Economy just inefficient. The income distribution is also ugly. The economic spoils are collected according to whatever the owners of capital and labour can extract, making full use of whatever monopoly powers they can build up. Not even lip service is paid to ideas of social equity.

So there is no unconditional case in favour of the market system. But there does exist a strong conditional one: private markets will be efficient provided that there are mechanisms to correct significant and genuine market failures. This suggests a logical and coherent role for the state. It should monitor economic performance for possible failures of the market. It should contribute to correcting these failures when the cost of doing so is less than the benefit from eliminating the original failure.

In terms of sensible national economic policies, the present chapter offers three conclusions. First, while an ideal market only uses resources productively, in practice markets may be wasteful. Second, since markets cannot deal with failings arising from their own nature, a non-market mechanism may be needed to stabilise the economy, maintain competition, adjust for spillovers, provide collective goods and improve information. Third, the need in a Dream Economy to directly tackle issues of social equity holds even more strongly for a Degenerate Economy.

There are two possible responses to the fact that private markets suffer important failures. One is to conclude that a smoothly-working market system is just pie-in-the-sky and can never be a realistic objective. I believe that this is to throw out the baby, the bath and the bathroom with the bath-water. The other reaction, appropriate to a pro-market social democrat, is to conclude that, where an economy is free from significant failures, the private market should be left to look after itself. But when these conditions are clearly and seriously breached, non-market interventions are needed to restore the market's high productivity and to improve its social equity. These two possible reactions could not be more different: the first seeks to dismantle and replace the market, the second seeks to fix it.

But who will do the fixing? How well placed is the state to tackle failures of the market? Does it suffer from failures of its own? These issues are taken up in the next chapter on the Decree Economy.

6

THE DECREE ECONOMY

Government Failure

From what we know of market failures, it might be expected that governments would have stepped in to fill these economic and social gaps. But this expectation rested on two doubtful assumptions.

First, it assumed that governments faced no technical barriers to carrying out whatever policy they wished.

Second, it assumed that governments would always pursue their declared objectives ("the national interest").

Recent decades have cast much doubt over both assumptions.

The Objectives of Government

Historically, government action was not motivated by the kind of economic arguments just presented about the Degenerate Economy. It was inspired by a belief in the *generalised* failure of markets. Not that markets left gaps, but that they produced a mess: they failed to deliver full employment, to develop strategic industries, to provide adequate health care and educational services, to offer protection against sickness and old age or to distribute incomes fairly. There was nothing markets seemed to do well. A simple contrast was drawn between the Great Depression of the 1930s and the successful harnessing of entire economies by state authorities during the Second World War.

But beyond these generalities, the case for increased government economic intervention was not specified in much detail. Thus there was no linkage between market failures and specific state programmes. Why bother with such theory-based arguments when the 1930s had seemed to provide satisfactory practical evidence? From this viewpoint, governments did not consider whether certain functions were most appropriate for the market and others best suited to the state's capabilities. Governments were willing to do everything.

When the private sector comprised three quarters or more of the economy, its failings were correspondingly prominent. But as the public sector grew to occupy half the economy in the developed world, its own failings and its limited ability to reach its objectives became equally apparent. As long ago as 1896, Alfred Marshall, a leading nineteenth-century British economist, warned of the danger of over-estimating the capabilities of governments. When asked whether he supported an expanded economic role for the state, Marshall replied: "Do you mean government all wise, all just, all powerful or government as it now is?"

That is the problem in a nutshell. If the government really possessed greater wisdom than private citizens, if it was really in a position to bring about any objective it desired and if it really operated to a higher moral standard than everybody else, then certainly it should be put in charge of the economy. For the good of the stupid, weak and venal citizenry, the government should plan their lives and businesses.

However, the state apparatus is staffed by people who, on average, are identical in their wisdom and morality to other ordinary citizens. The state has no advantage of knowledge or morals over the private sector. In judging the merits of institutions such as the market and the state, like must be compared with like. Institutions must be judged on their results, not their intentions. And certainly not the results of one compared with the intentions of the other. It is very satisfying to compare the ideals of one's preferred system with the practical failings of a rival one, but what matters are the successes and failings of each.

In the postwar years, the state has proved unable to deliver on its promises: full employment, sufficient public services at acceptable tax rates, adequate welfare benefits, and significant income redistribution in favour of the less well off.

The realisation began to dawn that the government was itself part of the problem. This prompted a more careful consideration of the fundamental issue: what was the nature of the advantage that the public sector was supposed to have over private activity?

If markets were failing, what was to prevent the public sector from failing too? Was there anything to ensure that the government acted as an independent guardian of the public good, or even that it acted efficiently? What would guarantee that its moral character would necessarily be very different from that of private organisations? The answer has turned out to be: nothing, necessarily. Governments, after all, are not gods.

Technical Barriers to Government Effectiveness
The first assumption on which the case for wholesale government intervention rested was that governments faced no technical barriers to carrying out their policies. This is not true. Governments face many limits. They have limited knowledge, they have incomplete control of the public bureaucracy, they are constrained by the political system, their citizens have proved adept at evading government initiatives, the costs of running the public sector are sizeable and difficult to control and the taxes to cover those costs can have some damaging side-effects. All this hampers the operation of government and restricts what it can do. Attempts to barge ahead with no regard to these factors have led to great inefficiency.

These technical barriers to state effectiveness are discussed next. Then, the question of whether governments pursue the national interest is examined.

Co-ordination and Information Problems
The state is staffed by rational planners taking the long view, right?

That's why Telecom Éireann, Bord Gáis and Dublin Corporation are famous for synchronising their cable-laying, gaspipe-laying and waterpipe-laying activities? That's why (in mid-1995) we still have three separate third-level education grant schemes? One run by the Local Authorities, one by the Vocational Education Committees and one by the European Social Fund. That's why, until the establishment of FÁS, Ireland had three agencies dealing with the labour force — AnCo, the National Manpower Service and the Youth Employment Agency? That's why, although T.K. Whitaker criticised the state's overlapping industrial development agencies in the 1950s, the Culliton report of the

1990s needed to make the same call for rationalisation? That's why, in the early 1990s, in almost the same breath in which it re-organised the IDA, the government established a parallel, dupli-cative grant-giver, the County Enterprise Boards?

Economic planning may seem superior to apparently chaotic markets, but the record shows governments to be very poor at co-ordinating their affairs. This is partly a question of size (large of-ten means rigid), partly a question of internal politics (obstruction may be in a bureaucrat's private interest), but mostly due to the difficulty of transmitting information within and between the di-verse parts of a large public sector.

Information does not spontaneously materialise. It has to be collected. Collection is costly. The cheapest way to collect infor-mation — as the Dream Economy shows — is through prices. But in a public sector using traditional non-market mechanisms, there are usually no prices. So often there is insufficient information to allow governments to engage in effective co-ordination.

Market prices reveal what it costs to make something and what consumers are willing to pay for a certain amount of it. Without prices, officials have only limited knowledge about the costs of providing public services and the amounts demanded by users. Elections are infrequent and imprecise measures of the public's policy tastes. Without information, it is impossible to match pub-lic services to citizens' wishes. To a considerable extent, the authorities are acting in the dark.

For instance, it is difficult for the authorities to know whether the resources they are devoting to non-market public activities are generating high or low output of public services. Although the problem of measuring unpriced output is tricky, it is not insolu-ble. Some ingenious measures have been proposed. FÁS and vo-cational training institutions could be paid according to the num-ber of trainees placed in jobs. Local authority funding could be linked to success in rent-collection or the turnaround time for va-cant houses. The justice system could be evaluated by public sur-veys. Builders could be required to state how many years they expect a road or a public housing scheme to last (and be held ac-countable for failure). Local authorities could be evaluated according to air quality, traffic accidents and complaints about public facilities.

Even without prices, it is possible to have performance and output measurement; it's usually just not done. Regular and open performance measurement would allow successes to be identified (and rewarded), failures to be discovered (and punished) and would bring the pressure of public opinion to bear on low performance.

In Ireland, the measurement of public sector activity is in its infancy. In the national accounts, the "production" of the government sector is measured by the costs of the resources used. The amount of education produced is approximated by the cost of teacher salaries, not by the results achieved. The amount of medical care is measured by the costs of running the health services, not by the state of health of the population. We can certainly make better measurements than these.

There is a further informational shortcoming which hampers efficiency in the public sector. The workings of the economy are only imperfectly understood. As a result, the full consequences of a policy action will often be incompletely understood. In some cases, a policy's consequences have turned out to be the opposite to what was intended.

One example is the package of grants and tax-reliefs offered to Irish house-buyers. Because this gives all buyers a bigger budget, it drives up house prices in general, so that much of the benefit has accrued to house-*owners* rather than to house-*buyers*. In terms of reducing the cost of housing to home buyers, this policy has largely been a waste, though it has been a great windfall to property-owners. The policy has also contributed to Ireland having one of the highest rates of home-ownership in the world, drawing investment funds away from more productive uses.

Similarly, companies in Dublin's International Financial Services Centre face special low taxes and can also use their rent bill as a tax deduction. Both rules are intended to reduce costs in the centre and encourage foreign companies to set up there. But what has happened? The owners of IFSC buildings have concluded that they can charge very high rents because the subsidies in the centre will still make it worthwhile to locate there! In 1995, it cost about £25 per square foot to rent in the IFSC compared to about £15 in Dublin generally. Much of the benefit of the subsidies have gone to builders rather than bankers.

Governments are not all-wise. They find it hard to marshal their countless departments and agencies in pursuit of their objectives. They lack information about their own costs and about what the public wants. They are not sure how a particular objective would be best pursued. These problems are not insoluble, but they do suggest caution when judging the state's capacity to intervene in the economy in a helpful manner. Increasingly, states are investigating whether new methods could supplement traditional non-market approaches.

"Free Goods"

In a market, costs and benefits are linked explicitly: you get only what you pay for, and you only pay what you consider the item to be worth. But many public services are made available to users on a "free" or subsidised basis and then financed separately through general taxation. This separation of costs (taxes) and benefits (public services) makes value for money harder to judge. The result can be an upward distortion in both the supply and demand of these services.

As an imaginary exercise, consider what the consequences might be if it were not conventional public services which were provided at a subsidised or zero charge, but rather supermarket shopping. Having paid our taxes, we could walk into the supermarket each week, put whatever we liked into our trolley and march out. Would our shopping pattern be unaffected? It seems unlikely. If shopping were "free" we would buy much more.

This may even be seen in the simple matter of plastic shopping bags. When supermarkets charge for these bags, people economise. Where the bags are free, there is no economising. And yet as the bags cost only pennies, we might have expected shoppers to use the same number of bags regardless. But we don't behave that way. What holds for pennies must be a lot more true of pounds.

We consume more of things for which there is no charge. But, sadly, in resource terms nothing can ever be "free". Whether or not money changes hands, the production of the good or service uses up raw materials and labour. These resources are gone forever, and they represent what it has cost society to produce the "free" good.

When they are "free", the demand for some public services is practically unlimited. There always seems to be a shortage of the service in question. No matter how much is spent on the health service or on education, doctors and teachers always maintain that they are underfunded. As long as services are offered for "free", these shortages are structural and permanent. Demand is always likely to outstrip supply.

If we paid directly (rather than indirectly) for these goods and services, we would compare costs (the price) with benefits (consuming the item in question) and decide — just as with marmalade or coal — how much we wanted to consume at the prevailing prices. Faced with prices and a fixed income, our budget constrains our demands. But without prices, the constraint is hidden, and we direct a never-ending stream of demands at the government.

A similar problem can occur when a group of people eat out together and divide the restaurant bill into equal shares. Collective financing — which separates the cost and the benefit — gives an incentive to consume more than would be chosen under private payment. Except for the bonds of friendship, there would be a temptation with shared billing to order lobster rather than chicken in the expectation of paying only part of the cost. If everyone behaved this way, a huge restaurant bill would result and everyone would pay more than they wished. Collective financing when there is no countervailing force such as friendship gives this process completely free reign.

How much "over-consumption" takes place when goods are free? It depends on how consumer demand reacts to the lower price. If responsiveness is low, consumers may use only a little more of a free good. But demand which is very sensitive to price may shoot up a long way.

"Free prices" also distort supply. Politicians are always tempted to offer more "free" services, and interest groups did not get where they are today by refusing enrichment.

Since public programmes are not free, it is only possible to say whether they improve or worsen community welfare when their costs and benefits are set side by side. To be able to make the comparison, in the absence of prices, the authorities need ways to measure the value of state-supplied goods and services. When this comparison is properly made, the public may well be persuaded that the government activity yields net benefits. But if politicians promise benefits without mentioning costs, or underestimate costs, the day of reckoning, when highly-taxed disenchanted chickens come home to roost, may undermine the whole ethos of public provision. "Self-financing tax cuts", as advocated by one Irish Taoiseach, and other such oases in the public finance desert, invariably prove to be a mirage.

A traditional public sector fails to put prices on its programmes — in politics, no one knows the price of anything. "Free goods" distort public demand and inflate political supply. As a result, old-style public programmes have often been wasteful.

Bureaucracy
Although the civil service and other public bodies are there to carry out the policies of governments, elected representatives have only limited control over what their officials do.

Traditionally, public agencies have been established as large bureaucracies. Inevitably, these have their own private agenda, involving increased power, size and perks. A reputation for shrinking from year to year is not one for which bureaucracies are famous. Nor do they often decide that their aims have been achieved and shut themselves down.

The Irish Land Commission redistributed half a million acres of land in one decade (1923-1932). It then staggered on for another six decades even though it had no further practical role to play.

The Bovine TB "eradication" scheme has been a much costlier saga. In 1958, Dr T.K. Whitaker wrote that "the limiting factor to the eradication of livestock diseases at present is lack of professional personnel". The number of professional vets was duly increased. Unfortunately, not enough account seems to have been taken of the fact that, unless vets' earnings depended on eradicating TB, not just treating it, successful eradication would actually cut vets' income. Few of us work hard to cut our own income. Bovine TB has not been eradicated and some people have come to the view that the limiting factor to eradicating livestock diseases is now the unsophisticated employment contracts the professional personnel have been offered.

A famous international example of an almost infinitely-lived bureaucracy concerns a special detachment created by the British military to watch from the cliffs of Dover for a Napoleonic invasion. The unit was set up in 1803. Napoleon died in 1821. The group was disbanded in 1927.

Public servants, including politicians, respond to the incentives they face. Public initiatives must be designed with this in mind. If the private interests of public servants conflict with their official objectives, it is only sensible to expect public servants to look after their own private interests as far as they can. In their place, you and I would do the same. Governments are not all-good.

The difficulty of controlling the public bureaucracy was initially misjudged because, during the Second World War, societies faced with great danger had put aside personal agendas and, in a "war-time spirit", worked selflessly for the overall goal of military victory. Unfortunately, such selflessness is not the norm in human societies, and it is unwise to devise social institutions on the assumption that something like a "wartime spirit" will always be available.

Governments' incomplete control over public bodies arises partly because politicians themselves often ask public bodies to carry out a multiplicity of inconsistent tasks. How then is one to know whether the costs of such public bodies are caused by their uneconomic responsibilities or simply by inefficiency? Without transparent accounts, the answer will never be very clear. But if inefficiency is present, it will hardly be in the agency's interests to provide transparent accounts.

CIE is expected to provide an efficient rail network in Ireland, but it is also expected to provide a service on lines which are entirely uneconomic. The money spent doing one cannot also be devoted to the other. RTE is expected to provide a high quality broadcasting service; yet it must also manage chronic loss-making activities such as its orchestras. The ESB is asked to provide electric power at a competitive price, but to continue to use grossly outdated regional power stations.

Governments' incomplete control over public agencies is also partly a question of information. Public servants are insiders whereas politicians peer in from the outside. When the early 1993 Fianna Fáil/Labour government brought Ministerial Advisers into office with them, with the intention and the effect of greatly strengthening the hand of Ministers vis-à-vis civil servants, the latter were very aggrieved indeed. Traditionally, the insiders have had a large informational advantage. Ministers come and go, public servants come and stay. Often, the Minister has no other source of first-hand data than what the public service itself supplies. This must leave a bureaucracy with a certain amount of discretion as to how it attends to its responsibilities. If a Minister asks teacher unions what pupil-teacher ratio is needed to raise educational standards, can she always necessarily expect to get an entirely objective answer?

Despite the well-known nature of bureaucracies, it has not generally been the case that public agencies have been designed with these shortcomings in mind, even though some, at least partial, solutions are known.

The problem of measuring output, for instance, could be tackled by giving explicit performance targets to each public body, civil service department and individual state programme. There would need to be agreement on how achievement of the target would be measured, and on a regular review of performance. Loyalty to the public interest rather than just to the public service could be improved by giving senior executives renewable fixed-term contracts linked to clear, measurable targets. Public servants would then face more appropriate incentives than they now do. An agency saddled with uneconomic objectives should be given a subsidy, whose proper size would be independently measured.

Bureaucracies are a potentially useful and an inescapable part of the modern world. But they are not staffed by saints. So bureaucratic structures need to be carefully designed. Traditionally, this has not been done and consequently the effectiveness of public agencies has been harmed.

Unanticipated Public Responses

Governments forget that state intervention (even the expectation of state intervention) can change the public's behaviour.

Governments are not all-powerful. People are not dumb animals that can be directed hither and thither. If you place a barrier across a lane, a line of sheep will no doubt shuffle to a stop. If you do something equally unsophisticated to humans, frustrating their wishes, they will quickly look for ways to evade the controls. This factor has to be taken into account at the stage when a public programme is being designed. But that has not always been done.

A well-known example of this problem concerns rent-control legislation. These laws had the very humane objective of keeping rents low, so that the poor would be able to afford housing. However, some disgruntled owners of rented property reacted to the controls by converting their buildings to other uses, thereby reducing the supply of rented accommodation. Other owners decided to provide lower quality accommodation to match the lower rents, so they spent less on maintaining the buildings. Neither of these effects was foreseen, and both harmed the intended beneficiaries of the policy. Policy-makers in many countries have since concluded that only carpet-bombing does more damage than rent controls to a city's housing stock.

The establishment or modification of a welfare system may likewise have unintended effects on wage demands. In an economy without welfare support the wages of workers are likely to be very cautious. Where there is a substantial safety-net, guaranteeing some income to those who may overestimate what a company can afford to pay, wage demands are likely to be greater. This does *not* mean that a welfare system is a bad thing. It means that in designing such a system, account needs to be taken of both the beneficial impact of the safety-net along with the possibility of undesired rises in unemployment because of greater pressures for unaffordable pay increases.

The welfare system is, after all, a type of insurance scheme. And private insurance companies are well aware that insurance changes behaviour. Once a customer takes out fire insurance they may become somewhat more careless about fire dangers in the home. Or, having purchased car insurance, the owner may be more willing to leave their car parked in locations they would not use if they had to pay the full cost of any theft or damage. Insurance companies have developed various means to try to reduce these behavioural changes, such as offering to insure only a portion of a claim so that the client is still motivated to take good care that the insured risk does not materialise.

If the state offers a mortgage subsidy, some people who previously rented a house will change to subsidised home ownership. If such behavioural effects are not foreseen, the cost of any particular public spending programme will be miscalculated. A startling Irish example was the seemingly innocuous Home Improvement Grant introduced by the coalition government in the early 1980s. The wave of applications under this scheme was so great that the Department of the Environment had to hire temporary staff to process the paperwork, and the total cost was some ten times larger than the initially-budgeted sum.

If the state offers farmers a subsidy on sheep it had better expect a sudden jump in sheep numbers. Between 1988 and 1993, the total number of ewes in Ireland jumped from 3.1 million to 4.7 million. This was associated with the introduction of an EU subsidy, worth £20 per ewe (in 1994) in disadvantaged areas.

If the state offers an old-age pension scheme, there could be a slackening in people's previous rate of saving. While the authorities should still succeed in adding to the incomes of those in retirement, the increase may not be as much as would be expected if the possible response of savers is overlooked.

This list could be extended to practically every public programme that there is. The lesson is clear. In deciding the degree of its involvement in any particular area, the state must take account of the extent to which existing behaviour may change in response to its involvement. These responses influence both the effectiveness and the cost of public programmes and cannot be neglected in designing state initiatives. Crude intervention may by quite ineffective or even yield unintended and perverse results.

High and Hidden Costs

A major problem with public sectors is their sheer expense. Traditional officialdom faces two cost problems. In the absence of competition, there is a tendency for costs to be higher than they need be. Secondly, the tax revenue on which the state is run does not merely transfer money from the taxpayer to the government. Its other (less visible) consequence is to discourage the taxed activity. Unsophisticated taxes can cause the economy to shrink, destroying jobs and lowering living standards.

Public bodies typically lack the pressure of competitive markets to root out waste, cut costs, and operate efficiently. Mostly, the consumer cannot signal dissatisfaction by changing to a new supplier. Furthermore, public bodies and companies are typically protected from the risk of bankruptcy by the willingness of governments to bail them out. This also lessens the incentive for high performance.

Lifetime job security for many public employees also makes it more difficult to penalise "slacking". It is no surprise that the 1992 Culliton Report concluded that the cost of many Irish public services was very high.

Furthermore, public spending requires that taxes be levied elsewhere in the economy to gather up the revenue to fund the spending. Therefore, in judging the net effect of a public scheme, allowance must be made not just for the benefits of extra schooling or improved medical care, but also the negative impact on those sectors of the economy which find additional taxes falling on them.

In recent years, the clothing industry in Ireland has seen value-added tax on clothes raised in several successive budgets. The increased tax revenue went, in part, to pay special pay rises to public servants. Another part went towards improved services for the mentally handicapped. In judging the overall impact of such a budget, the cash withdrawn from small clothing firms must be allowed for, as well as the better facilities made available to handicapped citizens. Of course, only the latter are announced.

A law which required an independent assessor — perhaps along the lines of the US Congressional Budget Office — to estimate the costs of additional taxation might facilitate a more balanced view of new spending programmes. In its absence, voters must themselves remember both sides of the equation and demand from public representatives that they do the same.

Besides, these are *hidden costs* of taxation. It is not widely understood that raising £1 million of additional taxation produces a dual effect. First, there is the effect on incomes. The taxpayer loses some money to the government, which uses it to provide more public services. Broadly speaking, these two flows cancel out. (This does not mean that everyone's satisfaction is unchanged, but that is a different question.) Secondly, there is some substitution away from the taxed activity towards a cheaper one. Some economic activities which were worthwhile in the absence of the tax now no longer happen. There is no offsetting gain elsewhere in the system, so this is a net loss to the Irish economy. In other words, to take an extra £1 from a taxpayer and put it into the public sector costs more than £1.

In the early 1980s VAT rates in the Republic were raised to levels much higher than in Northern Ireland. This had the same two effects. Consumers paid higher prices (lowering their income) but the government received extra revenue. These two flows would tend to leave total spending unchanged. But, in addition, retail outlets in the South lost business due to consumers switching some purchases to shops in the North. There were no gains anywhere else in the South to offset this loss of business, so this shrinkage of the domestic economy must also be considered a cost of taxation.

Taxes distort the economy and cause its potential size to shrink. How large are these losses for the Irish economy? One piece of research (by Patrick Honohan and Ian Irvine) published in 1987 (when tax rates were higher than now) concluded that for every extra £1 of tax revenue raised, the economy would shrink by well in excess of £1. In judging the impact of a tax regime, it is important to count both these sets of costs.

But the extent of the distortions vary: some taxes lead to much more substitution (away from the taxed good) than others. If there were no variability in people's response to taxation, it would not matter what was taxed. But because there is great variation in the possible response to different taxes, some forms of taxation are much costlier than others. In the examples already given of work and shopping, the response to the income and value-added taxes was large because people and shopping can be moved easily. Heavy income and goods taxes can be very costly in terms of reducing production and employment below what both would otherwise have been.

In contrast, property is immobile and the supply of residential property can be adjusted only very slowly. It is for just this reason that economists favour the levying of some taxes on fixed, immobile assets such as property rather than mobile labour, the quantity of which can be varied by employers and employees. Levying a property tax mostly transfers funds from the taxpayer to the government since little enough shrinkage of the stock of property is feasible, at least in the short run.

But even property is not fixed in supply and over-taxation would eventually damage its availability too. For that reason, the Commission on Taxation, which reported in the mid-1980s, advocated that consumption be the basis of a reformed Irish tax system. In that way, income, work and saving would not be taxed directly, but only the proceeds when they were used for consumption.

Ideally taxes should be levied where the distortions are least, that is, where there is less scope to reduce usage in response to the tax. The failure of the Irish tax system to take account of the distortionary impact of income and goods taxes implies that the size of the Irish economy, and the amount of employment it supports, are much less than their potential. A restructuring of the Irish tax system, to substitute more property taxation for less income and goods taxation, could leave considerable scope for the Irish economy to "unshrink".

Alcohol offers a relatively innocuous example of the kind of economic distortions that the present Irish tax structure can cause. Suppose you normally buy wine in a supermarket or off-licence. Imagine that one day your retailer asks you whether, the next time you want wine, you would be good enough to book a seat on an aircraft. He would accompany you on the flight and when the plane reached 30,000 feet you could have your usual wine order. Of course, it costs money to carry something into the upper atmosphere, so your wine will be dearer. You would think the retailer mad. Why would anybody (for no good reason) incur such costs to conduct a routine transaction? But this is exactly what people do in airport duty-free shops and on aircraft. The absence of the normal taxes and duties make it worthwhile to buy goods in what would otherwise be a very high-cost manner. For the parties concerned, taxes have made an otherwise very inefficient transaction worthwhile. One country may in this way scrounge a little extra tax revenue from another by inducing visitors to buy tax-free goods, but this gain to the Exchequer is likely to be marginal. For the economy as a whole, high-altitude retailing is daft.

Or consider some of the indirect costs of the Business Expansion Scheme. The BES is intended to provide funds to stimulate the growth of small firms. But it has other effects too. Because of the tax credit, such investments often cost only half of the sum injected. If the project performs dismally and just recoups its outlays, its economic return will be nil. But repayment of the face value of the investment to someone who (after tax) only put in half that amount, will give them a return of the order of 100 per cent. The tax system makes a wasteful project privately profitable. Since such investments are only affordable to the wealthy, such a tax regime flouts both efficiency and equity.

Despite this doomsday account of distortions, it needs to be restated that taxes permit expanded public services somewhere else in the economy, or increased income transfers to pensioners or the unemployed, or assistance for some other very deserving cause. Great care is needed to design tax structures so that economic distortions (like the above examples) are minimised. Otherwise, the tax regime can make the economy very inefficient.

In general, higher taxes lead to more economic inefficiency. There must come a point where the benefits of higher transfers or improved public services financed by the taxes are outweighed by the shrinkage of other parts of the economy. A balance has to be struck. Different citizens and governments will want to make different choices in this regard, but none can escape them.

In the early postwar decades, the importance of tax distortions was not as well recognised as it is today. The commitment to dealing with problems of hardship and poverty meant that the focus fell on the possible benefits from various public initiatives, with a tendency to disregard the impact on the rest of the economy of the taxes. Today, a failure to take adequate account of the trade-off between less private production (because of higher taxes) and additional public services (funded from the tax revenues) is no longer defensible. Unfortunately, the text of many

Irish Budget speeches is not often a source of reassurance on this point.

Taxation influences decisions from the cradle to the grave: it can affect the number of children a family has, whether they are looked after inside or outside the home, the amount of education they receive, their choice of job, their consumption pattern, in what form they hold their savings and at what age they retire. To look only at the impact of the government's spending decisions without allowing for the impact of the corresponding taxation will give a very incomplete picture of the government's actions.

Finally, government regulations, insofar as they raise costs, may also cause distortions that make the economy more inefficient. Many regulations concerning labour, health and the environment may be very desirable, but that is no reason to overlook the costs of such rules. As with taxation, there is a balance to be struck between the costs and the benefits. We cannot put our head in the sand and hope that an appropriate balance will simply happen.

For public activities to be more efficient and less wasteful, there is a need to strengthen the competitive pressures facing public agencies, to assess the costs as well as the benefits of public programmes and to design the necessary revenue-collecting taxes so that they least distort the rest of the economy.

Unproductive Lobbying
From the point of view of productivity, lobbying adds nothing to community income and, insofar as valuable energy and other resources have been used up, lobbying is wasteful.

A state grant redistributes income from taxpayers to grant recipients. A regulation establishing a monopoly raises prices and so redistributes income from consumers to producers. But these payments do not add to national income. On the other hand, lobbying does use up real economic resources that could have been used productively. After the 1994 Budget, the Minister for Finance stated that he had met with, or received written submissions from, no fewer than 70 interest groups. That was in connection with the budget alone; we must presume a much larger total of lobbying activity in a full year. Similarly, the amount of Irish government time and energy taken up with lobbying for the Structural Funds can only be imagined.

For historical and technical reasons, economists give the name "rent-seeking" to lobbying and all other wasteful ways of pursuing income-shifting.

Consider the following example. Imagine two Irish companies, SuperTech, a software engineering firm that writes computer programmes and SuperSuave, an accountancy firm specialising in tax advice. Suppose the firms are identical in numbers employed, turnover, profits, salary bill and payments to suppliers. Is there any difference between these firms except in the services they offer? Very much so.

SuperTech makes money for its staff and owners, thereby contributing to Ireland's total national income. The private gain is also a community gain. In contrast, some of the services which SuperSuave offers its clients involve ways to avoid the payment of taxes which might otherwise fall due. These gains to SuperSuave's clients are fully offset by a loss of tax income to the state. In other words, private income in one part of the economy is matched by losses elsewhere and there is no net community benefit. While the work of SuperTech has enlarged its own and the national income, that of SuperSuave has realised gains for the accountants and their clients but the community's income has only been redistributed.

This is not the fault of SuperSuave. It arises because of the complexity of the Irish tax regime. There would be less room for rent-seeking in countries with a straightforward tax schedule which was intelligible to the average taxpayer without the assistance of tax accountants. The danger in a tax regime of vast complexity is the scope it leaves for a large "industry" of tax advisers, who shift the tax burden around the economy, live fat on the proceeds but, economically speaking, spend much of their day in unproductive activity. A good tax regime would be based on clear rules, not on the discretion of administrators. The more discretion revenue officials have, and the greater the scope for bargaining over budget provisions, the more rent-seeking there will be. Ireland is a prime example of the rent-seeking society.

Naturally, it is not only taxation which attracts lobbying. A state administering large grants and other industrial concessions will also attract lobbyists. Imagine two firms making furniture for export. These identical firms begin with the same entitlement to grants from the state. But one firm is in a constituency with a government Minister, and successfully lobbies the Minister for additional grant aid. The other firm directs equivalent effort and resources into adding to its export sales. As a result, the income of both firms rises by £1 million. Does it matter how the two firms achieved the increase? Yes it does. In the second case, Irish national income is £1 million higher while, in the first, money is merely switched from taxpayers to the furniture firm.

Big government brings lots of lobbying. It is not by chance that there are thousands of registered lobbyists in Washington, nor that upwards of 2,000 organisations maintain representative offices in Brussels.

Even when lobbying does not involve direct public expenditure, there may be significant rewards to be had from persuading public authorities to introduce certain rules, or to modify existing ones. Examples include land rezoning, changing the number of taxi or pub licences, tightening or loosening restrictions on entry to professional courses and so on.

This is not an argument against *all* lobbying. Democracy would be a nonsense unless individuals and groups had the right to represent their views to politicians and to officialdom in general. However, as lobbying shifts income without adding to it, one would not want the rewards for lobbying to be so large that too much energy was attracted to it and away from productive economic behaviour.

How could lobbying be contained? By having public action guided by clear principles about when intervention is legitimate and when it is not. In those circumstances, a lobby might often be sent on its way. Such a risk would discourage lobbying in the first place. However, states that follow what they are pleased to call a "non-ideological", "pragmatic", "case-by-case" approach, have few economic principles to guide them and make much softer targets for wasteful lobbyists.

Do Governments Pursue the Public Interest? The Role of the Electoral System

The technical barriers to government action, just discussed, obstruct state efficiency. But aren't governments nonetheless pursuing worthy ends? Isn't the national interest being advanced? Aren't important social objectives being pursued? Isn't unemployment being lessened, aren't the poor being helped, aren't the disadvantaged being educated and the sick tended in public hospitals?

Yes, some of the time. But not always.

A poorly designed democratic structure can hinder the state's ability to pursue the national interest. Measures to oil the economy's wheels may simply end up greasing palms.

While economists and voters may be concerned about aspects of the national interest, such as productivity and social equity, politicians must concern themselves with electability. They have to focus on their constituency rather than on the country. Politicians will find it hard to resist anything that leads to the spending of money in their own area, whether the project is productive or wasteful. This is not because politicians are craven or corrupt, it is because they respond to the incentives created by the prevailing electoral system.

Politicians may face a conflict of interest. They will be tempted to justify expenditures on economic grounds when their real motive is the private political one of their own re-election. It is easy to see why in 1978 one TD told the Dáil as he realised the huge increase in public spending that was about to occur: "Happy days are here again". Well, no doubt his happy days were many. It's not so clear that the occasion should have been a cause of celebration for the younger generation, which has been left with the bills.

Between 1977 and 1987, the public elected governments which promised billions of pounds of benefits: rates were abolished, car tax abolished, house grants introduced, welfare payments raised, public salaries raised, increased subsidies offered to industrialists, to students, to farmers. The full list would fill pages. How was this financed? Mostly from public borrowing. This meant that repayment was left to future generations. In other words, the 1977-87 decision-makers engaged in a spending spree but left their children to pay the bill. Most people would be horrified by a family where the parents made their children pay for the adults' consumption. In economic policy, taxation without gestation is routine.

These public debts were incurred at a time when interest rates rose dramatically, putting further pressure on public finances. Taking the EU as a whole, the level of public debt has shot up from less than 40 per cent of GDP in 1960 to some 70 per cent in 1995. As we in Ireland well know, the deterioration in some member states has been dramatically worse. Until such time as these debts are repaid, the associated interest payments will continue to be a drain on the taxpayer. The damage wrought to national finances by the public spending policies of the 1970s will continue for decades to come. If it takes only twice as long to undo the harm as it took to make the mistakes, we will all be lucky. In the second half of the twentieth century, fiscal irresponsibility is probably the greatest area of government failure.

Industrial and economic development policies are particularly prone to conflicts of interest for politicians. A government may take two approaches to industrial policy: the economic or the political. The economic approach focuses on development: the public authorities seek to alter the structure of the economy in favour of expanding sectors and away from declining activities. Naturally, this is only possible if the authorities can successfully identify the sectors which will expand and decline in the future. Unfortunately, there is no reliable way to do this. While a magician may perform three impossible things before breakfast, it is best if a politician is not asked to try.

To achieve structural change the declining sectors must in fact decline and release resources of labour and capital to allow the expanding sectors to be able to expand. One way for this shift to occur is for earnings to fall (at least relative to the rest of the economy) in the declining sector. Lower pay costs mean that firms can try to hold onto their customers by offering lower prices while workers have a good reason to move gradually to better-paying sectors. Of course, this is not how it will seem to workers or shareholders in the "economically-challenged" sectors. They will demand "protection" from their political representatives, perhaps in the form of subsidies or import restrictions or some "special temporary reliefs" for the industry in question.

But we have now slipped from the economic to the political justification for government intervention. Propping-up a declining industry is the opposite to a national-interest policy of encouraging a switch *away from* declining sectors. It is negative and defensive. Such a policy may be supported on the grounds of giving the industry time to adjust. Yet once having obtained the subsidies, it must be in the interests of the workers and shareholders to try to have the assistance extended. If this is what happens, the eventual result would be to lock that sector into its existing position and prevent any structural change from taking place. The more the change is postponed, the more precarious will be the company's position and the greater than ever its dependence on public assistance.

Many Irish examples of this problem come to mind. The agricultural sector is the clearest and earliest example. Ireland has always had tens of thousands of farms which were too small ever to be commercial successes. Economic logic dictates that it would be better for most of these farmers to move to other parts of the economy and for their farms to be amalgamated into bigger units. If this process is prevented from occurring, three things happen. Commercial farming does not develop so land is wasted which would be productive as part of a larger farm. Thousands of farmers exist in a miserable limbo: unable to make a good living from farming, but receiving just enough welfare and subsidies to stop them from leaving agriculture. Finally, the uneconomic farming sector is a permanent burden on the taxpayer which is never lifted because the small farms remain trapped — by public policy — in a state of underdevelopment. Far from achieving economic development in the national interest, this policy reproduces underdevelopment at a considerable cost to the taxpayer.

The Irish Steel saga offers an industrial example. The original private company was bought by the state in 1947 for "strategic" (or perhaps electoral) reasons. The company went on to lose money almost every year since, particularly when account is taken of the special supplies of cheap ESB electricity which it obtained through further political arm-twisting. At the end of June

1995, the company had accumulated losses of £145 million. A small uneconomic steel plant received a gigantic stream of public funds without ever becoming a profitable entity or ceasing to require subsidies.

One reason for the steel plant's chronic losses is that there are "Irish Steels" in nearly every European country. Each government has built or subsidised steel mills, ignoring the actions of the others. This has produced a glut of steel driving down its price to the point where the steel industry in general is unprofitable. The national interest — that Irish Steel be shut down and the losses finally staunched — was not pursued by Irish governments. Once again, state industrial policy rewarded an economically unsuccessful and unproductive company by placing a heavy tax burden on commercially successful businesses, damaging their own viability. Finally, in late 1995, the Government sought EU approval for a deal to sell Irish Steel to an Indian firm.

The same happened in air transport; each government financed its own "flag carrier" creating a glut of aircraft seats and losses for many of these state airlines which then needed subsidies from the taxpayer to survive.

Would the public have voted for such policies if they had known the costs? It seems doubtful. But of course, single decisions are never put to voters in general elections. Although purchasing decisions are made individually by each household, voting decisions, except in referenda, are made in packages.

The problem which political constraints cause for economic policy-making arise from this fundamental difference between economic and political calculations. Economics asks whether a policy's gains exceed its losses *at the national level*; politicians ask whether they do so *at the constituency level*. If a policy gives a gain of £1,000 to 1,000 people but costs one million people £10 each, it is straightforward for an economist to conclude that the total gain comes to £1 million while the total loss is £10 million. This leaves the country as a whole with a loss of £9 million from that policy. Economically, this is a policy with a negative sum: total losses exceed total gains. But the political system may reach a different conclusion. Each individual politician must pay careful attention to the policy's impact on their own constituents; the national interest may take second place. A politician must weigh up 1,000 big winners (possibly in their constituency) against one million small losers, sprinkled far and wide. The losers may even be unaware of their loss. The politician may judge that the losers are not going to get worked up over £10, whereas the gainers may switch their votes. In that case, a policy which is against the national interest may nonetheless seem attractive to a politician. To repeat: this is not because politicians are slimy schmucks. It is because politicians' electoral responsibilities are local rather than national. If each politician thinks only of his or her constituency, the national impact of a policy may be forgotten. The present Irish electoral system *obliges* each TD to think first about their own constituency.

In small doses, the inefficiency of negative-sum policies will also be small. But if groups of public representatives horse-trade support for their own pet projects in exchange for supporting those of others', the impact on an economy can be very large. Ireland is a good example.

The Common Agricultural Policy is good for thousands of farmers but bad for millions of consumers. State subsidies to Irish Steel are good for a few hundred workers in Cobh but bad for millions of taxpayers nationwide. The Shannon stopover was good for tourism in Shannon but bad for everyone else. A large special pay increase is good for the public servants in question but bad news for taxpayers in general. "Free" university fees is fine for students and their families but the cost falls on the generality of Irish households. Nevertheless, re-election worries mean that TDs representing each of these constituencies will seek transfers for them regardless of whether the overall national effect is good or bad. The country has become locked into a pattern of negative-sum government interventions which are against the national interest.

No single TD, on their own, can escape from this political trap. To reject constituency parochialism would be to face electoral devastation while the political system itself would carry on exactly as before. It is we, the citizens, who are ultimately responsible for this political system. We have imposed it on politicians and it is up to us to modify it.

It is worth stating that the opposite electoral system to Ireland's present one, with all TDs elected from national constituencies (as in today's Presidential elections) and *none* elected locally, would produce the opposite problem. Policies with national benefits but severe and concentrated local costs would be supported without regard to their local impact. These considerations suggest electoral reform towards a system with a mixture of local and national voting.

Perverse political incentives become a more serious problem as the public sector gets larger. With a small public sector, the number of citizens dependent on it or substantially affected by its decisions is also relatively small. There remains a large body of disinterested citizens who are free to consider public policy proposals on their merits. But when the public sector is very large, the proportion of disinterested citizens drops, and public decisions are more likely to be made on the principle of "what's in it for me?".

Even if governments faced no technical barriers to doing so, they would not always pursue the public good. Certain electoral systems may cause politicians to pursue policies which are inefficient and against the national interest. Only political reform, designed to strike a better balance between local and national concerns, can resolve this problem.

Lobbying and the Public Interest

Unless lobbying can be contained, the state may not just damage economic efficiency but actually *worsen* social equity. In a system of representative democracy, where the majority is silent but affected minorities are vigorous in pursuing their interests, already-advantaged minorities can triumph over the public good.

Many people could accept some governmental inefficiency if social aspects of the national interest were being advanced by the government's activities. But unrestricted lobbying threatens the state's declared social aims.

Programmes that begin by being specific and targeted may become generalised and indiscriminate and end up shifting resources from the worse-off to the better-off. For example, the percentage of Irish farmland classified as "disadvantaged", and so eligible for larger Euro-transfers, has climbed relentlessly since we joined the EU. It is time to ask: "disadvantaged" compared to what?

Programmes launched with the intention of helping an under-privileged group may end up aiding the opposite social class. The road to socially regressive spending is triple-paved with sincere intentions. After 25 years of operation of the Higher Education Grants Scheme, a 1994 Department of Education working group found that some 50 per cent of the college-going children of *well-off* farmers were in receipt of grants, a regressive transfer if ever there was one. The scheme has failed to achieve much of an improvement in access to third-level education for the working class. Participation rates in the poorer areas of Dublin stand at around 3 per cent compared with rates of up to 50 per cent in some better-off areas. Of course, grants alone will hardly equalise access to higher education. But the scheme could be more effective if the available funds were better targeted.

Lobbying may also paralyse the state. The web of existing commitments to constituencies and to its own staff may leave the state unable to make any significant change to existing policies and programmes. The hullabaloo over the restriction on mortgage interest relief after the 1994 Budget was a telling example of the state flinching in the face of interest group backlash. The willingness of the beneficiaries of mortgage subsidies to call for the maintenance of these transfers in the name of "self-reliance" shows either extraordinary cheek or total self-delusion. There was a similar reaction to the proposal, during 1994, by the Minister for Education to include household assets (such as a farm) in the means-testing of the higher education grants scheme. Once again, the protest from the existing beneficiaries appears to have blocked this reform.

What can be done? Alan Blinder, the US economist, makes two specific suggestions to beat lobbying by vested interests. He calls them *linkage* and *revenue neutrality*.

First, policy reforms should be packaged. Consider the Common Agricultural Policy, on the one hand, and the semi-state companies, on the other. Government farming policy funnels subsidies in various guises to farmers, driving up food prices to consumers and leaving the taxpayer with a large bill. Government policy on the semi-state sector also involves large subsidies, high prices, poor service and a large bill for the taxpayer. Although both policies are national losers (national losses exceed national gains), they are winners for farmers and semi-state employees. Naturally, both groups defend their own ground when each policy is considered separately.

But both lose from *the other's* set of policies. Farmers have to buy expensive energy and costly communications. They pay high prices if they need to travel to Brussels, and were obliged to land at Shannon if they wanted to go to the US. Meanwhile, semi-state employees are forced to purchase expensive food, even though far cheaper supplies are available from producers outside the EU. And heavy taxes are paid to finance farm grants and the likes of headage payments.

Suppose these two policy packages were considered for adoption or rejection together? Even if the abandonment of these two particular schemes did not leave the great majority of members of both groups better off, it is certainly easier on a packaged basis to devise a set of economic reforms that would do so. As Alan Blinder puts it: "If a proposal offers genuine net benefits to society as a whole, it should be possible to package it in a way that leaves few losers." In the area of Irish tax reform, for example, this is the only approach which offers even modest prospects of success. And that is the path along which reform should attempt to move.

Furthermore, Blinder suggests that interest groups looking for increased government expenditure should be required to suggest a matching proposal to cut government spending elsewhere. The combined effect would therefore be to leave total government spending and taxation unchanged (revenue neutrality). Critically, the legislature would be required to vote on the two proposals as a package.

Linkage and revenue neutrality would transform the problem of schemes that are economic losers seeming like political winners. Linkage should make it possible to devise a reform programme that would allow politicians to escape from the present paralysing effect of interest groups. With a large enough and carefully-designed package, the number of net losers from the total set of changes would be much smaller than from item-by-item changes.

Today, no interest group seeks to cancel public programmes, only to extend them. But would early-retirement for teachers have been sanctioned in 1995 if the *teacher unions* had had to specify where to cut spending to finance their better pensions? Revenue neutrality would mean that the costs of making a concession to an interest group, previously spread out in small doses over a large population, would come back into sharper visibility. Interest groups would be pitted against one another, rather than against the community interest. Revenue neutrality would apply to politicians as well so they could not, as now, sanction a scheme which disproportionately or exclusively benefited their own constituents without openly specifying the cost and where it should fall. These two changes would cut a major part of the ground from under the lobbies.

Other ways to contain lobbying would be to place a ceiling on private donations to political parties and to have spending limits on election candidates.

Many interest groups, in making strident demands for additions to public services, often present only the sketchiest indication of the benefit to the community from the additional expenditure. As a result, they leave themselves wide open to the charge that they are mainly concerned to boost their own earnings, working conditions or benefits, with little real concern for the public interest.

Doctors and health workers call for more funding for "essential" treatments, but no matter how many hundreds of millions of pounds we spend on health (and we spend a very great deal), resources are never considered adequate. Teachers too have a long shopping list; in recent years, they have stressed reductions in pupil-teacher ratios and early retirement for themselves. The Educational Forum in 1993 sought, as a minimum, an extra £500 million spending on Irish education, even though the number of students in education is now in decline. County councillors demand improved roads in their area. And so on. Each group complains that "the government" is not doing enough, that other governments do far more, and that the nation's economic development or civilised standards require this urgent step. Of course, "the government" never pays, only the taxpayer, but a more sympathetic hearing can be expected to a demand made on the government than for one made on the general taxpayer.

We should be sceptical of promises by politicians, or demands by interest groups, about new or extended public provision, when there is no precise statement of the benefits to the community from the measure, and of the way it is proposed to pay for it.

Lobbying is not merely unproductive in itself. It can be contrary to social equity if already-advantaged groups use it to stack up additional advantages for themselves. The public authorities must be careful not to be an easy target for income-shifting towards the better-off.

Conclusions

Market failure, though real, does not necessarily justify state intervention which can prove in certain circumstances to be no better. Likewise, government failure does not on its own justify unmitigated liberalisation; markets are quite unable to achieve certain economic and social objectives. What we need to know are the ways in which different systems are suited to different tasks and to rearrange roles accordingly.

There are technical barriers which make the state inferior to the market at economic co-ordination. As noted, self-imposed absence of prices leads to information shortages. Limited knowledge leads to policy mistakes. There is excessive (wasteful) demand for "free goods". A poorly-designed bureaucracy can be spendthrift. The costs of operating the state sector are high, especially when the hidden costs of tax distortions are included. The unanticipated response of the public to government initiatives can inflate programmes' costs and reduce their effectiveness. Each of these factors impedes the effectiveness of the state.

Besides, there can be electoral incentives for politicians to be more concerned with the local than the national interest. An electoral regime can make the destination of the benefits of public programmes more important that their size. And behind-the-scenes lobbying by the well-organised wealthy can pervert the state's declared aim of improving social equity. Such a public sector is not well placed to improve the life of its citizens.

Today the serene confidence of the early postwar decades in public sectors staffed by well-intentioned and well-informed experts, and led by benevolent, competent politicians has faded almost without trace. As the naïve cult of the expert has died, it has been replaced by a generalised mistrust of both expert and political leader alike. Quite possibly, the pendulum has now swung unduly in the direction of jaundiced cynicism.

But it would be quite mistaken to conclude that there is no role for the state in the economy. In this chapter the focus has been on the state's failings. But, as the last chapter showed, markets too are subject to failure. Each institution has a role in a well-organised Designer Economy, according to the simple principle that each should do that which it is best at, and try to avoid other tasks.

There are roles for the state in providing law and order and in outlawing anti-competitive business practices. And in supplying infrastructure, environmental protection and training. It has a social role in tackling poverty and guaranteeing education and health care. Such a state is going to have a major place in the economy and society. This line of thinking offers a coherent role for both the state and the market and suggests a boundary between what it is sensible to ask the state to do and what should be left to the market. The state does not, in general, have a role in regard to ownership of the economy, in regard to direct production activity or in regard to setting detailed controls and plans for the rest of the economy.

As for how much to provide in the way of activities that are appropriate to the state, that can only be decided on the basis of comparisons of the costs and the benefits of the different possible programmes. This calls for much more measurement of the value and effectiveness of state programmes, in other words, for professional cost-benefit calculations of state initiatives as a matter of course.

Without coherent boundaries to its activity, the state may neglect the very functions where it does have an advantage and become involved in tasks where, because of the government failures just discussed, it is at a disadvantage.

The key question is the *design* of government intervention. That is the subject of the next chapter. If government activity is to correct failures and not add to them, it must carefully select the tasks it seeks to carry out and carefully design the interventions it decides to make. Provided that is done, the state can indeed improve the performance of the economy and of society. But the public sector should not be thought of as inherently better than the private. It is the quality not the size of the public sector that matters.

Good economic performance requires a coherent set of economic principles. The above review of government failures suggests the following four conclusions. First, the state can fail: it is not all-wise, all-powerful or all-good. Second, public programmes are worthwhile only if the benefits they create exceed the costs of providing them; this assessment should be made at the margin. Therefore benefits and costs must be measured, whether by market or non-market procedures. Third, without political reform, to strike a better balance between the local and the national interest, politicians will continue to pursue policies that may be good for their constituency but bad for the country. And fourth, without political reform to contain lobbying for regressive public spending and regulation, the net effect of government may be to diminish social equity.

We now have the conclusions drawn from the Dream, the Degenerate and the Decree Economies. Let's apply them to the Designer Economy.

7

THE DESIGNER ECONOMY

Four Designer Principles

We know that producers, consumers and public officials alike, are attentive to their own private interests. Therefore, after democratic debate and discussion, a community needs to adopt a legal, political and economic "architecture" which gives citizens an *incentive* towards behaviour which is socially and not just privately beneficial. Mainstream economic research has shown the best such "architecture" to be a market economy, corrected for important and valid market failures. I have christened this combination the Designer Economy.

How is the Designer Economy designed? According to the following four principles. First, in the market sector, competition must be safeguarded. Second, in the political world, the electoral system should allow balanced consideration of the national and the local interest. Third, governments should have clear and explicit objectives. Finally, public services should be reformed to put the consumer, not the producer, first.

A Designer Economy would be unambiguously founded on **competitive markets**. This would require powerful competition laws, a strong Competition Authority and a better understanding by the population of the importance of fostering competition. It would also require regulatory agencies to oversee competition in "natural monopoly" utilities like energy, water supply, and telecommunications.

Second, to allow the political system to focus on national objectives, **political reform** is needed to achieve a better balance between national and constituency concerns.

Third, **government intervention** in the economy should be directed at two clear goals: the correction of important *market fail-*

ures and the promotion of *opportunity and social equity*. To tackle
market failures, the state needs to establish where in the economy
they are found, and the most effective way of reducing them.
Likewise, it needs to assess the scale and nature of social disadvantage, and to investigate the most effective policy responses.
An independent Audit Office should review existing public programmes, and assess new ones, for their compatibility with these
targets. The public authorities should divest themselves of those
responsibilities which do not advance either of the state's core
functions, or indeed which are in conflict with them. Propping-up
lame duck industries and expanding "middle-class welfare"
would be two examples of the latter.

Fourthly, many public services require substantial **institutional
reform**. To lessen government failures, traditional systems should
be reorganised on the principle of putting the consumer first.

Such a social market of competitive and "corrected" markets
would deliver more equitable and productive results than either
non-competitive (Degenerate) markets or non-market (Decree)
economies. These four designer principles are discussed in the
remainder of this chapter.

A Competition Authority: Safeguarding Market Competition
A Designer Economy would give the highest priority to fostering
competitive markets, knowing that unless the laws of the land
promote competition and arrange for it to be rigorously policed,
nobody else will.

Firms will find it more profitable to reach cosy market-sharing
agreements. If these are not forthcoming, the firm with the deeper
pockets can charge loss-making prices which will bankrupt its
rivals and leave it in sole command of its market. The mere threat
of such behaviour will often be enough to bring rivals hurrying
into a smoke-filled back-room to hammer out an agreement
keeping prices high and sharing out the profits. Consumers are
too dispersed and unorganised to be able on their own to mount
an effective defence of their position. Consumers' interests are
best protected by competition in the marketplace. For European
states, this objective is increasingly being organised at a Union
rather than a national level. European competition policy goes
back to the earliest days of the Treaty of Rome. Article 85 of that

treaty prohibits agreements by companies to restrain or distort competition while Article 86 prohibits abuse of a company's dominant position in a market.

Competition was also at the heart of Jacques Delors' plans to relaunch the EU in the mid-1980s. The key idea of the Single Market was to remove remaining national barriers to trade within the EU. Many of the benefits of the single European market — faster economic growth, more dynamism, lower prices — were expected to arise precisely because of intensified competition. The Delors report of 1989, which placed Economic and Monetary Union on the political agenda, made competition policy one of the key characteristics of economic union.

The Maastricht Treaty continues in the same vein. It aspires to an economic system in which "competition in the internal market is not distorted" and it stipulates that the "Member States and the Community shall act in accordance with the principles of an open market economy with free competition". The importance given to competition and competition policy in the overall legal architecture of the EU should not be doubted.

Similar objectives exist at the national level in many states. Germany has a Monopolies Commission and a Federal Cartels Office which intervene if any single company controls more than one-third of a market (or if any three companies control more than one half of the market). Britain has a Monopolies and Mergers Commission and an Office of Fair Trading. In the United States, the competition laws are more than one hundred years old. Each national regime is operated somewhat differently, but in their various ways each seeks to promote competition.

What happens when there is no institution to safeguard competition or when firms manage to evade the competition laws? The last few years provide plenty of international and Irish examples.

In 1982, the US competition authorities taped the following exchanges between two US airline presidents (American Airlines and Braniff Airways). The conversation was later printed in the *New York Times*:

A: I think it's dumb as hell for Christ's sake, all right, to sit here and pound the **** out of each other and neither one of us making a ******* dime.

B: Well . . .

A: I mean, you know, goddamn, what the hell is the point of it?

B: Do you have a suggestion for me?

A: Yes, I have a suggestion for you. Raise your goddamn fares 20 per cent. I'll raise mine next morning.

B: Robert, we ...

A: You'll make more money and I will, too.

B: But we can't talk about pricing!

A: Oh ****, Howard. We can talk about any goddamn thing we want to talk about.

Executive A was mistaken. In the US, it *is* illegal for two companies to discuss pricing and the airline president ended up before the US courts.

In the early 1990s, there was a bitter dispute between British Airways and Virgin Atlantic. The smaller airline accused British Airways of using "dirty tricks" to steal its customers. Virgin is pursuing BA in the US courts for damages of $1 billion.

The giant software firm, Microsoft, was investigated at length by the US competition authorities for using long-term licensing agreements allegedly to block rival software products from the personal computer market. A settlement was reached with the US Justice Department in 1994. In 1995, Microsoft attracted further attention from the Justice Department because its Windows 95 package incorporated an Internet on-line facility which allegedly represented a move by the company to dominate the electronic commerce and on-line entertainment market.

In July 1994, during controversy about the profits earned by privatised water companies in the UK, one British newspaper wrote:

State monopolies are thoroughly discredited. We know their faults. But when you turn to private monopolies to do a job, you regulate them with chains, and where necessary beat them with rods, lash them, kick them and confine them. Do all that or they will take you for everything you've got.

What newspaper said this? Could it have been the *Morning Star*? No, it was the *Financial Times*, actually.

The EU competition authorities fined 33 European cement producers a total of nearly £200 million in 1994 for operating a cartel. Irish Cement's share of the fine was nearly £3 million.

Irish Ferries' attempt to open a route to Brittany ran into difficulties with the port authorities in Roscoff. The same port is used by Irish Ferries' main rival, Brittany Ferries. The matter has since been brought to the attention of the European Competition Directorate.

Efforts by companies to douse down competition are the norm, not the exception. Unless a Designer Economy maintains a powerful and vigilant competition agency, creeping monopolisation and a slide towards the Degenerate Economy will be the result.

In Ireland, the Competition Authority (established in 1991) blocked the 1994 take-over of the Cooley distillery. In 1995, it issued a report which found the Independent newspaper group to have abused its dominant position in the newspaper market.

These two findings were hailed as "landmark decisions", indicating the novelty for Ireland of conducting surveillance of marketplace competition. There is a long way to go yet. In terms of Designer institutions, we need a still-tougher Competition Act, a much-strengthened staff to support the Authority's work, as well as a full set of investigative powers (along the lines of the Brussels Competition Directorate) to allow the Authority to enquire and explore into areas of business behaviour where anti-competitive abuses are suspected. Such machinery on the private side of the economy logically requires that Irish governments should press ahead with liberalising the commercial semi-state company sector also.

Political Reform: Protecting the National Interest
The way in which an electoral system could place sectional (often producer) interests ahead of the national (consumer or taxpayer) interest was discussed in the last chapter. A Designer Economy

would reform overly-local voting systems to give more weight to national concerns. Some national public representatives would continue to be elected from local constituencies but others would now be chosen from a single national constituency. This second group of politicians would have to be attentive to the overall national interest. A specific form of this proposal, adapted to Irish circumstances, is set out in Chapter 9.

An Audit Office

Most of the argument over public services centres around what is spent, rather than what is produced. Each autumn, Ministers fight over their budgets. Teachers, doctors, Gardaí, county and city councillors, social workers and others, all call for more money to be spent. Yet what matters to citizens are results — learning, state of health, crime levels, municipal services and social services — and whether the money (the input) being spent is generating a matching level of output.

Such measurement is not always welcomed by those whose work is being assessed. A recent head of the UK's Audit Commission, Howard Davies, described his work as "engaging in guerrilla warfare with some hitherto untouchable parts of the public sector".

During the 1980s, the UK Audit Commission, responsible for evaluating local government (which in Britain includes education) and the national health service, issued comprehensive examinations of local authority services, social services, the police, schools, and hospitals. The studies found services to be producer- rather than consumer-driven. There were large discrepancies in the level of service provided for the same money in different areas, but no consequences flowed from low-performance or non-performance. There were few (if any) incentives to cut costs or raise output. There were no criteria of success or failure; it was assumed that everyone would just do today whatever had been done yesterday in the way it had been done yesterday. Staff payments were not performance-related. Professional staff, such as hospital consultants, had taken effective control of managerial tasks in many services. Very adept with arguments about protecting standards and horrified at the mention of anything as indelicate as money, these vested interests were fierce in guarding their terms, their conditions, and their closed shops. There was little independent lay assessment of public services. Consumers could exert no leverage over these systems since they were offered no choices within it; those who could afford to, opted out.

Under the independent scrutiny of the Audit Commission, there has been some progress in improving the efficiency of British local authority and health services. Market-type reforms have been introduced into most areas other than the police force.

In a 1992 pamphlet, Mr Davies advocated further steps: an improved financial framework, clearly defined outputs, an effective separation of the purchaser function (seeking value for money) from the provider function, market-testing, competition and customer choice, independent collection and verification of performance data, strong lay management and outside inspection and auditing.

In Ireland, recent years have seen the Office of the Comptroller and Auditor General undertake a more ambitious evaluation of public services than in the past. But the scale of this activity is still modest when set against the fact that in Ireland governments spend almost one pound out of every two.

A Designer Economy should establish a powerful Audit Commission, with a wide remit, modelled on the UK organisation. It would have the task of evaluating current public-sector performance and promoting the use of best international practice.

Designer Government: Where to Act?
If the economic role of a Designer government is to tackle market failures, where are these to be found? The appropriate areas can be shown to be six: health and education services, social insurance, public administration, infrastructural provision and environmental protection.

Health care suffers from several market failures. First, there are spillovers. In the case of infectious diseases, the community cannot afford to leave health care to possibly careless individuals whose neighbours will bear part of the price of any carelessness. Admittedly, except for AIDS, there are few serious infectious diseases in the developed world today, but presumably this is testimony to the public health care programmes of the past. Second, there is a problem of local monopolies: except in large urban centres, there will often be just a single hospital in any one locality. The user is thus denied the benefit of competition between health care providers and the lower medical bills that would come with competition. A third failure concerns information. We can all judge whether a supermarket is selling good-quality oranges, but, at least in the case of complicated procedures, what layperson can be sure whether a doctor is providing good health care?

Aside from economic considerations, there are social grounds for public surveillance of the distribution of health services. Any society aspiring to notions of equal opportunity must monitor whether its people have access to reasonable medical care. A society concerned to alleviate the effects of poverty will want to ensure that being poor is not a delayed-action death sentence.

If the private market is inadequate, governments' traditional answer has also been flawed. States have established inefficiency-inviting monopoly public health systems, lacking competition, profit measurement and prices. A Designer government would look in other directions. The state could pay for health care without directly providing it. A national insurance scheme could finance medical services while leaving provision to competing hospitals and health centres. Naturally, the state would encourage citizens to deal with those hospitals which (perhaps now by employing fewer costly doctors and more economical para-medical staff) were able to offer good quality health care more cheaply than rival institutions.

For instance, in the US, people may join a scheme of "managed" health care. In return for an annual fee, paid into a fund, a team of doctors arranges medical care for members. Critically, this changes the incentive facing doctors. Their income (the residual, after outgoings on members' health care have been subtracted from payments into the fund) no longer depends on treating illness but on maintaining health. Health funds also increase competition since the fund now bargains with local hospitals to get better value. Such schemes have led to big savings in medical costs, and are spreading rapidly in the US.

Alternatively, medical procedures could be divided in two. One set, deemed essential, would be covered by public health insurance. The other would consist of procedures considered nonessential or exorbitantly costly or with a very low success rate; these would fall outside the state health care system. In the early 1990s, the US state of Oregon consulted the public on the priorities to be given to each of the available 709 medical treatments. Then, given the state's health budget and the cost of the highest-priority procedures, the Oregon legislature voted to fund publicly the top 587 treatments and to leave the remainder to private payment. (The decision has since been challenged in the courts.)

In a Designer government's health care system, the state's role would be to set health *policy*: to see that the *whole population* had insurance cover, to encourage *competition* and allow consumers to choose their doctor and hospital, and to publish *information* on hospitals' charges and "success rates". But the state would not itself operate the system. This task would be decentralised to individual hospitals and medical centres which would be accountable for their results. The state would be free to concentrate on prevention rather than, as today, on repair.

Education and training are also services in which market failures are found. There is a clear-cut spillover problem in a world of changing technology. Companies need to give their staff up-to-date training. This can be expensive. A company that believes it may lose many of its trainees to rival firms (who are saved the training costs), will undertake less training than it would like to provide. If many companies see themselves in this position, there will be too little training in the overall economy.

Intervention in the market may be justified here, but it depends very much what form it takes. The traditional approach is to establish a state training monopoly — this has all the standard drawbacks of a monopoly. A Designer government would be more inclined to turn to the solution adopted in Germany, which is collective without being statist. Germany has local (not centralised) training councils which bring firms together under the auspices of the chamber of commerce. Their basic function is to ensure that the local economy's capacity to upgrade its skills is not undermined by the temptation towards inter-firm poaching of trained staff.

In general, the German model of the social market locates collective mechanisms, such as the famous supervisory boards and works councils, *within individual firms* rather than making them part of the state apparatus.

Spillovers may also exist in education itself: the community may benefit from its citizens' education over and above the private benefits that the citizens themselves reap. Too little education may be undertaken if individuals ignore these community benefits. But caution is advisable. The private incentive to pursue education is far from weak and spillover effects may be small. So, while educational spillovers are a possibility, their presence and size need to be established rather than simply assumed.

A further motive for intervening in the market's supply of educational services is social. Democracy amounts to very little unless citizens receive an education permitting them to understand and to participate in the political process. Furthermore, an objective of equal opportunity is that young people receive an education reflecting their inherent abilities rather than their parents' income.

The Decree Economy has responded to these problems with a centralised, hierarchical, slow-moving educational system. School calendars still date from the harvesting requirements of the nineteenth century farms! Not many industries still use the same basic production structure as 200 years ago.

In contrast, a Designer government would give the state the role of determining educational *policy*: to see that schools meet national *standards*, that all the population have *access* to education and to publish *information* on schools' performance. But the state would not itself operate the system. This would be decentralised to individual schools, between which parents would *choose*. With choice, school performance would matter. Schools would be accountable for their results, so they would be obliged to reward teacher success and to tackle teacher failure. The state would be free to focus on learning (the output) rather than on teaching (the input).

A Designer Economy would also need to provide schemes of **social insurance** because many important risks which individuals face are not privately insurable.

First, private markets will not insure unless the customer is left with an incentive to continue to behave prudently afterwards.

There is no private unemployment insurance because there would be little to stop some policy-holders voluntarily choosing unemployment, after being insured, if the payments from the policy were generous enough. Also, without a prohibitively expensive system of inspection, the insurer would find it difficult to know whether a claimant was really unemployed.

Second, markets do not provide insurance against catastrophes (acts of God). No private firm can offer insurance for an event in which everyone (or an unpredictably large number of customers) could simultaneously try to make a claim on the policy. Examples include war, famine and, in the economy, inflation and economic recession. The private sector does not offer insurance against these risks. Unless state schemes do so, no safety-net will exist.

The problem faced by private insurance markets is the familiar one of information. Only under the idealised conditions of a Dream Economy would firms be able to distinguish responsible from irresponsible people in order to charge each an exactly appropriate premium. (This is the same as the problem of distinguishing good from bad plumbers, discussed in an earlier chapter.)

Although sufficient private insurance is not available in a Degenerate Economy, Decree Economies have sometimes reduced information even further. Until recent years, financial companies were permitted to keep secret the commissions they paid to brokers who sent them business. And pension funds are permitted to quote notional retirement payouts based on hypothetical investment returns; these are little more than fiction.

In addition to the economic (market failure) reasons for intervention, there is the social justification. Those who care about providing a minimum-income standard below which citizens cannot fall, regardless of whether they are at work, unemployed or retired, will want social insurance to be available to those unable to make private arrangements.

A Designer government has no easy solutions to the technical problems facing the provision of many kinds of insurance services. The very information which private firms lack about their potential customers — such as who behaves prudently and who likes to go bungee-jumping — is generally also hidden from the state. Still, as with the services already discussed, a Designer government would establish a national *policy* for insurance cover, to see that financial firms meet *supervisory standards* and to provide *information* to the public about companies' costs and performance. But direct provision of insurance would be left to competing suppliers.

Spillovers and information shortages are the main economic grounds for intervention in the markets for health, education, training and insurance. In addition, services such as **public administration, national defence**, and **law** and order are pure *collective goods*. They are provided to everyone or not at all. The private sector would not be able to provide services where non-excludability would allow people to take a "free ride" without payment. And yet, without these services, a civilised and well-managed society is difficult to imagine.

Infrastructural provision can also suffer from market failure. Physical infrastructure has some of the features of a collective good. For instance, some transport and communications networks are provided to everyone who wishes to use them (within the capacity of the system). Secondly, economies of scale may make it cheaper to provide a single national network than several local ones. Thirdly, there may be spillovers: some of the benefits of less traffic congestion and pollution accrue to members of the community who do not themselves use public transport. For all of these reasons, it might be difficult to generate an appropriate amount of private investment in infrastructure. A Designer government could ease that problem by funding some infrastructure from general taxation.

In the 1990s, a type of infrastructure which will need careful public policy consideration will be the new information systems: computers in general and the Internet in particular. Issues of future national productivity as well as of general community access arise.

Finally, **environmental protection** for current as well as future generations can also be an area of market failure. Environmental damage, like pollution, is a spillover which can impose very large costs on third parties. In a Degenerate Economy, these costs will not be borne by those who caused them, so the responsible parties have no reason to minimise them. The reaction of the Decree economy is often to ignore pollution — witness the overloaded sewerage systems in many Irish towns at present. When it does respond, it typically deploys centralised *controls* and regulations overseen by a state bureaucracy. In contrast, a Designer government would use decentralised *incentives* such as effluent fees.

Economic analysis suggests that (in addition to competition and stabilisation policies) carefully constructed interventions in the above areas could improve the economy's performance. Correspondingly, the state should seriously question whether to continue to be economically involved in areas where it is tackling no clear market failure.

Effective Policies to Promote Opportunity
Today, most people feel that it would be as objectionable to make access to education and health care — the stepping stones for effective participation in the community and the workforce — completely dependent on income as it would be to link voting strength to income.

Nonetheless, access *is* very unequal because many incomes are very low. A 1994 ESRI report, *Poverty and Policy in Ireland*, stated that approximately "one in five Irish households in 1987 were on relatively low incomes, experiencing deprivation of a quite basic kind". (For example, not being able to afford new clothes or a warm overcoat, or going into arrears or debt to meet ordinary living expenses.)

The ESRI authors proposed three main sets of policy measures to make a start in tackling Irish poverty. These relate to education, the labour market, and the malign interaction of the tax and welfare systems. (Discussion of labour market issues is postponed to the next chapter.)

In regard to education, the researchers pointed out that those with a poor education risked subsequent poverty, unemployment, and low pay (if at work). They argued for educational resources to be concentrated at primary level, on disadvantaged schools and especially on schoolchildren who were likely to leave school without formal qualifications. Those who had dropped out should be offered second-chance education.

As regards the welfare system and its poverty traps, the study noted that some aspects of the present Irish system were biased against work. In particular, unemployed adults receive additional dole payments for each of their children, as well as medical cards, other non-cash benefits and help with housing costs. But these receipts are lost on returning to work. This loss of income is a disincentive to work. The researchers propose that, instead, child benefit (payable regardless of whether the parent is at work) be increased substantially. To keep down the cost of this measure, the benefit should be taxable, thereby automatically clawing back a good deal of it through the tax system from well-off households. These changes would allow the child-dependent part of the dole payment to be scaled back and eventually abolished. The ESRI authors conclude that this measure would be "the most effective single way of attacking the unemployment trap while improving the situation of poor families". The 1995 Budget, in fact, made a beginning in introducing this change.

Social spending today is facing something of a worldwide crisis. A vastly complicated and costly system has grown up in an ad hoc fashion. There are countless programmes, separately administered. In some cases, poorly-designed welfare payments have trapped people in poverty. These problems raise detailed technical issues of welfare design which go far beyond the scope of this book. Here it must suffice to say that a Designer government, committed to efficiently meeting its social equity targets, would draw on professional research to discover whether the effectiveness and costs of existing programmes could be improved.

In Britain, a thorough review of its welfare system was undertaken in 1993-94 by a (Labour Party-established) Commission on Social Justice. The Commission had a membership of sixteen, a staff of six, and professional research support. It received some 450 submissions, visited 11 UK cities, issued 2 interim reports and 13 working papers. A serious welfare review would require resources on that scale.

Some of the Commission recommendations indicate the likely direction of forthcoming reform in the European welfare state. The report advocated a welfare system that would move away from payments which required the recipient to be out of work, towards schemes that would actively help current welfare claimants to earn their way out of poverty. This "welfare to work" strategy would also seek a better balance between citizens' rights and responsibilities.

Other Commission proposals related to education, including the provision of universal pre-school education, stronger emphasis in primary education on the provision of basic skills, and an expansion of higher education financed by a sophisticated graduate tax. There were also proposals for wide-ranging pension reform.

Some Irish social spending perversely benefits the better off. A study by four researchers at the ESRI (Breen, Hannan, Rottman and Whelan), writing in 1990, noted that Irish public expenditure on education "has been primarily directed towards the benefit of the middle classes" and that "equality of opportunity, despite being a goal of state policy, has never been actively pursued".

The existing welfare system is poorly organised and costly. It has unintended work disincentives built into it. A Designer Economy would want to review and redesign its social programmes and its welfare spending to ensure that they actually and cost-effectively met the intended objective of lessening inequalities in society.

Designer Government: Stopping Institutional Failure
Even if we knew *where* intervention may be needed, that does not tell us *how* the intervention should be undertaken. Collective action need not be old-style state provision. There have been some recent innovative ideas about reforming traditional public sectors to avoid or minimise government failure.

For example, 1993 saw the publication of *Reinventing Government*, probably the first text on public administration ever to enter the US bestseller lists. It prompted the Clinton administration to establish a commission headed by Vice-President Al Gore to undertake a national performance review based on the book's ideas.

Reinventing Government offers an inspiring message for the cynical 1990s: government, if reformed, can make society a more civilised, productive and equitable place. But to do so, government must change. Sceptical public officials should note that *Re-*

inventing Government is a public servant-friendly book: it rightly blames bureaucracy not bureaucrats.

Its authors, David Osborne and Ted Gaebler, point out that US public sector institutions were designed for the earliest years of the twentieth century, against a prevailing background of political patronage and corruption. At the time, the solution appeared to be bureaucracy: a cadre of public servants, independently appointed, professionally managed and working under clear rules. To minimise the scope for political interference, public servants were to be left with little discretion. Everything was to be decided according to the rule book.

In the slow-moving, standardised and hierarchical world of the early- and mid-twentieth century, this "one size fits all" public sector was not too inefficient. But today it has become very costly. Rule-driven bureaucracy is ill-suited to the fast-moving 1990s.

Osborne and Gaebler argue that, today, government needs to be *entrepreneurial*. Whether a person behaves entrepreneurially depends on the institutional structure in which they work. Merely raising or cutting spending, without altering incentives, will leave behaviour, and therefore effectiveness, unchanged.

After examining a wide range of public organisations and activities across the US, the authors extracted ten common threads to dynamic and effective public action:

> Most entrepreneurial governments promote **competition** between service providers. They **empower** citizens by pushing control out of the bureaucracy, into the community. They measure the performance of their agencies, focusing not on inputs but on **outcomes**. They are driven by their goals — their **missions** — not by their rules and regulations. They redefine their clients as **customers** and offer them choices — between schools, between training programmes, between housing options. They **prevent** problems before they emerge, rather than simply offering services afterwards. They put their energies into **earning** money, not simply spending it. They **decentralise** authority, embracing participatory management. They prefer **market** mechanisms to bureaucratic mechanisms. And they focus not simply on providing public services, but on **catalysing** all sectors — public, private and voluntary — into action to solve their community's problems.

Traditional public service programmes are failing, say Osborne and Gaebler. They are driven by constituencies, not customers; by politics, not policy. They use commands, not incentives. They create centralised but fragmented delivery and provoke wasteful turf-wars. They lack self-correcting mechanisms to keep them on course. And they never die.

In contrast to this old-style non-market orthodoxy, Osborne and Gaebler list the advantages of market-oriented government as follows: the market is decentralised and customer-driven, it de-politicises demand and supply, it responds more quickly and flexibly to changes in the overall environment and it is based on voluntary response to incentives. But the market on its own is not enough. The public authorities need to step in to empower communities: to set rules, to provide information, to devise market-type institutions to fill private sector gaps, to share risks, and to invest in infrastructure and people.

Some of the main proposals of Osborne and Gaebler are set out below. They have the common theme of giving the consumer a greater say: by direct empowerment, by giving improved (budgetary) information, by seeking out citizens' opinions, and by channelling funds to individuals (as vouchers) rather than to institutions. Indirectly, consumer power could be increased through decentralisation and more competition.

Decentralisation: An Answer to Information Shortages
Governments lack the necessary information to attempt detailed management of the economy. The answer is for the state to structure the marketplace and then allow decentralised suppliers to compete for business. Governments are better suited to setting policy than to providing services, better at overseeing the activities of others than at direct delivery.

Osborne and Gaebler suggest that governments should do "more steering and less rowing". Rowing rests on brute strength; steering on intelligence. A rowing organisation focuses on implementing a programme mechanically; a steering organisation tackles the underlying problem. For instance, the Irish Bovine TB scheme focused on injecting cattle — TB eradication depends on extinction of the disease.

Governments need to separate policy-making from the provision of a particular service. They need to commission work from competing providers, leaving suppliers to concentrate on using resources as productively as possible, on being flexible and innovative and on satisfying the consumer — all things which governments have traditionally had difficulty in doing.

Osborne and Gaebler give an example, particularly pertinent to Ireland, of the consequence of bringing information about costs out into the open. In New Zealand, the postal service was converted in the 1980s from a civil service department into a public authority. Only then was it revealed that almost half of the country's post offices were losing money. The board wished to close the post offices but the politicians were nervous. However, when the public learned that it would require a subsidy of NZ$42 million to keep the offices open — or almost NZ$100,000 per post office per year — public support evaporated and 432 post offices were closed. This released NZ$42 million to be spent more productively.

Decentralisation is especially important in an uncertain world. The best answers to any problem are not known for sure. It is better to let many varied private solutions be attempted. The ones that succeed will, in doing so, reveal the correct solution. A traditional public sector, in contrast, puts all its eggs in one basket.

Osborne and Gaebler show that the best response to government's endemic information shortage is decentralisation.

Better Budgeting: An Answer to Cash Accounting
Osborne and Gaebler propose several budgetary reforms. Probably the most radical is accruals-based rather than cash-based accounting.

Today, Irish governments prepare their accounts on the basis of cash received or cash paid. This means that a debt incurred today but which does not fall due this accounting period is simply ignored. The results can be perverse. For example, if PRSI is extended to a new class of beneficiaries who will be entitled to certain benefits (for instance, a state pension) only after a delay of several decades, the government's finances can seem to improve (because more PRSI premia are paid today) even though the measure may cost the state money over the long-term. This is daft accounting. Likewise, the appearance of the Irish government's finances can be affected by whether certain cheques from Brussels arrive on 31 December or 1 January. Depending on which it is, one year's accounts are improved and another's disimproved, although the true underlying position is the same regardless.

A second problem with cash accounting is the treatment of assets. For instance, if you own two houses and sell one, your total assets (cash plus houses) are unchanged, even though your money holdings have risen. Not so with cash accounting. If the government sells a semi-state company and obtains £250 million, the value of its assets (to a first approximation) are unchanged but the £250 million will appear as increased government income. No such increase has in fact taken place unless one chooses to ignore the asset sale.

The orthodox system of government accounting is dangerously flawed since it frequently ignores the known future effects of today's decisions. It may be noted that cash accounting would not be tolerated in the accounts of a private company. Better budgeting would make public accounts more transparent. Accruals accounting has recently been adopted in New Zealand and Australia, and the UK government has announced its intention to follow suit.

Empowerment: A Response to Traditional Officialdom
The traditional purpose of public bureaucracies is to service dependent *clients*; recall the descriptions from the Combat Poverty report in Chapter 1 about life in unemployment-wasted Kilbarrack. Osborne and Gaebler recommend a radical shift towards empowering *citizens*. This phrase has a nice ring to it, but what does it mean?

It means returning control of public services to citizens: parent-run schools, resident-run public housing estates, community-run hospices, neighbourhood-managed policing. While communities cannot be forced to take charge of schools, housing or neighbourhoods, they certainly can be given this option. Despite the instincts and training of many professionals and experts, numerous communities in the US have been found to take up such offers.

Osborne and Gaebler list the advantages of citizen empowerment over public bureaucracy: improved flexibility and creativity, greater commitment to the community, better understanding of community problems, a focus on solving the underlying problem not mechanically delivering a public programme, and an emphasis on positive capacity not negative deficiency. A community can manage itself much more effectively and less wastefully than can distant officials or professionals.

Osborne and Gaebler also believe in the empowerment of public officials. They argue for what they call mission-driven not rule-driven organisations. Officials should be told the objectives to be met, not how to meet them. This leaves the organisation free to find the best way to meet its targets. Compared to highly-regulated organisations, mission-focused agencies are more flexible, innovative and effective and they sustain higher staff morale. They explain in detail how participatory management can gain the support of initially-sceptical unions and employees. They say: "efforts to improve productivity [alone] usually undermine both productivity and morale; efforts to improve morale by empowering employees usually heighten both morale and productivity".

A refocusing on missions rather than rules means clearing away obsolete regulations and programmes. To achieve this, Osborne and Gaebler recommend "sunset laws" (a date by which a programme or regulation dies, unless it is expressly renewed), review commissions and zero-based budgeting.

Finally, politicians are public officials too and face most of the same incentives as other public servants. Since 1990, laws to limit the number of terms that a politician may serve in Washington have been proposed in over 20 US states, although in 1995 these were ruled unconstitutional by the US Supreme Court. Such laws might be too extreme a step. But they would certainly change the incentives facing politicians! With a restricted period of office, politicians would be less inclined to sacrifice long-term objectives to short-term re-election considerations. At a stroke (as it were), politics would be less attractive to the kind of person who plans to carve a career out of clientilist cronyism without any consideration for the long-term concerns of the country.

Traditional officialdom — the Decree Economy — has many shortcomings. Osborne and Gaebler show that citizen empowerment, mission-orientation and political reform can help to tackle these defects.

Citizen Enquiries: A Response to the Lobbies

There are many ways for the state to discover the wishes of its citizens rather than just to accept the sectional claims of well-funded and well-connected lobby groups. Governments and public bodies could conduct surveys and interviews, put senior officials periodically in open public offices, offer customer-service training to staff, offer quality guarantees, test-market new pro-grammes, send out undercover inspectors, appoint ombudsmen, request suggestions on free-phones and by electronic mail.

But interest group lobbying can ultimately be addressed only by reforms to the political system. There will always be private benefits to those who advocate public action, and private benefits to those who resist public action; this is the most plausible motive for each group to exert itself. Consequently, groups that demand extra public spending need to provide reliable evidence that there are society-wide (not just private) benefits from this public spending and they should be required to specify how the new spending will be financed. Lobbying needs to be brought out into the democratic sunshine.

Vouchers: One Answer to "Free Goods"

Frequently, the proceeds of taxes which are levied on citizens are passed directly to producers (schools, universities, hospitals, training agencies, research institutes, social welfare centres, refuse collectors, fire services, etc.) who then provide services "free" to households. Inevitably, the public agency is unresponsive to the user, who has no power, but highly attentive to politicians and public officials who determine the agency's budget.

But nothing obliges public services to be organised in this old-style way. It is possible instead to channel funds directly to the user and allow them to select the supplier with whom they are most satisfied. For instance, customers could be given vouchers to be used at the supplier the customer chooses.

These ideas are already in use. Tax relief on mortgage interest, on private rental payments and on insurance products are all equivalent to vouchers. The customer chooses the bank, the landlord, or the financial company they wish to deal with, and the state then subsidises the cost of the service in question. We would quickly object if mortgage relief were only available for loans offered by one particular bank. Yet, this is exactly the restriction we face, while hardly noticing, with most public services. Many of these could also be financed through voucher schemes.

After the last war, the US passed the GI bill which allowed American soldiers to go to college. No "GI colleges" were built (although Veterans' hospitals were). The former soldiers were simply given vouchers which were usable at a host of accredited institutions. The soldiers were left to pick the institution they were happiest with.

The advantages of a voucher scheme are the usual ones that flow from customer power: accountability, de-politicisation, innovation and reduced waste.

Traditionalists claim that vouchers would damage equity. Osborne and Gaebler show that this depends on how the scheme is designed. Take education as an example. There are three possible ways to deliver education while seeking to promote equity. One way is to offer public education to everyone. But indiscriminate subsidisation leaves the rich free to "top up" the budgets of their schools thereby maintaining inequality. A second path is to leave the rich to finance themselves and concentrate public funds on schools to which only the poor are admitted. This discriminates in favour of the poor, but at the price of social class-segregation and the creation of educational ghettos. A third way is to finance individuals, not institutions, using a system such as vouchers. There is no stigma and the value of the voucher given to poor households could be raised to compensate for the extra money well-off households would be able to add to their smaller voucher.

The old-style approach to public service provision — "free goods" financed from general taxation — turns citizens into supplicants before civic officials who in turn have to please politicians rather than the population. A well-designed voucher scheme can help to upright such upside-down accountability.

Competition: An Answer to High Costs
The biggest step towards reducing the costs of providing public services would be to replace state monopolies with competition.

Education, for instance, is a service which could benefit from a well-designed competitive framework. But can there be decentralisation with accountability? Actually, this is exactly what competition offers. Each educational institution is given maximum autonomy, but unless the organisation uses that autonomy to satisfy the community's educational ambitions, it will be left with no pupils.

Would competition harm equity? The current system of monopoly supply of education is already highly segregated: those with resources use private schools or settle in affluent suburbs. This is the status quo. Well-designed competition could improve on it. First, all parents, rich and poor, would have to be supplied with adequate, reliable and independent assessment of schools' performance. (This appraisal would be done *after* taking account of the average calibre of a school's pupil intake; in other words, value-added should be measured.) Second, competition would put pressure on unsatisfactory schools. These would have to pull up their educational socks or face decline and closure as pupils moved to other schools in the neighbourhood or to newly established schools offering a better service. Today, low-performing educational institutions with guaranteed state grants can and do carry on delivering poor performance.

Not only in education, but across a wide spectrum of public services, competition could contribute to improving efficiency and equity. Even in areas where public bodies provide services not to the public but to one another, competition can still help to sharpen performance.

Osborne and Gaebler argue that public employees would not suffer from a carefully-managed change-over to competition. In fact, they should gain. It is hard to be happy working in a lumbering, inefficient organisation which is deeply unpopular with the general public. It is a lot more satisfying to work for a dynamic, well-regarded and well-run organisation. Most people are prepared to work differently and to work harder in order to move from the first situation to the second.

A second way to contain the costs of operating the public sector would be to give organisations "block budgets" to support their mission, leaving considerable discretion in the internal allocation of that budget. This would reduce the current waste produced by the end-of-year rush to spend budgets. This would also simplify the political process, leaving public representatives to concentrate on policy rather than voting on organisational budgets.

If, in addition, organisations could keep a fraction of unspent funds, every employee could have an incentive to save money rather than to spend it mechanically in line with a budget. And managers could build up an investment fund to improve the organisation's effectiveness.

Thirdly, Osborne and Gaebler argue that governments should not only spend money, but they should be allowed to earn it. Because public bodies rarely think in terms of making money, they often accumulate considerable assets — land and buildings — which are left unused though they could be earning money and funding an improvement in the public services that are their owners' main responsibility. For instance, schools could be rented out for other uses during the summer, much more than happens at present.

Finally, it would sometimes be appropriate to contain the cost of public services by charging fees. Examples would be rubbish collection, water and sewer services, recreation facilities, parking, police services at special events, building inspections and so forth. In the US, polls have shown that the public often finds it reasonable that the user should be expected to pay for a service rather than having a tax indiscriminately levied on users and non-users alike. Osborne and Gaebler note that three conditions need to be satisfied for user-fees to be appropriate. First, where there are spillovers, where some of the benefit accrues to those who do not necessarily use the service, the user should not be charged the full cost of providing the service. Second, equity can be secured by offering vouchers or fee-waivers to target groups so that user-fees do not curtail access for disadvantaged groups. A third requirement is that it must be possible to collect the fees efficiently.

Fees have two advantages: they raise funds and, like any price, they reveal which services the community values (is willing to pay for) and which services are only demanded because they are "free".

Osborne and Gaebler show that the traditional high costs of public sectors organised on non-market principles could be lessened by a combination of competition, budget reforms and user-charges.

Conclusion: The State and the Market

In discussing Designer government, this chapter has drawn at considerable length from the Osborne and Gaebler book because while it offers a damning critique of orthodox public sector activity it presents a dazzling package of suggestions for revitalising contemporary government. The broad thrust of *Reinventing Government* has been supported by the US think-tank the Brookings Institution, although it warned against hoping to solve overnight problems that have developed over a century. In overall terms, it underlined the need for a *culture of performance* to tackle the current *performance deficit* of public sectors. More generally, the Designer Economy offers a clear role for both the public and private sectors built on four principles.

First, once competition has been safeguarded, the private sector should be left to produce such normal goods and services as the population wishes to consume and is willing to pay for. Second, where necessary, there should be political reform to ensure that national parliaments can carry out their primary role of defending the general interest. Third, governments should concentrate on two central tasks: promoting economic opportunity and ensuring that any gaps left by the market (in areas such as health, education, training, public administration, infrastructural provision and environmental protection) are filled, without necessarily engaging in their direct provision. Fourth, public services need to be "reinvented" to make them more responsive to the consumer.

In this way, public action and the operation of the market are carefully integrated: the private sector is left to do what it is suited to doing, while the state makes good the market's omissions — but without attributing to the state exaggerated notions of competence, knowledge or virtue.

It is a mistake to debate the roles of the private and public sectors in the traditional all-or-nothing way. As Osborne and Gaebler put it:

> The truth is that the ownership of a good or service — whether public or private — is far less important than the . . . incentives that drive those within the system. Are they motivated to excel? Are they accountable for their results? Are they free from overly restrictive rules and regulations? Is authority decentralised enough to permit adequate flexibility? Do rewards reflect the quality of their performance? Questions like these are the important ones — not whether the activity is public or private.

The 1991 Development Report of the World Bank came to a very similar conclusion: "It is not a question of state or market. Each has a large and irreplaceable role."

This is now the consensus across most of the political economy spectrum. The public perception of bitter ideological disagreements between economists of different political persuasions, although more true at one time, is today about twenty years out of date. In the words of the British economist, Professor Nicholas Stern, writing in 1989, many researchers:

> would now place equal or greater emphasis on government failure relative to market failure in the balance of the argument, than was previously the case with earlier writers, who concentrated heavily on market failure. The scepticism is born of experience but one must be careful not to be too sweeping. We have learned much about what governments can do effectively as well as where they are likely to perform badly. Whereas it is possible that they may be damaging to efficiency and growth if they try to exert detailed and universal control of production decisions, governments can be effective with direct action to raise standards of education, health and life expectancy, and in improving infrastructure such as water supply, roads, power . . . . Further, we should not assume that all government involvement in the production process is doomed to fail. The South Korean example suggests that careful integration of state intervention with private sector initiative can produce most impressive results.

In a similar vein, the American economist Professor Joseph Stiglitz wrote in 1988:

> Today, among American economists, the dominant view is that limited government intervention could alleviate (but not solve)

the worst problems [of market failure]: the government should take an active role in maintaining full employment and alleviate the worst aspects of poverty, but private enterprise should play the central role in the economy.

These are balanced up-to-date statements of representative economic thinking on the way to foster economic development, in the first or any other world. Both the market and the state can fail. Quite a lot is known, on grounds of both logic and evidence, about the areas of greatest relative strength and weakness of these two types of social institution. We have come a long way from the image of a government seeking out the public good and soaring free above a private sector hamstrung by money-grubbing motives. While some contemporary assessments of public intervention may be too pessimistic, one would not want to return to the naïveté of the saintly monk perspective.

The way forward therefore is to be clear about the respective strengths of the private and public sectors and to reorganise public and private responsibilities accordingly. It is a question of carefully integrating the public and private sectors. There will continue to be a major role for the state in the economy; those concerned about this point can sleep easy.

This renewal, although improving the position of the community at large, would be resisted by some traditionalists. But the case for reform is so strong that the public and even many present supporters of the status quo could be won over by the argument for a Designer Economy. That is a task for political leaders.

8

PRODUCTIVE JOBS FOR A DESIGNER ECONOMY

Introduction
Since unemployment is the most critical economic problem facing
Ireland, discussion of designer economics would be very incomplete without considering what its principles imply for tackling
joblessness.

There are three different aspects to promoting employment and
tackling present-day unemployment. First, there is the need to
minimise recession-related joblessness; this is the cyclical element
of the problem. Second, the long-term unemployed need to be
helped back to work; that is the structural part of the problem.
Finally, there is the wider issue of how to stimulate economic activity so that the economy and employment levels expand rapidly.
Each of these is considered below.

Cyclical Unemployment
One of the best things a Designer Economy could attempt at the
end of the 1990s would be to avoid the macroeconomic policy errors and public finance disorders seen in the 1970s and 1980s. The
lessons are clear. A Designer Economy should, over a *medium-term*
horizon, use interest rates and public spending to nudge the
economy in the direction of economic expansion or contraction in
a way which would dampen booms and recessions. This could
help to keep the economy on a path of relatively smooth economic growth, and would offer a stable national economic background for other decision-makers in the economy. Compared to a
utopian ideal, such an economic policy seems modest; compared
to the record, it is challenging.

Note that such a counter-cyclical policy does not give the state a role as an engine of job creation. Nonetheless, in an economy like that of the US (where unemployment moves up and down between, say, 5 per cent and 7 per cent), even reducing unemployment by an average of just one percentage point would be a big fall in average joblessness. Of course, in the parts of Europe where unemployment touches 15 per cent or more, a purely counter-cyclical policy, although helpful, would clearly be a quite insufficient response to mass unemployment.

Structural Unemployment
What of the structural part of unemployment? A very large part of today's unemployment is long-term joblessness which is only weakly related to the economy's cycles of growth and recession. Starting from a point where a high level of structural joblessness exists, an end to recession would not bring such unemployment to an end.

However, the state's traditional response to structural unemployment — an expansion of the public sector — is also flawed. Regardless of their intentions, governments lack the capacity to be efficient producers. While government counter-cyclical policies may be able to lower the average level of unemployment over the economic cycle, direct job creation initiatives have rarely been successful.

Could a Designer Economy do better, perhaps by focusing on improved education and training systems? If resignation in the face of long-term unemployment is a counsel of despair, better education and training is something of a counsel of perfection. Successful education and training programmes do increase the availability and productivity of workers in the economy. (The qualification "successful" in the last sentence is important; what matters is learning rather than teaching and the second does not necessarily deliver the first.) But, in addition, there must be a demand for the newly-trained workers from employers, otherwise much of the training will be wasted.

Before establishing new training programmes, a Designer Economy would attempt to discover why so many present programmes fail, with large numbers of young people leaving the secondary school system without basic qualifications. According to the European Commission, only 42 per cent of Europeans of normal school-leaving age emerge with a qualification from secondary education. The Designer Economy would first want to get the basics right at primary and secondary levels, so that all its citizens leave education with the essential skills for entry into society and working life.

Secondly, a Designer Economy would want directly to address today's long-term unemployment and prevent tomorrow's before it can happen. It would therefore be sympathetic to a system of life-long education and training for its population. This would help to achieve what the London think-tank Demos calls "secure flexibility". Change in today's economy is unpredictable and fast-moving. The individual feels insecure and is apt to resist the changes. Flexibility would be more forthcoming if those needing to change jobs, or change the kind of work they do, could turn to a revamped educational service and extended in-company training schemes. Also, a welfare system redesigned on the principle of a ladder rather than the traditional safety-net, and a trade union movement committed to helping the unemployed into work rather than just protecting union members in existing jobs. The report of the UK Commission on Social Justice recommended, along similar lines, the creation of a tri-partite financed Learning Bank. Workers, employers and the state would contribute funds to the Learning Bank. Then, at some point over their post-school life, each citizen could fund the equivalent of three years' education and training.

What of *existing* structural unemployment? A major intervention by a Designer Economy is clearly necessary. However, the record of existing broad-based retraining schemes is poor. Reports prepared for the National Economic and Social Forum show that the greatest successes have come from decentralised schemes with a large element of local design and control in which detailed locally-available information (about both candidates and jobs) is put to use. Professor Richard Breen of Queen's University, Belfast, who has prepared a number of studies of Ireland's labour market programmes, has commented that "the most efficient strategy would be to adopt the most cost-effective measures and expand their provision. [But] as things stand, we do not know which, of all forms of government expenditure on job creation, is the most cost-effective." Without routine assessment of programmes, the weak ones cannot be weeded out and the successful ones expanded.

Painful though it is, the long-term unemployed must also have realistic expectations about their short-term prospects. A low-skilled person can choose to work at a relatively low-paid job or, in all probability, not to work at all. Over the long term, everybody tries to improve themselves and to do better. This slow struggle cannot start until a person has one foot on the jobs ladder. A failure to get onto that ladder makes it difficult for one's children to get onto it either, with potentially horrendous long-term personal and social costs. Consequently, a job is definitely better than no job, especially for young and first-time job-seekers who can reasonably expect to climb a promotional ladder over time.

If it were possible to smoothen economic cycles and to have well-trained labour forces, the remaining question is where, in a Designer Economy, the *engine* of direct employment growth would be found? This brings the discussion right back to the distinction between productive and unproductive economic activity with which this book began.

Productive Job Creation

There are two ways to create employment. One approach focuses on productivity, the other settles for "job creation". The first policy means that more goods are made, using more people. The second policy means that more people are used but only to produce the same goods as before. There is only one way to create the first kind of job but unfortunately there are many, many ways to create the second.

An episode from Irish history offers an especially stark example of unproductive employment creation. The de Valera government's policy of "self sufficiency" led it to impose heavy taxes (tariffs) on imports. In order to get around the trade barriers, some foreign companies set up factories in Ireland. One UK car manufacturer established a car assembly plant in Ireland. How did this work out? Actually, cars continued to be made in Britain exactly as before. Then, those for the Irish market were taken to one side of the British factory and dis-assembled. The parts were arranged in a ready-to-assemble kit. The kits were sent to Ireland. In the Irish "factory" they were re-assembled into cars. Thus were jobs created.

The catch is in the price. On top of the UK cost of the car, the extra labour needed to dis-assemble and re-assemble the cars had to be added to the Irish price. Furthermore, the Irish factory had a dominant position in the Irish car market. For both these reasons, the Irish price of identical car models was a lot higher than the UK price. Irish car workers gained but Irish car buyers lost heavily. Those who continued to buy cars now found themselves paying twice: the UK price plus the cost of employing unneeded car assemblers. This latter payment was effectively an income transfer — a kind of welfare payment — from car buyers to car workers. In addition, some previous buyers were simply unable to afford a car at the higher price.

If duplicating a car assembly line were genuine job-creation, why not keep going? Of course, dis-assembled-re-assembled vehicles would soon become so costly to "make" that practically none could be sold. Either the business would collapse or it would have to receive a direct subsidy to allow it to reduce the selling price of cars to a level consumers found affordable. This would be another income transfer to the project.

In the end, the whole population could be employed dis-assembling and re-assembling, dis-assembling and re-assembling, the same set of cars. Full employment would have arrived, although since the entire economy would now be producing only a handful of cars, national production, income and living standards would have collapsed.

This kind of "economic activity" is exactly on a par with digging unnecessary holes in fields and filling them in again. Nothing of value is created. However, costs are raised in a fashion which transfers money from one part of the community to the other. And, at these higher prices, fewer consumers can afford to buy the product.

Unproductive job creation redistributes national income without any *extra* output obtained in exchange. This is the road to rags. If the economy's production can instead be raised, the proceeds from its sale — a net increase in national income — are then available to those who expanded production, without any offsetting loss elsewhere.

Aside from the other objections, those who work at some unproductive jobs know well enough that little is being made. This has a predictable effect on their self-esteem. Unproductive schemes contribute neither to economics nor to happiness.

Compare all this with a productive business, say a furniture factory. The factory converts timber and labour into more valuable furniture so the economy's production is expanded. The difference between these jobs and those in the car assembly plant is that furniture is something of value, unnecessary cars kits are not. Consequently, the factory makes money, can stand on its own commercial feet, and does not need to be subsidised by the community.

So how can we encourage productive business? We first need to know why such firms exist. Does the furniture factory exist to "create employment"? That is not the likeliest explanation. After all, if "employment creation" were all that were intended, it could have been achieved with less bother by simply getting people to engage in pointless activity, like dismantling and rebuilding cars. As we have seen, this would have been sufficient to create "jobs". The reason the factory exists is because it makes money for its owners, its managers and its employees. Nobody intended to "create a job" although this is what happens when businesspeople set out to make money and workers look for someone to sell their labour to.

In order for productive businesses to exist, along with their output and employment, businesspeople must make money from employing others and workers must make money from being employed.

This basic fact is sometimes overlooked in discussions of job creation. A Designer Economy could not afford to and so would focus relentlessly on the *productive* kind of jobs. It would nurture business creation and business expansion. It would structure its operations to offer the minimum hindrance to the owners, managers and workers of a business. It would raise the incentive for the population to be entrepreneurial: to take business risks by establishing, managing, expanding, investing in, or working for productive businesses. A Designer Economy would promote economic vitality in its citizens in a general economic environment marked by adequate economic incentives and well-functioning competitive markets. There would be broad freedom of entry to markets for new firms or individuals. For an economy starting from a position of very high unemployment, any doubts about the scale of the entrepreneurial rewards necessary should err on the side of generosity.

Adequate rewards for expanding businesses and employment are needed not only to raise productivity in the economy but also because technological developments and intensified European and global competition will continue to lead to changing job requirements at home. We must ensure that individuals and companies are rewarded for meeting these new challenges.

This is far from being a new message. A litany of reports about Irish economy policy have all consistently recommended that Irish citizens be given the incentive to get on with productive economic behaviour.

Back in 1958, the Secretary of the Department of Finance wrote that "a great and sustained effort to increase production ... is necessary to avoid economic decadence". He argued that "further economic development ... is not so much a question of obtaining capital as of securing the necessary enterprise ... the real shortage is of ideas ... these are likely to fructify only if domestic conditions and policies are favourable to profit-making" and that "no programme of development can be effective unless it generates increased enterprise and saving on the part of a multitude of individuals".

More recently, the mid-1980s report of the National Planning Board argued that Ireland needed economic policies which would "encourage and sustain growth of output and employment ... by inducing private persons and agencies and public enterprises to use their time, talents and other resources more productively in Ireland." In particular, the objective of tax policy should be "to increase the incentive to work, save, invest, take commercial risks and innovate".

The 1992 Culliton Report stated:

Enterprise means accepting risk and that many risky ventures fail. Until a sufficiently large cadre of people in Ireland are prepared to undertake the risks associated with business and are adequately rewarded for success we will continue to experience only modest progress.

A similar call was made by the General Secretary of the Irish Congress of Trade Unions in a 1993 Thomas Davis lecture on unemployment. He argued that "the key element that makes [capital, materials and workers] come together is enterprise and entrepreneurship. . . . We need an entrepreneurial revolution in this country."

In the end, it is up to each of us to act. Better still, as a society we must place incentives before citizens to make it worthwhile for them to act.

At the present time, the rate of job creation is not remotely rapid enough; this is especially true in Europe. The industrial countries' think-tank, the Organisation for Economic Co-operation and Development (OECD), recently drew attention to the fact that, since 1960, the United States in an average year added nearly 2 extra jobs for every 100 jobs in existence, whereas Europe added less than half a job.

Tackling unemployment means making business and work more rewarding. But we must also be clear about what it does not mean. It does *not* mean trying to slow down technological change, restricting foreign imports, introducing mandatory job-sharing, or significant expansion of the public sector. These popular "solutions" to unemployment are discussed next.

Unproductive Job Creation

Work-sharing would reduce joblessness only if there were people ready to earn less in return for working fewer hours. In the example of the furniture factory, job-sharing might mean that a piece of furniture would be made by two workers, each working half of a week, in place of one worker working a full week. It is true that this doubles the number of people employed (while leaving, at this stage, the number of full-time posts unchanged). But what is each person to be paid? If their pay is cut in line with the reduction in hours, then we have raised employment only at the very considerable price of halving income per person. Job-sharing has become *income-sharing*. The latter concept is much less popular than the former and, correspondingly, the demand for work-sharing might be much reduced when its implications for earnings are spelled out.

On the other hand, if pay is not cut one-for-one with hours of work, this will raise the cost of an hour's work to the employer. The two workers between them are supplying only a week's work but, if their pay is less than halved, the cost of this labour to the firm will have increased. But we do not buy more of something because it becomes dearer. We cannot expect to lower unemployment by making jobs costlier, so work-sharing in a form that made work costlier could well raise unemployment instead of lowering it.

The scale of *voluntary* work-sharing, once its impact on earnings is realised, might not be very large. Opinion poll surveys indicate that the numbers would not make a serious dent in unemployment. On the other hand, *imposed* work-sharing in a form that raised labour costs might actually add to unemployment. Besides, there is a further objection to work-sharing for countries like Ireland with a low proportion of people in the workforce. To support their populations, such countries need more income — above all for those out of work — not a division of existing income in a different way.

Could the government push down unemployment by directly employing more people? Or by raising its day-to-day spending and boosting demand? After all, to meet this extra demand private businesses would have to increase production and to employ more people. This is true but it is not the full story. The initial effect of government spending would be to lower unemployment. This happened in Ireland in the late 1970s. But how is the government to pay for its extra spending? Sooner or later, it must collect extra taxation of an amount equal to its higher spending (or more, if debt interest has accumulated in the meantime). These new taxes will cause household and company spending to fall by an amount equal to the rise in government spending. Total spending, and total demand, would be unchanged and likewise employment. When this second unavoidable aspect is included, government spending is seen to have only a temporary role in reducing unemployment.

For Ireland, there are two further reasons why stimulating public expenditure would not be an effective way to reduce unemployment. If we were starting from a clean slate with very little public debt, we might contemplate some additional government borrowing. But that is not the position today. Our outstanding stock of debt is already enormous, mainly because of previous failed episodes of demand stimulation funded by borrowing. Our public debt position is still too fragile to engage in another bout of expansionary public spending. The mistakes of yesterday have tied the hands of governments today. Besides, Ireland is one of the most open economies in the world. A very large part of an expansionary spending programme would flow away into foreign imports, possibly lessening unemployment in Shanghai more than in Shannon. A Designer Economy would not make the mistake of thinking that the hose of public spending was always the solution to the fires of unemployment.

Furthermore, it would scrutinise its own activities to ensure that neither its taxes nor its spending programmes were exacerbating an unemployment problem. Taxation can itself cause job losses. Suppose that in our furniture factory labour taxes rise. Someone must pay the extra tax. But who? There are two principal candidates — workers and owners. Workers might accept this fall in after-tax pay. Or, they might seek an exactly compensating pay rise which, for unchanged sales, would cause a corresponding fall in company profits, shifting the burden of the tax onto shareholders. It can be shown that, in either case, the result would be lower employment.

If workers accept the fall in after-tax pay, the rewards for an hour's work (relative to an hour's leisure) will be reduced. This is unlikely to produce any *wholesale* change in willingness to work. But at the margins, there would be reduced labour on offer from borderline people for whom paid employment is only slightly more remunerative than the value of working in the home, or collecting potential welfare receipts. In other words, some existing jobs will go. Indeed, if labour taxes are very high, these effects may not be so small, especially where workers can move without inordinate difficulty to jobs in lower-tax jurisdictions. In any case, labour taxes do reduce employment.

Suppose workers try to offset the tax by pushing up wages and transferring the burden to profits. If the profit fall persisted, investors would want to shift their money out of this lower-profit activity into better yielding businesses. Investment would fall, the business would contract and so would its need for employees. This process has been observed in many countries. Mobile firms have steadily shifted production out of countries where total labour costs (inclusive of labour taxes) are high to places where costs are lower and, as a result, profits are higher. The production of Waterford Glass products in Eastern Europe is one example.

The effect of a tax cannot be evaded. Either pay is reduced, in which case less of it will be offered, or the business earns lower profits and some investors will switch to other firms. Again, the need for labour will fall. Even if an attempt is made to shift the burden onto consumers (by means of a price rise), higher prices will mean fewer goods sold, so fewer need be made, so less labour is needed. The job-destroying effect of a tax cannot be escaped.

A Designer Economy should be very slow to raise taxes above current levels. It would almost certainly want to reduce them, especially for the low-paid. It would also restructure taxes away from jobs, which are scarce, towards things which society would be more happy to see discouraged, such as environmentally-damaging activities.

Obviously, the welfare system plays a complicating role here. It is self-evident that, for it to be worthwhile to work, a person must be better off in work than out of it. While some people have high earning power others, with limited skills, will have only a modest capacity to earn income in a market economy. A welfare system would do the unemployed no favours by offering them cash and other benefits (medical cards, cheaper fuel, lower rents) in excess of their potential market earnings. This risks trapping such potential workers in a state of unemployment for life.

Of course, if you believe that "work is dead" or some similar statement, the picture would be different. The public authorities might then believe there was a choice only between people who were better off or worse off, but in either case unemployed. In that event, welfare levels might be set above what the recipients could earn at work, without worrying about the likelihood of the un-employed re-entering work. Public authorities should be quite certain that the proposition "work is dead" is true before estab-lishing a welfare system that would *guarantee* that the low-skilled would be permanently cut off from jobs.

Work-sharing and public spending are non-solutions to un-employment. Similarly, proposals to stall technology or to stamp out imports only create unproductive jobs. Technological change is not the cause of unemployment, *provided* an economy is flexible enough to respond to technical changes.

Suppose that, in the furniture factory previously considered, better machinery allowed a worker to make two pieces of furni-ture per week instead of one. Would this cause unemployment? Not unless you believe that the demand for furniture is fixed, in which case, naturally enough, the number of workers needed to supply a static market would fall to half its previous level.

But, for two reasons, neither the size of individual markets nor of the overall economy is fixed. First, the amount of something which consumers wish to buy — the size of the market — *varies* with the price charged. At high prices, we buy less; at low prices, more. If technology improvements allow more products to be made for the same wage bill this implies that each product can be made at a lower wage cost. If some of this saving is passed on to the customer, the lower price will enlarge the market. Meanwhile, the balance will raise incomes in the firm; higher incomes also expand the economy.

In any case, it is a matter of simple fact that economies across the developed world have been growing for several hundred years. How could this possibly be, if there were only a fixed num-ber of things to be made and economies were of a fixed size?

Technical progress would only cause massive unemployment if the workers released from a shrinking sector could find nothing else to work at. But this has *not* been the experience of human history. Human wants have not yet shown the least sign of being saturated. Nor has human ingenuity at devising new products and businesses come near to being exhausted, as long as it is adequately rewarded. In the last fifteen years, massive brand-new electronics and information technology manufacturing and service industries have been created from scratch, not incidentally making billionaires of some of the relevant entrepreneurs. These industries, along with new financial and other services, have mopped up millions of workers being made redundant in other sectors of the industrial world.

There is no arbitrary upper limit to the size of an economy which, along with technology, determines how many people can work. It is the reverse: the productive power of a country's working inhabitants determines the size of the economy and of their income. The extent of this productive power is set by the population's skills, their other resources, their ingenuity and the degree to which they are rewarded for being enterprising and inventive.

Nonetheless, at some point consumer tastes for a *particular* good or service may stagnate. Once a particular market's size stops growing, thereafter further technological improvements do mean that less labour is needed to produce that particular good. But even here, as long as an economy is able to create new jobs in new areas, technological change itself will not be a source of unemployment. For example, the share of agricultural production in the overall economy has fallen sharply over the last century. Consumers, getting steadily better off and having pretty much satisfied their food needs, switched demand to industrial products, especially labour-saving devices for the home. In more recent times, this process has extended to industry itself. Demand has been moving over to services like education, healthcare and entertainment.

Restraining technical change would be the unproductive form of job creation, keeping more people than were actually needed in a given part of the economy. It should be resisted in a Designer Economy.

Nor would restricting imports create productive jobs. (We have already seen the car assembly example of this.) Trade allows a country to export as well as to import. Logically, therefore, a country should specialise in producing those products which it is able to produce cheaply and buy from other countries the things which they make cheaply.

After all, this is what each family does in its private life. Few families aim for self-sufficiency: building their own house, making their own clothes, growing their own food, and so on. Instead, we "export" from the family what we specialise in making and "import" into the family products and services that others have specialised in making.

None of us becomes unemployed because, we spend our incomes on buying things that others provide, instead of making everything we need ourselves. The reverse is true: our community is better off because we each specialise at the task at which we are best. We could make everything ourselves, just about, but such "self-sufficiency" would lower our living standards.

Would the family of a farmer who stopped buying clothes and instead made them at home have "more jobs"? The farmer's decision would reduce the income of clothes-makers, and their spending would fall — including spending on food. The farm family would have gained clothes-making employment but lost some farm work. Moreover, when all the effects were added up, the community would be worse off because total production of clothes and food would be lower. Why? Shifting some work from specialists (farmers at farming, clothes-makers at making clothes) to novices (farmers making clothes, clothes-makers growing food) would mean that the tasks would take longer. In a given working week, the total supply of food and clothes in the community would be reduced. A farmer could not make as many clothes in a day as could be obtained in exchange for the food made in a day, had the farmer concentrated on food production. So the farmer is worse off.

Likewise, international trade is just a cross-border swap. So import restrictions designed to promote import-competing jobs have negative effects on jobs in exporting industries. If Ireland stops buying cars from Japan, Japan loses the Irish pounds earned on its car sales which permitted it to buy tourist and other services from Ireland. Creating jobs in import-substituting sectors is offset by job losses in exporting sectors and overall living standards are lowered.

Would we be richer or poorer in the morning if the government banned certain imports? This is not a hard question for Irish people to answer. Ireland followed this path from the 1930s to the 1960s. De Valera-style self-sufficiency duly impoverished Ireland and more than half a million people gave their verdict with their feet. It must be better to permit imports — allowing the home economy to obtain cheaper goods — and instead to have the domestic labour force produce goods and services which consumers, at home or abroad, are willing to buy.

Unproductive job creation damages economic efficiency. It redistributes income from consumers or taxpayers in a way not necessarily related to social equity. In contrast, productive economic activity raises employment without cutting living standards. Since international trade is not the fundamental source of unemployment, the Designer Economy would favour liberalised trade.

But Where Will the Productive Jobs Come From?

If we resist the unproductive path to job creation and rely solely on stimulating enterprise and productivity, where are all these wonderful new jobs to come from? Will they really be called into existence by something as seemingly feeble and intangible as economic incentives and rewards? Believing the answer to this question is the really big intellectual challenge. The truth is that no one can know *what* the jobs will be or *where* they will occur. Future jobs depend on future profitability. And only prophets would know for certain the location of future profits. Everyone else must take their chance. Many businesses will make an attempt. Some will succeed, some not. We cannot foresee which will be which. The same applies to jobs and careers. The main thing is that there be an adequate reward to compensate for the risks associated with the attempt.

But isn't it true that work is dying? So many gurus say so. They do; but the facts are against them. Outside Europe, there is no sign whatever of work dying. In North America, 35 million jobs have been created since 1973. And 10 million in Japan. Even in Europe, 10 million were created. In the developing states of Asia, jobs are expanding at exceptionally rapid rates. Right now, in China, millions of new jobs are coming into existence. Many of these jobs have unattractive features but, as long as they keep arriving, it is nonsense to claim that work is dead.

But can we be *sure* that there will be something for Ireland to make? Defeatists believe that very little can successfully be produced in Ireland and, accordingly, that we must lower the trade shutters, fling sand in the gears of technology, divide a fixed stock of jobs amongst the population and expand the public sector's role as a social employer of the last (and sometimes the first) resort. But I know of no reason — no sensible reason — to believe this tale of woe. Besides, the full implications of its being true would be overwhelming. If it were true that Ireland could make nothing, then the national goose would really be cooked. There would be no reason to do anything. No economic strategy could save us if some jinx condemns Irish people, alone of all the nations on the globe, to be unable to turn a profit from mundane business tasks. If those who say that "Ireland cannot compete" believe their own words, why do they bother opening their mouths? Why protest about imports or newfangled equipment? Nothing matters anyway in an Ireland that is doomed to decay.

Living Standards, Employment and Wages
To raise living standards, we all wish to see wages rise rapidly. But, as wages are also linked to employment, it would be counterproductive to raise pay without regard to productivity increases. Furthermore, starting from a point of high unemployment, any serious commitment to lowering unemployment means the monies provided by higher productivity should first be committed to investment and job expansion before being directed to raising the pay of those already at work.

Wages are the link between people and jobs. In order for this mechanism to work — for wages to bring people and jobs together — two things are required. First, wages must be high enough for employment to be something which earns good money for workers. Second, wages must not be so high that employers and investors cannot also make good money from the business. Overly high wages leave many workers too costly to employ and unable to find work; overly low wages would, in several different ways, cause workers to drop out of the labour force and leave employers unable to find the staff they needed.

What does it mean to say that "labour is too costly to employ?" It has to do with productivity. If hiring a person costs more than the value of what they produce, it cannot be profitable for an employer to recruit them, and so they won't be employed. Therefore, if a job is to make money for the employer, workers must be paid in line with the value of their work.

Without productivity increases, wage rises simply move a company's expenditure away from non-labour costs into the wage bill. Since overheads and debt interest and suppliers must still be paid, this really boils down to turning some profits into wages. There is a limit to how far this process can be taken. If taken too far, it would ultimately not be worth the owners' while to continue operating the business. Far from having raised incomes, the company would close and wages would vanish. A related risk is that profits would be reduced to the point where they were no longer sufficient to permit adequate re-investment to secure the future of the firm. In this case too, wages could be raised temporarily only eventually to fall to zero. These considerations highlight the way in which profits and wages are mutually dependent.

If a company is not making good profits, its employees should be as worried as its owners. Any attempt to push up pay without a corresponding rise in company income can only shift money around the company with distinct dangers for the long-term health of the firm.

But what of the other half of the equation? Will the wage which allows an employer to make good money from hiring someone be enough to allow that worker also to make good money from working? Well, that depends very much on the person's productivity. In private medicine, the value placed on the services of brain surgeons permits the charging of fees which are enough to make a profit for the hospital as well as leaving the surgeons financially well provided for. Employer and employee are both satisfied. But office cleaners or labourers who perform simple manual tasks with a low economic value will be paid correspondingly little if the business is to make any money for its owner.

Aligning pay with productivity is fine for highly productive people, but it means the low-skilled will be low-paid. There are two genuine answers to this problem and one false one. The false approach is to force a company to remunerate its workers by more than the value of their work; this makes the business lose money and eventually it will close.

One helpful part-answer is that a community motivated by social equity could transfer some income to the low paid, in addition to their market earnings, through the tax-and-welfare system. In this way, the welfare system would make payments to people in work rather than paying them not to work. Realistically speaking, the scale of such transfers is likely to be modest.

Since productivity determines wages, the long-term answer to low-pay is to raise the productivity of the workforce.

How can productivity be improved? Productivity is raised by the use of a great deal more machinery in conjunction with higher-skilled workers to boost output per person. It therefore depends on three kinds of capital. There is business capital (plant and machinery) provided by firms, public capital (infrastructure) provided mainly by the state, and human capital (the quality of labour) which is provided by workers in the context of the prevailing education and training system. Raising productivity means maintaining the incentive to invest in these three kinds of capital.

Take agriculture as an example. Better technology — improved education and more machinery — has dramatically raised the average Irish farmer's capacity to produce. In 1980, some 100,000 Irish farmers produced agricultural products worth about £1.5 billion. In 1950, when Ireland had 400,000 farmers, agricultural output (in the prices of 1980) amounted to, let us say very approximately, £900 million. So over those 30 years the value of farm production *per farmer* has jumped from £2,250 to £15,000. When this output is sold, the proceeds raise farmers' incomes. Farmers' living standards are so much higher now because the average farmer is producing so much more today than in earlier decades.

A different way to look at these facts would be to say that technology and productivity "destroyed" some 300,000 jobs. Well, we could have had 400,000 farmers in Ireland in 1980, or indeed 4 million for that matter. But since, on its own, this would not increase the size of the market for agricultural produce, per-farmer incomes would have to fall by three-quarters from £15,000 to £3,750 (£1.5 billion divided into 400,000 shares). This would be the high price of unproductive "job creation".

Of course, new technology could be resisted. Tractors and fertilisers could be banned in farming. But, then, the higher incomes would be lost too. Technology and living standards are the two sides of a single coin. One cannot be had without the other. Rising living standards are very popular but they are unobtainable without technology-driven increases in productivity. Living standards, wages and employment are all connected.

But suppose, as in the mid-1990s, that tremendous numbers of people are already unemployed? What then for wages? Well, the higher revenue which a company obtains from higher productivity may be spent in three ways: raising pay and dividends, to the benefit of workers and investors; cutting prices, to the benefit of customers; or, using the extra resources to expand investment and employment.

From the viewpoint of the unemployed, price cuts and investments are better than wage growth. Wage increases make jobs more expensive, which is not good news if you're looking for work. In contrast, price reductions stimulate consumer demand for the product and are positive for employment in that industry. Similarly, investment to expand a business is good for employment especially if, at the time the decision is made, workers are not becoming more expensive compared to machines.

Current levels of Irish unemployment exist in the context of national wage bargaining. Given the connection between wages and employment, the European Commission's 1993 *White Paper on Employment* advocated that any "new gains in productivity would essentially be applied to forward-looking investments and to the creation of jobs" rather than as an income increase to those already at work. This objective could be pursued, within a national pay bargaining framework, by having a percentage gap by which *average* wage increases would be below *average* productivity increases. The European Commission recommended that agreement be sought to keep "hourly wage increases below the growth of productivity". A figure of one percentage point of a gap was mentioned. But Irish unemployment is the second-highest in Europe, so the gap should be considerably larger here.

Under such a proposal, wage increases would not be as rapid as otherwise. But everybody would still gain. Each person moved from the dole queues into a job lowers the need for taxes to finance dole payments, so after-tax living standards rise in all households across the community.

Conclusion

To promote employment, a Designer Economy would pursue relentlessly the *productive* kind of jobs, supporting projects and policies only if they passed the productivity test. This would mean rejecting trade restrictions, technological restraints, mandatory work-sharing and public sector "job creation".

A Designer Economy would strive never to make the entrepreneurship of workers or employers less rewarding because of the state's own behaviour. In an economy like Ireland's, the rewards for entrepreneurship need to be greatly increased.

A Designer Economy, in the interests of the labour force, would not make labour more expensive. State action, such as budget provisions, should be checked for their impact on the cost of employment. In the interests of the unemployed, labour use should be made cheaper by shifting some of the burden of taxation away from scarce work towards property and environmentally-harmful activities. The Culliton Report's (1992) proposals for radical tax reform would be a good place to start.

A Designer Economy would revamp education and training to encourage life-long learning and to support "flexible security". It would make welfare services more active and less passive.

These principles are quite general. But that is what principles are. It is up to policy-makers and decision-takers to flesh them out into specific policy proposals.

9

INSTITUTIONAL REFORM

Introduction

Ireland suffers from important institutional failings that leave it some way from being a Designer Economy.

First, economic policy is not guided by coherent principles. As a result, economic responsibilities are not properly divided between the state and the market. If productivity and social equity were the goals, then direct production, under competitive conditions, should be the task of the market. The state's duty should be to close the (closeable) economic and social gaps left by the market. But this is not the allocation of responsibilities we see in Ireland today.

Second, the private sector does not make the best use of its resources: the known weaknesses of the market economy — limited competition and unequal opportunities — are not sufficiently acknowledged or tackled.

Third, the public sector also fails to make the most effective use of its resources. Here too competition is deficient. In addition, the state apparatus is outdated, poorly designed and, in places, breaking down.

Fourth, the present Irish electoral system gives too much weight to the constituencies rather than the country, paralysing national economic management and postponing economic reform.

One factor holding these various failings in place, rather like an ice-cap, is the "consensus" which has shaped Irish economic policy-making for the past decade. This status quo consensus receives a very uncritical press in Ireland. But not every consensus is desirable. One might be a virtuous coming together of different interests to subordinate sectional concerns to the welfare of the nation. Another might just be collusion by insiders against the public at large. A consensus might start as the first and degenerate into the second. The content of the consensus matters as much as its existence.

A central plank of the present Irish consensus is the need for a balance between economic and social objectives. So far so good. But, on the assumption that more public spending is the only way to promote social objectives, pressure is applied to keep public spending rising at least in line with overall economic growth. No fundamental reassessment of public and private responsibilities is possible in such a framework, which freezes the tasks and the shares of each sector as they are now.

Irish institutional reform means taking a sceptical look at the present consensus. To protect the interests of the unemployed, we should consider a procedure like the clause in the 1989 Belgian competitiveness law. This requires that if there is a fall in export share, or if wage rises exceed those of trading partners, a review of the prevailing pay agreement is triggered to reverse the loss of competitiveness. No such mechanism exists in Ireland, even after the currency crisis of 1992-93 revealed the costs of inflexible national pay bargaining.

A Cartelised Private Sector
The great failing of the Irish market sector is the absence of sufficient competition.

There are just two main retail banks, one very dominant newspaper group, one dominant beer producer, one beef baron, a dominant spirits manufacturer, a dominant video rental company, a dominant building materials' firm.

Competition between booksellers has been restricted by adherence to the Net Book Agreement, competition between grocers by the Groceries Order, competition between car sellers by exemption from EU competition law. The large mark-up on magazine prices (flexible when the Irish pound weakens but rigid when the Irish pound strengthens) is a sign of weak competition in retailing.

The two largest retail banking groups have been allowed to amass control of 70 per cent of the banking market between them. The *Financial Times* reported in September 1994 that the return on equity of AIB and Bank of Ireland, at 40 per cent in their Irish domestic operations, was double that achieved by the most profitable European banks. The bank officials union has used its own monopoly power to extract high pay for its members. Until very recently, the banks' management went along with this, since the cartelised conditions in the industry allowed the cost to be passed on to the consumer.

The newspaper industry is dominated by the Independent newspaper group. One notable difference between the US and Irish economies is that when Dr Tony O Reilly wishes to make $1 million in the babyfood business he must do so in the teeth of commercial competition. But to make a fortune in the Irish market, he is permitted simply to swallow his competitors. And for all that they object to the Independent group, its Irish newspaper rivals are quick to close ranks and to give vent to the crudest beating of the nationalist drum when it is a question of protecting their cosy world of high newspaper prices from foreign competitors.

Competition has been eliminated from nearly all of Irish agriculture. Prices are set in Brussels, production is regulated by quota ceilings and "producers" are even paid to set aside (i.e. waste) land. Although farmers see themselves as staunch supporters of the "free" market, this is true only insofar as it applies to property. When it comes to production, farmers want the market kept as far as possible from them. The Irish Farmers Association proposed in 1995 that east European farmers be kept out of the EU for a further twenty years. There have also been calls for farmers alone to be eligible for forestry grants.

Entry to the Irish professions is heavily restricted. Until the mid-1990s, a handful of Dublin stockbroking firms earned large risk-free commissions on government bonds. An *Irish Times* investigation of dental treatment in 1994 found the cost of the same procedures to be three times higher in the Republic than in Northern Ireland. The enormous earnings of millionaire medical consultants is partly related to entry restrictions. Only a tiny handful of pharmacy graduates emerges from the Irish university system each year.

The legal professions agitate to prevent any capping of their lucrative earnings from insurance claims but there is a £0.25 million ceiling on claims against the Law Society compensation fund. The infamous expenditure on the Beef Tribunal indicated the scale of inflated charging for Irish legal services. The "daily rate" paid to the legal millionaires-to-be was twice that paid to British barristers who worked for the Scott Inquiry in Britain. Did the Irish inquiry need quite so many barristers for quite so many days for quite so much more money per day?

An interesting detail to emerge from the 1994 resignation of Mr Harry Whelehan as President of the High Court was his inability to resume his career as a barrister without the Bar's permission, as expressed in a vote by member barristers. In what other business does re-entry depend on a vote of incumbents? Irish restrictive practices are far from confined to such organisations as the Aer Lingus craft unions.

State licensing directly restricts entry to the taxi business, to many other kinds of transport service and to the pub trade. Dublin has hardly more pubs today than in 1900. Even though the population is much larger and incomes much higher, the Dublin beer market is still divided between an almost fixed number of pub-owners. No wonder Dublin pubs look like barns and that some can reach a selling price of a million pounds a go.

Some of these trade restrictions are in conflict with others. Restricted pub licensing means fewer pubs so drinkers must travel further. But restricted taxi licensing means fewer taxis so drinkers choose to drive — in breach of the drink driving laws. It would be comic if it weren't tragic.

In the trade union movement, competition for members is outlawed by the ICTU's policy of no "poaching", which gives union officials a quieter life but is a dubious proposition for union members.

Post-1987 national pay bargaining has been conducted by the greatest cartel of them all: big unions, big business and big government. The agreements have delivered substantial real pay rises to the employed and lots of extra spending power to politicians. But for those outside the club, principally the unemployed and emigrants, the benefits are harder to see.

As a result of these anti-competitive practices, Ireland has a highly cartelised domestic economy which is inefficient, stagnant and inequitable. Without the threat of commercial rivals, dominant businesses have lax management and inefficient work practices. These higher costs have to be borne by the consumer. Furthermore, the domestic economy stagnates. (The British Nobel Prize-winning economist, Sir John Hicks, once remarked that "the best of all monopoly profits is a quiet life.") Inefficient firms find it difficult to export to other economies, so the domestic economy comes under siege as freer trade rules extend foreign competition deeper and deeper into the home market. Social equity is also reduced. Privileged producer groups with monopoly power can boost their incomes, not by supplying something new or better, but because they are able to restrict supply and keep up prices.

Anti-competitive business practices must be an important consideration, although not the only one, in explaining the record of the Irish economy. Unlike some other factors, this one is under our own control.

Individually, none of the interest groups which gain from anti-competitive practices will co-operate with the loss of these benefits. The only chance for reform would arise with a general striking-down of such arrangements. That approach would allow the benefit of everyone else's loss of privileges to be traded for the loss of one's own advantages. But any attempt to tamper with producer privileges one by one inevitably brings forth forecasts of the end of civilisation as we know it.

For instance, in the late 1980s, the vintners successfully stymied the effective extension of drink licences to restaurants by getting sympathetic politicians to insert so many "safety" conditions into the new law that many restaurants would practically have had to be rebuilt to qualify for a licence. At the time, the vintners conjured up a vista of increased underage drinking and the end of the family pub if more competition were allowed.

Similarly, lobbying by solicitors succeeded in 1994 in overturning proposals in the Solicitors' Bill to allow financial institutions to carry out conveyancing and probate work. The then President of the Law Society told the *Sunday Business Post* that competition was fine for supermarkets but not for legal services which were not like "the selling of cornflakes".

IBEC claimed, in October 1994, that a failure to renew the Groceries Order (limiting competition in the grocery sector) would raise prices, eliminate 19,000 jobs and lead to something it called "commercial terrorism".

Irish garages have sought to thwart imports of second-hand Japanese cars by appealing to issues of alleged safety, filling the airwaves with advertisements about cowboy car salesmen.

In its 1993 survey of the Irish economy, the Organisation for Economic Co-operation and Development (OECD) zeroed in on competition. The OECD judged the Irish legislative machinery (up until then, the Restrictive Practices Acts and the Fair Trade Commission) to have been flawed, weak and often irrelevant. The report contrasted the competitive foreign-owned export sector with the domestic service sector where "competition law has been weakly enforced and restrictive practices have been allowed to flourish".

The OECD drew a direct link between high Irish unemployment rates and lax competition laws.

The clearest sign of weak competitive pressures in the Irish economy is to be found in the high level of Irish prices. Although by European standards Ireland is a relatively poor country, in 1985 the price of Irish private consumer goods was 5 per cent higher than the EU average and 8 per cent higher than in Britain. This is quite remarkable. Since Irish incomes are lower than the European average, the labour which goes into Irish production is cheaper than on the Continent. So how then is the resulting output dearer? The OECD suggests the answer lies in anticompetitive arrangements which keep prices high.

By 1990 Irish consumer prices had moved slightly below the EU average but they were still 10 per cent higher than in Britain. The deviations were particularly pronounced in the domestic service sector, one of the most sheltered parts of the Irish economy.

In 1990, food prices in Ireland were 10 per cent higher than the EU average, beverages were 80 per cent dearer, transport services were some 10 per cent dearer, communications were 30 per cent more expensive and medical and health care was also some 10 per cent above the EU average. The OECD reported that, in both 1985 and 1990, Irish prices were higher in nine out of the twelve categories of household consumption spending. Only rent, clothing and footwear, and education and recreation were decisively cheaper than on the Continent.

In the case of some goods, part of the explanation for high prices is undoubtedly high Irish goods taxes. But this is not the whole story. After all, between 1985 and 1990 there was a dramatic fall in the relative cost of Irish transport services — from 70 per cent above the EU average down to 10 per cent — at least partly due to the arrival of competition in Dublin-London air travel.

The OECD found competitive pressures to be especially weak in the Irish wholesaling and retailing sectors. For every 50 retail businesses in Ireland there are only 6 wholesale outlets. In France there are 8, in Germany 16 and in the UK 25.

In the early 1990s, the basis was finally laid for a possible improvement in the laws governing competition. A Competition Act was finally adopted in 1990, one hundred years after the equivalent US law. This machinery, though welcome, is in its infancy. Mr Patrick Massey of the Competition Authority argued in mid-1995 that, up to then, the new Act had made relatively little impact because the Authority could not, on its own initiative, investigate cases of possible anti-competitive practice. This inexplicable omission was rectified in a 1994 amendment to the Act. But the amended legislation still does not specify the fines or penalties for non-compliance. Furthermore, the likelihood of detection is too low to deter many law-breakers. So far, the impact of the Act has been nothing like as great as it might be.

To address the problem of anti-competitiveness we need a new institutional structure of more *domestic* openness and competition, but also a changed attitude to anti-competitive behaviour by private businesses. Increased competition and reduced cartelisation can only be achieved by strengthening laws in that area. The market cannot police itself. But historically the Irish state has failed to provide a tough "competition policy" to regulate private firms.

A Monopolised Public Sector

No less than the private sector, a lack of competition bedevils the Irish public service. Educational, training and health services are overwhelmingly state monopolies. So are domestic electricity, gas and peat energy supply, postal and telecom services, rail transport and city bus services. The state is dominant in broadcasting, health insurance, certain kinds of banking and in forestry. For many years, a state airline and a state shipping line relied on monopoly privileges. Harbour boards and airport management are state-controlled.

Telecom Éireann and RTE are allowed to own the country's main cable television company, preventing others using the cable network to provide competing services. In 1995, Bord na Mona bought out its direct competitor, Coal Distributors Ltd. RTE snuffed out a rival to the RTE Guide by refusing to supply the Magill Guide with details of its broadcasting schedules. (It has taken Magill almost a decade in the European courts to have this action deemed illegal.) Community rating will strongly discourage foreign insurance companies from challenging the VHI in the market for health insurance.

Until the late 1980s, state bodies were actually exempt from the Restrictive Practices Acts, itself an interesting commentary on official attitudes. This omission allowed companies to exploit their monopoly position in their own and their employees' favour, to the detriment of customers. The 1993 OECD review of the Irish economy described the semi-state sector as one in which the "principles of competition have been subordinated to more social and collectivist goals, leaving consumer interests at risk from relatively inefficient public sector monopolies and excessive regulation". Despite some recent improvements, the OECD judged reform of the commercial semi-state bodies to be "partial and incomplete".

What have been the economic results of this wholesale monopolisation in the state sector? Without a full-blooded audit to measure state sector performance, only fragmentary information is available. But suppressing competition cannot in general be conducive to high performance.

A 1995 OECD study found that in Irish primary and secondary schools, the standards of basic reading, maths and science were lower than in many other developed countries. Amongst the weakest students, the gap was more pronounced still. The short Irish school year was considered to be a crucial contributory factor to the general standards gap. The OECD also found the performance of individual Irish schools to be much more uneven than in other countries and that almost one-quarter of students do not complete a full secondary education.

A 1993 ESRI report for the European Commission remarked in passing that Telecom Éireann was the highest-cost telecom company in the EU and probably in all of the industrial world. A former chairman of Telecom Éireann, Brendan Hynes, wrote in early 1994 that the average Telecom customer's phone bill was 30 per cent more than the European average and that this was because "Telecom Éireann is very inefficient".

In the mid-1990s, An Post was bombarded with criticism over late delivery of post. No very elaborate technical assessment is needed to judge the quality of the services provided by CIE.

One snapshot test of the effectiveness of state broadcasting services is that the credit for exposing the beef industry scandal and the Fr Brendan Smyth extradition delay goes to UK and Northern Ireland television documentaries.

Such evidence as there is does not indicate high performance levels in the monopolised state sectors of the Irish economy. The state is failing in one of its key functions: ensuring competitive conditions in the economy at large.

Instead, the state has taken responsibility for direct production tasks that are best left to the private sector (aircraft maintenance, steel making, sugar manufacturing and turf cutting). With some qualifications, the same is true of telecom services and electricity supply. The private sector is best at performing these tasks because competitive markets force firms to work hard, root out waste, cut costs and meet customers' needs.

State efforts at direct production are hamstrung by three obstacles. First, the public authorities are reliant on the companies they are supposed to be managing for the very information needed to conduct good management. The companies will not always have an incentive to be frank and forthcoming. Second, the monopoly rights and political safety nets granted to these businesses validate poor management and inefficient work practices. Thirdly, political control brings chronic problems. Consumers and voters are interested in value for money, politicians are concerned with electability. So public representatives deliver "regional policy" by compelling planes to land in their region. They deliver "jobs" by overstaffing public firms. They deliver "public accountability" by appointing political associates to semi-state boards. They deliver "low inflation" by refusing to sanction merited price increases. And they deliver "investment" by shelling out taxpayers' money for semi-state equity. In these circumstances, it is no wonder that semi-state companies are eventually brought to their knees.

A commercial orientation — serving customers rather than constituents — requires an arms-length relationship with local political worthies. In practice, that means private ownership.

While attempting countless tasks to which it is utterly unsuited, the Irish state fails to attend adequately to responsibilities that it alone can deliver, especially the tasks of rooting out anti-competitive business practices and promoting opportunity.

Public Policy Incoherence
Why does the Irish state fail to carry out properly the tasks which it alone can accomplish but struggle to achieve objectives which are best left to the private sector? Because its actions lack the guidance of explicit and consistent principles. Without such principles, like productivity and social equity, action is inevitably incoherent.

If productivity were the guide, the state would have taken on fewer direct economic responsibilities but more supervisory functions. If productivity were the guide, competition in the private and public sectors would have been policed much more strictly. If productivity were the guide, the state would offer transitional finance to help workers in declining industries switch to viable businesses, not to prop up uneconomic ones. If productivity were the guide, the state would not impose a job-destroying combination of high labour taxes and low capital taxes.

If social equity were the guide, the state would not just pay out welfare passively but intervene to stop a spell of unemployment being extended to chronic long-term joblessness,. If social equity were the guide, the state would channel finance towards disadvantaged primary schools, not third-level colleges which the disadvantaged will almost never reach. If social equity were the guide, the state would stop artificially inflating the incomes of big farmers. If social equity were the guide, the state would not subsidise Hollywood film moguls as part of a risk-free tax shelter for the wealthy in Ireland.

In general, if productivity and equity were the guides, the state would seek to fill those economic and social gaps left by the market which were amenable to state action, judged on a realistic assessment of state capabilities.

But productivity and social equity are not the dominant guides to state action in Ireland today. Much of what the government now does rests on no national economic or social justification but can be explained only as parish-pump politics, often of the most short-sighted and inefficient kind. Consider the 1994 budget. It was littered with measures that lacked a demonstrated economic or social justification: special tax treatment for loss adjusters employed by insurance companies, for VAT payments on certain luxury coaches and for elderly brothers and sisters sharing the family home; a building grant to the Sheriff Street youth club; a plan to co-ordinate World Cup tourism; and a pilot initiative to encourage people to live in the upper floors of business premises in the centre of certain cities.

But why should we need separate tax provisions, not just for luxury coaches, but for *certain* luxury coaches? Why should we need special measures for elderly brothers and sisters with certain accommodation arrangements? Should Ministers really be free, without further ado, to subsidise youth clubs and sports stadia in their own constituencies? And if the owners of city-centre properties want more people to live in them, couldn't they try charging low rents before looking to taxpayers to subsidise them?

Most recent economic assessments have recommended that Ireland abolish — not extend, as in 1994 and 1995 — its endless fiddly little tax breaks. This would allow lower tax rates to be applied to a wider income base. But no such vision motivates Irish tax adjustments of the 1990s.

After the 1995 budget, the extension of tax relief from house mortgage to house rental payments was defended by politicians on radio talk shows on the grounds that people who rent accommodation were "the only people who get no help from the state". If this means bestowing gifts like Santa Claus, it is a hopeless guide to public policy. The government is not Santa Claus, it cannot *simultaneously* help everybody: any money it spends on Peter it must collect from Paul. It should treat comparably citizens in comparable circumstances. That, in fact, offers a perfectly coherent justification for tax relief on rents: to equalise the tax treatment of owned and rented accommodation, leaving households to make the arrangements that suit them best. But these were not the efficiency grounds on which the measure was defended, so presumably these were not the grounds which motivated the change either.

If the state's role, in a Designer Economy, is to fill the (economic and social) gaps left by the market, two questions should be asked about each public policy and programme. Does it enhance productivity (by resolving some market failure)? Or does it improve social equity (by increasing the opportunities of the disadvantaged)? Only by asking such questions could a coherent policy package be developed.

In the case of the EU structural funds, two ESRI researchers, Patrick Honohan and Philip O Connell, argued in 1994 that it was hard to find a market-failure rationale for many of the spending programmes. The authors felt, for example, that too many projects were driven by EU environmental Directives of an overly Rolls-Royce character. And they pointed out that if Irish firms lack private finance to set up or to expand, more government grants would just eliminate any incentive for the financial services industry to plug such a gap. There is a good case for directing structural spending towards tackling the low qualifications of the unemployed. However, the ESRI researchers noted that the gravest form of this problem — educational drop out — is not part of the National Development Plan at all.

Like the budgetary and industrial policy measures, the spending of the structural funds also seems not to derive from a coherent set of principles. Given the murky rationale for many state interventions, it seems inevitable that funds could be more effectively used if spent on programmes with clear objectives.

But perhaps public initiatives are directed elsewhere? Perhaps they are aimed at improving opportunity and social equity? Unfortunately, many recent policy measures do no such thing. On the contrary, the mid-1990s have witnessed numerous redistributive policies which take income from the poorer to give it to the richer. Examples include the 1994 pay rise of up to 17 per cent for senior civil servants, other VIPs (and originally government ministers). The 1995 abolition of fees for third-level education. The 1995 scaling-back of residential property tax. And the 1995 proposals to allow some teachers to retire on an enhanced pension after less than full service.

All of these measures overwhelmingly help the already better-off: middle-class civil servants, middle-class students, middle-class property owners and middle-class teachers. In fact, a home-owning civil servant or teacher with children in college could benefit from three out of the four proposals. Social redistribution, proposed as a Robin Hood policy, seems to have degenerated into a Sheriff of Nottingham scam.

The scale of such transfers can be enormous. Abolishing fees could save a family with several children who go to college a sum of the order of £20,000 (and possibly much more) over a period of years. No government would ever stand for election on an open platform of taxing all families in order to make a gift of the proceeds to a small number of families. Yet, this is what governments without goals find themselves doing.

It is impossible to have coherent policies without coherent principles. These seem to be lacking in Irish public policy today and it cannot therefore be surprising to find a cartelised private economy and a monopolised public sector.

A Growing Crisis in the Public Sector
Since about 1990, signs of public sector crisis and decay have come fast and furious.

The problems began with a wave of financial scandals affecting Ireland's "political-industrial complex". First, the beef industry was accused of serious malpractice and of having an overly-close relationship with the Department of Agriculture and with politicians and political parties. Shortly after, accusations were made against executives of the former Irish Sugar Company. The convoluted financial engineering surrounding the purchase of a site for a new Telecom Éireann headquarters then led to a further scandal. Long and costly public investigations followed, but some of these were decidedly inconclusive.

Meanwhile, the EU-inspired dismantling of their traditional monopoly privileges had prompted a crisis in other parts of Ireland's semi-state sector. Only enormous taxpayer subsidies to Aer Lingus, Team Aer Lingus and Irish Steel prevented their closure in the early 1990s. In 1995, Bord na Mona received a huge write-off of its debts. Shielded by "derogations" from EU laws, Telecom Éireann, An Post and the ESB have moved to restructure and cut costs now that Irish phone, postal and electricity users will no longer be at the monopolies' mercy.

But the crisis is far from being confined to the semi-state companies. Much more worrying have been the criticisms which have touched central government departments and other important state institutions during the first half of the 1990s. Sharp controversies have affected the Department of Finance, the Department of Agriculture, the Central Bank, the Central Statistics Office, the Army and the Gardaí, the Office of Public Works, the Blood Transfusion Services Board and Dublin Corporation.

The 1992 currency crisis did not show the managerial capabilities of the Department of Finance or the Central Bank in a particularly good light. Days before the 1993 devaluation, the Department of Finance issued a public statement about the dire consequences of devaluing. Seven specific claims were made, ranging from the highly dubious to the utterly false. No serious ex post account of the currency crisis has been provided by these highly-secretive agencies, despite the hundreds of millions of pounds which the crisis cost the Irish economy. The report of a committee which studied the affair was never published.

The picture of the Department of Agriculture which emerged from the Beef Tribunal was somewhat less than flattering. This, after all, was the Department which had congratulated one of its officials for confusing a Dáil deputy. In 1989 the Department had received an inquiry from a TD as to how the insured quantities of Irish beef exports to Iraq could greatly exceed total Irish beef exports to Iraq. The official who dealt with the query was reported to have given the Dáil Deputy "factual" information which would "probably confuse" him and was praised for handling the phone call "with considerable skill given the invidious position in which he had found himself". Agriculture was also the Department, as Fintan O Toole has related in *Meanwhile Back at the Ranch*, which had taken no action over the "widespread" theft of intervention beef by factories, which it had known about since 1980.

Economic figures produced by the Central Statistics Office have been subject to unresolved controversy for ten years. The national accounts have been periodically and substantially revised, most recently in early 1993. Current trade and growth figures are the subject of open ridicule.

In 1994, international consultants Price Waterhouse produced a deeply critical report on the Irish Army, describing the defence forces as "badly structured, too old, poorly trained, inappropriately equipped, over-manned, over-ranked and too widely spread in too many barracks and locations."

A corporate strategy plan for the Gardaí, announced in 1993, led to a performance, development and review (PDR) report on the Gardaí. This criticised the force for being too autocratic and for having no real culture of performance. Few members of the public needed any such reminder after the 1994 Lansdowne Road riot, the 1995 Brinks-Allied robbery and the seeming inability of the Gardaí to tackle the rising drugs menace or to apprehend gangland bosses.

Attempts by the Office of Public Works — for long exempt from the state's planning laws — to build a set of highly controversial interpretive centres plunged the OPW and the affected local communities into years of dispute. In the end, very large expenditures of public funds sometimes led to nothing but community division, bad will and a large hole in the ground.

An audit of the Blood Transfusion Services Board, leaked in March 1995, referred to blood being stored in a "filthy outbuilding" and to "totally inadequate" record-keeping. This was in the wake of the shocking 1994 discovery that contaminated blood products had been distributed by the Board. Tests of more than 50,000 women have to date identified some 1,000 with hepatitis antibodies, about half of whom have the virus itself.

In 1993, a Lord Mayor's Commission on Housing in Dublin reported that the less favoured tenants of Dublin Corporation were being housed in "intolerable" living conditions. It also called for thorough-going reform of the Corporation Housing Department, identifying problems with excessive costs, poor service and restrictive practices.

Any one of the above controversies would be quite serious. That such a blizzard of them should sweep across the public sector in so short a time, and reach so deeply into the managerial heart of the state, has to be considered worrying evidence of major *structural* shortcomings in the design of the Irish public sector.

Outdated State Machinery

One reason for the problems in the organisation and management of the public sector is the great age of Ireland's state apparatus. Much of it dates from pre-1922 British practice and therefore from the middle of the nineteenth century. At independence, we re-labelled institutions but we did not reshape them. When Seán Lemass and T.K. Whitaker set about modernising Ireland in the 1960s, it doesn't appear to have occurred to them that along with policy changes, it might also be necessary to reform the Dáil and the civil service or to review economic legislation. Under the Lemass-Whitaker formula, the state took a dramatically larger role in the Irish economy. However, the instruments by which economic development was to be directed — such as the Cabinet, the Dáil, the government departments — were hardly altered at all. This was like trying to put new wine into old skins — so it may not be a complete surprise that some of the results have turned sour.

Famously, the 1969 Devlin Report proposed considerable modernisation of the government apparatus but these changes, which would not have suited traditional civil servants nor traditional politicians, were never implemented. T.J. Barrington, the first Director of the Institute of Public Administration, blamed that failure on "the inertia of the civil service management and the narrow selfishness of civil service unions".

However, in mid-1995, a new study of civil service reform, (*Strategic Management in the Irish Civil Service*) was published. This document, written by a group of senior civil servants, is part of a wider review of public sector performance (the Strategic Management Initiative) announced in February 1994. The officials' report examined radical 1980s reorganisations of the Australian and New Zealand public sectors. It found evidence that the reforms had significantly improved productivity and caused a release of energy, dynamism and creativity. The Irish civil servants concluded that the paramount goals of public policy were being better met in these jurisdictions than in Ireland. They deduced that there were valuable lessons for Ireland from the Australian and New Zealand reforms, which were potentially transferable to Ireland. Inevitably, the officials had cold feet about some reforms (such as written contracts between Ministers and Departments) which they found "too radical to be accepted in the circumstances of Irish political and administrative structures and culture". However they did endorse principles such as greater devolution of authority and responsibility in the Irish civil service, clearer and more exacting accountability (including a proper accruals system of record-keeping), more concentration on departmental and individual performance, terminable employment contracts, improved medium-term goal setting and systematic evaluation of the effectiveness of individual spending programmes.

All these measures — if they are implemented — would be Designer Government-type innovations. The report contained a host of further detailed suggestions, indicating the very challenging scale of reform now acknowledged by senior civil servants themselves to be necessary in Ireland today.

The Role of Localism in "National" Politics
Perched on top of a cartelised market sector and a crisis-ridden public sector stands the Irish political system. It is disinclined to tackle these pressing problems.

Patrick Honohan, a former Taoiseach's economic adviser, has written of the 1980s how it almost seemed that "as the policy problems have grown, the size of the policy steps actually taken has shrunk". Numerous commissions and review bodies reported (on taxation, social welfare, the public finances), but governments fudged in the face of measures that would provoke the electoral wrath of a major interest group. Since no serious change could be made without alienating some interest group, the result was a long period of paralysis.

Although today the 1980s public finance crisis and prolonged stagnation seem over, urgent economic problems remain. Commissions and reviews have continued to report during the 1990s, in many instances urging large-scale economic reform. But action along such lines is not being contemplated. Today it almost seems that as long as the international economy grows and the structural funds flow, the multinationals come and the emigrants go, the captains of the ship of state will not try to change course.

The reason is the same as in the 1980s: Irish political captains and crews are more *local* than *national* representatives. The electoral system obliges them to care more about how the ship of state can help their constituency rather than about the condition of either the ship or the state.

For this reason, two former Taoisigh, Mr Haughey and Dr Fitzgerald, have called for consideration to be given to reforming the Irish electoral system of proportional representation in multi-seat constituencies.

In October 1991, Mr Haughey suggested that "mature consideration" be given to a combination of single-seat constituencies that would elect a proportion of Dáil members, together with a list system to elect the balance. Essentially the same formula was proposed by Dr Fitzgerald in April 1995.

In an *Irish Times* column, Dr Fitzgerald presented a lucid description of some key shortcomings of the present Irish electoral system. First, TDs (most of whom are serving county councillors) and Ministers (most of whom regret that they are not) devote too little time to their national duties. Second, despite Ireland's tiny size, a Taoiseach choosing a Cabinet must pay more attention to the geographical spread of Ministers than to their individual suitability for high public office. In a small country, drawing on a small pool of political talent, this is ridiculous.

This local over-attentiveness derives from the fact that all the members of the Dáil are elected from local constituencies. Without representatives elected at a national level, the overall interest can only be of theoretical concern to "national" politicians.

Multi-seat constituencies exacerbate the problem. In such constituencies, larger political parties run more than one candidate. Therefore TDs — including Ministers — are at risk of losing their seat to a rival from within their own party, typically an ambitious local councillor free to cruise the constituency while the TD languishes at meetings of the Dáil or the Cabinet. To compensate, TDs and Ministers want to spend a lot of time in their bailiwicks. As a result, it has been traditional for the Dáil proper to sit only Tuesday to Thursday — a three-day week.

(Political rivals within a single party have little room to compete on policy, so multi-seat constituencies drive them to compete on local spending promises and other forms of clientilism.)

Dr Fitzgerald acknowledged that the reason voters are so anxious to have a local TD at the Cabinet table is because voters believe — often rightly — that Ministers will abuse their office to deliver as much public spending as possible to their own constituency. For instance, Ministers seem to be completely free to dismantle government departments — like pieces of Lego — in order to relocate some of the building blocks in their own constituencies.

Dr Fitzgerald concludes, like Mr Haughey, that Ireland should follow Germany and introduce a two-tier electoral system. The Fitzgerald formula would work something like this.

Voters would receive two ballot papers, one for the local and one for the national constituency. On the local ballot paper, they would vote for *candidates* as they do now. On the national ballot paper, they would cast a vote for one political *party*.

Half the Dáil would be elected from the one-seat local constituencies. On its own, such a system, even with a transferable vote (voting 1, 2, 3 as now), would give large parties a higher percentage of Dáil seats than their share of the national vote. So, a second set of TDs would be selected from the national constituency. Each party's share of the national vote would be calculated by counting the second ballot papers. Then, an appropriate number of the highest names on each party's electoral list (previously presented to the voters) would be deemed elected in such a way as to make the composition of the Dáil proportionate to each party's share of the national vote. Dr Fitzgerald argues that this system could meet the requirements of "eliminating the undesirable features of the present electoral system, while ensuring continued proportional representation of parties in the Dáil".

But something more is needed. To change the electoral system would require a referendum. But for citizens to have a chance to vote in a referendum, the TDs *elected under the present electoral system* would have to agree to abolish the very mechanism that had brought them into the Dáil. Not all might be happy to do so. This reluctance could be assuaged, Dr Fitzgerald suggests, by having a transitional period during which the TDs selected on the list vote would be chosen from amongst the best-performing but unsuccessful candidates in the constituency votes. Over time, more and more of the list-seats would be filled on the basis of national constituencies and fewer would be reserved for unsuccessful candidates from the local constituencies.

Eventually Ireland would have a fully-fledged part-list part-constituency electoral system. Crucially, this would leave at least half the members of the Dáil with an electoral incentive to be mindful of the national interest. Furthermore, politicians could specialise as local or national representatives.

There are two further aspects to political reform in Ireland. First, party lists should be filled openly, perhaps by a vote of party members. Lists should not be drawn up by backroom party managers.

Secondly, while these electoral reforms would curtail the abuse of public spending programmes by parish-pump-priming Ministers, supplementary measures would help too. Comprehensive auditing of public expenditure to judge its compatibility with explicit policy objectives would restrict the ability of Ministers to discriminate in favour of their constituency.

The present Irish electoral system, by giving too much weight to the constituency rather than the country, has undermined coherence in national economic management, allowing a cartelised economy and a decaying public sector. A switch to a two-tier electoral system is much overdue.

Conclusion: Institutional Failure and Institutional Reform

The Irish economy suffers from important institutional failings. Public policy is not guided by coherent principles such as productivity and social equity. As a result, there is too much state involvement in production and too little in regulation and promotion of opportunity. Furthermore, efficiency is neglected in both the market and the state. Finally, the present electoral system hampers the formulation of a coherent national response to these problems.

The public sector should be rededicated to its core roles of administration, regulation, resolution of serious market failures and advancing social equity and opportunity throughout Irish society. Direct production should be left to the private sector. Commercial semi-state bodies should become commercial non-state firms.

Institutional reform is needed within both the market and the state sectors. The private sector needs revamped competition laws and modern enforcement agencies and procedures. The public sector needs redesigning to give it clear objectives, professional management, performance measurement, effective outside inspection, a separation of purchasing from providing, and a strong voice for the customer, preferably by giving the customer the option to switch to another supplier.

Finally, reform of Ireland's multi-seat PR electoral system is long overdue.

These are the principles of Designer Government. They should guide sustained, widespread and rapid institutional reform in Ireland.

10

CULTURAL REFORM

Introduction
An important aspect of the Irish Disease relates to the culture and ideas through which we interpret the world around us. In Ireland, these contain several unhelpful elements.

In fact, a parallel could be drawn between Irish attitudes and what American feminist Naomi Wolf calls "victim feminism". There is no better phrase to sum up a common Irish attitude than "victim Irishness" which rationalises and justifies sluggish performance. Nothing is more urgently needed than its replacement by the opposite attitude of "power Irishness". To change our performance, we must also change our ideas.

The culture in which individual Irish people are raised and live gives a low weight to principles such as merit but a large importance to "victim" attitudes. Irish people see a weak relationship between rewards and effort and behave accordingly. Victim Irishness underlies our traditional negativity and defeatism, our record of emigration, our downplaying of merit, and our preference for dependent political clientelism over independent civil citizenship.

Victim Irishness
The following are some of the components of victim Irishness:

Failure: we identify with the powerless, the underdog and even with failure itself. We blur the all-important difference between sympathy for and being part of the Third World. From Cuchulainn to Pearse, we have many myths of heroic defeat but very few of triumphant success.

Helplessness: refusing to accept our share of responsibility for our present predicament, we see ourselves as victims of foreign aggression in the past, foreign multinationals today and, no doubt, a "foreign" European super-state in the future. We imagine ourselves as an oppressed and disadvantaged group, petitioning politicians for entitlements, instead of as responsible individuals capable of fashioning our own fate. Peripherality is as much a state of mind as a fact of geography.

Assurances: we seek tidy certainties, mainly from politicians, in a world which, outside the kindergarten, offers only probabilities. Abroad, we routinely look for special concessions, amounting at times almost to a general "derogation" from the challenges of modernity. Unfortunately, no one owes us a living.

Anti-market: we suspect ourselves to be failures at commerce and in the marketplace so we adopt an anti-commercial stance and, in line with Yeats' graphic phrase about those who "fumble in a greasy till, and add the halfpence to the pence", we portray money, money-making and money-values as suspect.

Fantasy: we seek growth without change, solutions without costs, Continental living standards without Continental behaviour or attitudes.

Timidity: we lack confidence, have a poor self-image, often expect the worst, and meekly accommodate the second-rate and the mediocre. But in this life, the meek inherit nothing.

Zero-sum values: we have a fixed-cake mentality, believing that there is only so much to go around, so one person's achievement must mean a loss for someone else. Our understanding of fairness stresses guarantees for those who might do badly rather than adequate rewards for those who strive to do well.

Collectivism: our rhetoric stresses the community over the individual, upbraiding the upstart and the self-starter, implicitly requiring that everybody stay in his or her appointed place.

The recurring themes of victim Irishness are negativity and defeatism, migration and mediocrity. Fortunately, these dark elements are not the only ones to be found in Irish culture. They are emphasised here only because of their negative economic effects and because, if we could lessen them, it would brighten the overall cultural picture.

Negativity

Especially on returning to Ireland after spending a period on the Continent, one is struck by the negativity which pervades this country. We seem to be *against* so much more than we are *for*. Against rod licences, against chemical factories, against interpretive centres, against wind-farms, against fish-farms, against radio masts, against ESB pylons, against gold mining, against any mining. If there is something to be stopped, we can mobilise faster than the Israeli army. But our swords are one-edged. Almost nobody shouts go. Starting things is somebody else's responsibility. The government. The IDA. The employers. The EU. Always *duine eile*. At the international level, we systematically resort to the EU for money, to the US for enterprise and the UK for nearly everything else. We act at times as though without Brussels, Big Business and Britain we'd be banjaxed.

Many Irish people seem to believe in a Star Trek theory of economic progress. Development will somehow be "beamed down" on Ireland without so much as a blade of grass being moved. Jobs will waft through the air, leaving our bays, our valleys, our countryside, our rivers, our streets and our air untouched. So far, there hasn't been much sign of such jobs, and in the meantime it is our population which is wafting away. Away to places where there are jobs without Ireland's static conception of the environment.

In 1993, the World Bank published a report on the economies of East Asia. It had two glossy photos on its cover. The top showed terraces of rice paddies, green and idyllic-seeming. Underneath was a booming seaport, grey and ugly. Unfortunately, no one has yet found a way to build a shipyard or a steel plant in an undisturbed rice paddy. Since it is not possible to have both at the same time, one must be chosen over the other. If we reject development, then we must be prepared to live with the consequences of underdevelopment. Jobs have a cost, but so does unemployment. Less development and fewer of its costs means more of the costs of underdevelopment. We cannot escape both. We cannot expect our politicians and policymakers to find a formula offering wealth but no waste. There simply is no such formula.

There can be no development without change. Not all changes are for the good. Some developments do spoil the physical world.

But lack of development spoils people. Modern mills are not dark and satanic, but even if they were, the alternatives of idleness and exile are hardly bright and celestial. We must choose. If we reject the spoliation that goes with economic development, then we must accept the delights of the dole queue and the bill for house alarms.

If we mean it when we say we want jobs, then we have to be selective about preserving everything exactly as it is now. We can keep some valleys and bays "unspoiled", but also unproductive, while making others available for economic development. We can decide what air or water quality we would accept in return for a higher level of employment. We can decide what countryside to retain for agriculture and tourism and what to devote to housing. It's time to stop always shouting stop. For jobs to come first, many other desirable things must come second.

Defeatism

The Irish are too inclined to defeatism. Seán Lemass complained in 1960 that the main weakness of the Irish character was "an undue disposition to be sorry for ourselves". Peter Sutherland said in 1990 that "we have a capacity for excessively admiring noble failure. . . . We seem sometimes to be inured to coming off worst and almost to wallow wilfully in this".

We are accustomed to painting ourselves as a long-downtrodden people who have struggled heroically against terrible odds but — the position being hopeless — have eventually succumbed. However, you can become too accustomed to losing. And if you are convinced you're going to lose, it is almost impossible to win.

There are examples of other small countries, also with big neighbours, whose experiences — and attitudes — have been very different to ours. Switzerland comes to mind. At different times in its history, the Swiss had a border with Napoleon to the west, Bismarck to the north-east, various Austro-Hungarian Emperors to the east, and Hitler and Mussolini on absolutely all sides. They were not an island. They retained their independence by their own unaided efforts.

That might be too energetic for us. We are happier to think of ourselves as underdogs. We respond sympathetically to the description in *The Commitments* that the Irish are the blacks of Europe. To believe this, you would have to be colour-blind.

If we look around us today, it is not hard to find people and countries that have real problems. The list would be a long one. It might, in fact, cover most countries in the world and certainly those in Eastern Europe, in the former Soviet Union, in large parts of Asia and above all in Africa.

But not Ireland. In 1990, according to World Bank figures, we had an average income of some $9,500, far above the income of most of the world's population. The average income in Sub-Saharan Africa, in China and in India was about $350 in the same year, and only around $2,000 in Latin America, the Middle East and North Africa. It is a sobering thought that Ireland and Egypt generated approximately the same total income, something over £30 billion, in 1990. But we divided it up among 3.5 million people while the Egyptians divided it among more than 52 million people.

There are many things that can be said about Ireland, including the fact that it contains lots of poor people, but it can not be said that we are a poor country. Daniel Ortega, leader of the Nicaraguan Sandinistas, when he visited Ireland in the late 1980s, was seen one day to look out a window at the rich green Irish fields outside and to mutter: "If only we had land like this in Nicaragua".

Because we believe the béal bocht blarney about being deprived and handicapped, we expect others to swallow it as well. We do contribute very generously to causes in the Third World but we also expect our EU neighbours to transfer significant amounts of income to us. In 1994, total Irish aid to developing countries would have been of the order of perhaps £100–£200 million. Aid receipts from our EU partners were measured in billions. We give small, receive big and, on both counts, clap ourselves on the back.

Since national "debates" about European Community matters revolve primarily around grants, subsidies and handouts, it must seem to many Irish people that the letters EC stand for European Charity. The latest Structural Funds are the fifth postwar set of transfers to Ireland. We obtained Marshall Aid, cutely, without even having fought in the war. In the early 1970s began the Common Agricultural Policy. Compensation for EMS membership followed at the end of the 1970s and now we have had two helpings of Structural Funds.

To date none of these transfers has lessened our appetite for still more aid. We may think that this situation will carry on merrily into the future, but the EU is certain to tire of our Oliver Twist approach to Community funds. Do we propose to find ourselves, later this decade, jostling with Poland, Hungary and the Czech Republic for Community grants? Have we no sense of who is more and who is less deserving?

Irish defeatism is not justified. We have the resources to address our difficulties. Plenty of land, plenty of space, much infrastructure, a healthy and reasonably well-educated population. In short, a starting point that many countries would be happy to think of a destination. It is not that we are starting far behind, rather, that we could make so much more of what we have. At present we lack only the institutional framework to take us further on our way.

Migration and Modernisation — To Run or To Roar?
Irish history has been strong on flight. To resolve our problems, we need to stay grounded.

This is not to deny that some emigration is good and that much of it is inevitable. For reasons of language and history, emigration is *available* to Ireland on a scale that is just not possible for other countries. There is nothing we can do about language and history now. What we can address is our employment record and the gap between Irish and foreign living standards, which provide further motives for the exodus.

Irish emigration has always been a substitute for change and reform. In the past it has permitted non-industrialisation without economic collapse, uneconomic farms without destitution, large families without starvation and, in general, economic failure without revolution. As emigration continues through the 1990s, it delays change once again.

If there had been no net migration from the 26 counties since the Famine, and the natural increase in the population had nonetheless been the same, the people of the Republic alone would have numbered about 18 million by 1986. Clearly, it would not have been enough just to stop emigration. We would also have needed a huge boost in Irish production. And, of course, the two things go together, just as the absence of employment in good jobs at home goes hand in hand with emigration today.

But emigration has been "good" for Ireland only in the sense that the Famine was "good": each reduced the population of the country nearer to the level that could be supported by the extent of economic activity which prevailed at the time. But surely we should consider this to be merely addressing the symptom — overpopulation — rather than the disease: underdevelopment?

When emigrants pack their bags and clear off, they continue with a cycle in which the conditions which gave rise to emigration in the first place are just reproduced in Ireland, again and again, as they have been for 150 years, with no solution in sight. I sympathise with the view that at least graduate emigrants bear part of the responsibility for this country's backwardness. It is hardly surprising that a problem from which people perpetually run away remains perpetually unsolved.

Fintan O Toole of the *Irish Times* put it well when he wrote that the Irish can adapt to anything except change. We are prepared to rip ourselves out of our local communities, leave our families and friends, move thousands of miles away to a completely new and strange land to look for a living there. But we don't address the alternative, which is to tackle and solve the factors in Ireland which give rise to such exile.

Foreigners are often puzzled by our fatalism. In 1988, at an international academic discussion of the Irish economy, the French economist Charles Wyplosz made a comment which, in the light of Irish history, was deeply ironic. He had just had our debt, unemployment and emigration problems explained to him. His response was to express puzzlement at the apparent lack of nationalistic feelings in Ireland where people prefer to leave rather than to make the sacrifices needed to tackle economic problems head-on.

We all claim to care deeply about emigration. But are we prepared to make sacrifices in support of economic reform? There is no painless solution. If the problem is to be solved, one generation is going to have to take the responsibility for making the changes in Ireland — in our attitudes, our institutions and our general performance — that will at least slow the emigration rate to tolerable levels. Will it be this generation? Or will the task be left to *duine eile*? The emigration problem needs a collective solution. Unless it is tackled jointly, each individual may as well follow the well-worn trail abroad.

Forty years ago, Dr T.K. Whitaker noted the absence of a magic solution to Irish economic problems and called for Irish people to "have sufficient patriotism and realism to accept the standard of living produced by their own exertions here — even if it continued for some time to be lower than the standard available abroad — otherwise the basis for economic progress simply would not exist". He insisted that the eventual success or failure of his reform program "will depend primarily on the individual reactions of the Irish people. If they have not the will to develop, even the best possible programme is useless". This remains true today.

Values: Merit or Mediocrity?
In addition to negativity, defeatism and migration, a further important element in the Irish culture is the value system underlying victim Irishness. Merit is downplayed and mediocrity is excused. There is a spirit of "twill do" rather than "can do".

The meritocratic idea is that of a *fair contest*. A race in which rewards go to the best contender, regardless of birth or budget. But a *fair* race, in which everyone has a chance to participate to the limit of their ability.

In Ireland, however, the idea of treatment on merit — recruitment on merit, payment on merit, promotion on merit, and dismissal on demerit — is not a value that guides public attitudes or official policies. Nor is equal opportunity, the notion of the entitlement of all to be present at the starting block.

Poor productivity is simply not penalised in either the private or public sectors. Weak competition offers protection against underperformance. This is not an accidental weakness. It has been engineered through the political system, which monopolises wide stretches of the Irish economy, or through cartelisation of markets in the private sector. Numerous examples have already been given. The result of not rewarding according to merit is underperformance.

In the political world, for example, merit is the last thing on the minds of parties who invite a member of the family of a deceased TD to stand in the subsequent by-election.

In the civil service, Professor Joe Lee, in characteristically pungent language, has noted that "high-class achievers jostle cheek by jowl with high-class dossers", implying a considerably non-meritocratic civil service. The 1995 report on *Strategic Management in the Irish Civil Service*, written by civil servants, admitted that the "Irish public service has not seriously tackled the issue of what to do in cases of underperformance".

In the teaching profession, only in 1995 is the problem of underperformance being acknowledged (without yet being tackled). But the proposed solution — early retirement on an enhanced pension — is far from meritocratic. Essentially, better pension terms are to be offered to inferior teachers than to excellent ones. What lesson will pupils draw from this?

In the financial sector, there was a telling contrast between the UK and the Irish sequel to the currency crises of 1992-93. In Britain, "Black Wednesday" prompted a complete institutional overhaul of the Bank of England. Significant numbers of managers were forced into early retirement. But in Ireland, no institutional review was undertaken, and the Irish Central Bank has carried on exactly as before.

Nor do the numerous scandals of the late 1980s and early 1990s — Beef, Greencore, the Telecom headquarters, the Davy's share purchase — seem to have led to much punishment. Long and costly public investigations followed but some of these were decidedly inconclusive.

In the public sector, it is unheard of for senior managers of public companies, no matter how loss-making, to be called to account. None of the senior executives responsible for managing companies like Irish Steel, Aer Lingus or TEAM, which went on to make huge losses, were even called before a Dáil Committee to explain themselves.

Although a French scandal over contaminated blood led to criminal proceedings, in Ireland the hepatitis scandal is not the subject of criminal investigations to ascertain whether any prosecutions might be warranted.

In the private sector, no one was held accountable for the collapse of the AIB-owned Insurance Corporation of Ireland in the mid-1980s with losses which totalled hundreds of millions of pounds. No resignations followed in AIB. There was no investigation to establish whether there had been any regulatory failure by the Central Bank.

If merit is to matter, mediocre *performance* must be punished. But in Ireland, nothing is allowed to fail. Whatever the price, the walking dead are helped to keep on walking forever. This is usually defended on the grounds of unspecified "social" objectives. The Army doesn't need many of its barracks for military purposes, but they are still kept open on "social" grounds. The level of business doesn't justify the existence of many post offices, but they are still kept going for "social" reasons. Subsidies to Aer Lingus and Irish Steel were often defended, not on air travel or steel industry grounds, but on "social" grounds. Merit never gets a look in.

For many Irish institutions, firms and individuals merit doesn't matter. For our future to be brighter, this must change. In terms of performance, we must show mediocrity no mercy. There should be no surprise that Ireland has failed to produce more enterprise when its economy fails to penalise underperformance.

The Silence of the Shepherds: (Lack of) Accountability and the Irish Public Finance Debacle

A striking example of the absence of merit in Irish public life relates to the public spending debacle of the 1970s and 1980s, for which nobody was held accountable.

The control of public expenditure is a paramount goal of public policy. The civil servants admit this themselves in their 1995 report *Strategic Management in the Irish Civil Service*. There was a gross failure to achieve this goal in the decade 1977-87. But nobody wants to talk about that today. No insider will account for the mistakes. None will apportion, let alone accept, responsibility. A remarkable silence on the whole subject extends throughout the upper echelons of politics and the public service. It was all a mysterious accident, for which nobody involved was responsible.

In November 1993, Mr Maurice Doyle, then Central Bank Governor, made a speech about Irish unemployment in which he described the Irish economy as one "afflicted by a severe case of sclerosis". Fundamental restructuring was needed, in taxation, social welfare, wage bargaining, restrictive practices, education, training, industrial policy and competition law.

Mr Doyle's speech was one of the most savage broadsides ever delivered at Irish economic policy. Many people would sympathise with Mr Doyle's diagnosis. But wasn't Mr Doyle one of the chief architects of the economic structure that he now condemns? Before Mr Doyle arrived at the Central Bank — partly as a result of a restrictive practice that confines the Governorship to senior Finance officials — he spent decades at the highest levels of that Department, executing, on behalf of various governments, the very policies that he now denounces.

When did Mr Doyle realise that Irish economic policy was producing sclerosis? While he was implementing the policy or only afterwards? As arrangements now stand, we have no way of knowing whether he fought tooth and nail against this sclerosis, or cheerfully went along with its construction. And, although mandarin resignations might not have altered the economic course governments were determined to follow, was there no point that civil servants would have refused to go beyond?

Mr Doyle does not tell us since, in fact, he says nothing about his own role in this affair and merely observes that the way in which the economy came to be afflicted by sclerosis is "a matter for conjecture". Presumably he himself doesn't need to rely on conjecture, and it would be nice if we didn't have to either. That would allow senior public officials to be held accountable for their economic tenure during recent decades. But on the issue of responsibility, his and others, Mr Doyle is silent.

Nor is he alone. Dr Garret Fitzgerald pens a weekly column for the *Irish Times*. He too is frequently scathing about the economic status quo in Ireland. For example, he described our tax system as "economic and social lunacy" (January 1994), he called for the phasing-out of mortgage interest relief (July 1993), he criticised the over-centralisation of the Irish state (February 1994) and he urged Dáil reform and a new code of conduct for the civil service (August 1994).

We must suppose that Dr Fitzgerald never raised taxes in his life but strove to abolish mortgage interest relief, to decentralise the Irish state, to reform the Dáil and to have the strictest code of conduct for the civil service. Clearly, the Dr Fitzgerald of the *Irish Times* cannot be the same Dr Fitzgerald who spent decades as a TD in Dáil Éireann, ten years as leader of the second-largest political party in the state, four years as Foreign Minister and nearly five years as Taoiseach.

As with Mr Doyle's speech, you would never think from Dr Fitzgerald's newspaper columns that he himself had any hand, act or part in the creation of the economic status quo that he now repudiates.

Another leading member of the same generation is Mr Padraig O hUiginn who spent many years as Secretary of the Taoiseach's department. In November 1993 Mr O hUiginn was interviewed about the Irish economy on RTE's *Marketplace* programme. It was put directly to him that, as one of the country's most senior civil servants for many years, he bore some of the blame for Ireland's unemployment record. Mr O hUiginn's reply was the memorable observation that "a calculation had been made" which showed that if Ireland had the average European rate of labour force growth, unemployment would be only half its present level. This reasoning, in Mr O hUiginn's estimation, established that Irish unemployment was substantially due to demographics. But one could equally say that *if* jobs growth had been ten times stronger, then unemployment *would* be much lower. Or, *if* we all had a gold mine in our gardens, then average income in Ireland *would* have overtaken the European average.

Surely we employ politicians and civil servants to tackle the actual problems the country faces, not to tell us that if the problems weren't there, their own record would be much better. Why are senior civil servants who profess powerlessness in the face of a problem not asked to stand aside in favour of less-fatalistic replacements? Like Mr Doyle and Dr Fitzgerald, Mr O hUiginn is silent about his own role during recent decades.

In a meritocratic public service, senior officials asked to carry out directions they believed to be against the national interest would have a channel to bring such information promptly before the public. And they would be held accountable, if their decisions bequeathed sclerosis to the following generation. They would not get away, as they now can, with erroneous excuses, selective silences and well-padded pensions.

The Irish public finance debacle is a clear-cut example of the absence of meritocratic reward and punishment in Irish public life. But it merely reflects the shortcomings of the value system in the wider Irish society.

Cultural Reform: Power Irishness

To adapt Naomi Wolf's terminology, we need to evolve away from victim Irishness towards what might be called power Irishness. Power Irishness would comprise:

Responsibility: we must take responsibility for solving the problems we face as a people. Howsoever we may have arrived where we are, it is up to us to engineer the escape. Our own choices, individual and collective, will determine what happens to us. We are actors, not passive spectators of the world we live in.

Self-confidence: we must apply our intelligence to the situation confronting us, in the belief that if we marshal our resources and power, we can compete with the best and win. We do it in sport, we do it in music and literature, we can do it in other areas too.

Merit: a strong community is composed of strong individuals, so we need to encourage and reward the efforts of individual Irish people to advance themselves. Our sense of fairness must be extended to mean not just looking after losers but also adequately rewarding those willing to try hardest.

Aspiration: we must refuse to take a national vow of poverty, and aspire unapologetically to better incomes and better times, so that we may improve our position and that of our community. We must not sentimentalise underdevelopment which we know is not glamorous, nor green nor good.

Commerce: we must accept the need for commerce and money-making, and believe that it is as perfectly Irish to wish for fame and economic success as it is to strive in artistic or sporting endeavour.

Realism: we must recognise the need for practical compromises between preserving the way Ireland is now and modernising it for the future.

Core values: we must hold to a set of core values. This book has advocated productivity and social equity.

Naomi Wolf argues that groups looking for power and success should follow the strategy of immigrant communities arriving in a foreign country:

> Immigrants do not believe that all must be at the same economic level in order to work together; they pool and pass on resources because all seek to raise their status and multiply their access. They do not expect to believe the same things; they merely expect each other to honour the basic social contract of giving back to community organisations. And they are ... intent on raising the status of the group within the life of the larger society.

Given Ireland's emigration record, these ideas should be especially compelling to an Irish audience. In reforming Ireland, we can learn from the successful patterns used for generations by Irish people moving to foreign economies.

Civil Society

To move away from our traditional clientelist dependence on politicians, we need to build a stronger *civil society*.

Civil society is a newly rediscovered idea. One of its recent origins lies in the Eastern Europe of the 1970s and 1980s. Under totalitarian governments that wished to destroy all independent organisations, East European "dissidents" (i.e. democrats) sought to rebuild civil society underground. They organised unofficial markets, political debating clubs, "samizdat" magazines, and a host of other activities to keep alive some semblance of citizenship and civil society. In Poland and Czechoslovakia, the Solidarity and Civic Forum movements consciously dedicated themselves to restoring an independent civic infrastructure. The name "Forum", recalling the direct democracy of ancient Greece, was also used by the East German (New Forum) and Hungarian (Democratic Forum) movements.

A strong and healthy civic culture would combat the vices of victim culture and would foster the development of a capable, responsible and active citizenry. Through a variety of organisations, people would take more responsibility for themselves and for their society's overall development. It can hardly be denied that today in Ireland civic culture is weak, civic standards are low and our political culture is positively sick.

In the late twentieth century, with its large government sectors, civil society might most easily be described as the "non-state". It is the enormous mosaic of individuals and autonomous associations constantly grouping and regrouping in the form of sports clubs, leisure activities, housing co-ops, gay, lesbian and other collectives, trade unions, debating societies, neighbourhood watch schemes, publishing ventures, childcare networks, parents associations, women's centres, churches and religious bodies, credit unions, residents associations, political movements in support of racial and gender rights, environmental protection and innumerable other activities besides.

What these groups have in common are their independence, their pluralism and their self-government. They operate on a small scale and in a local, decentralised fashion. In these settings, people can actually practice their constitutional right to free speech and to participate as equals in decisions affecting them. Citizens can exercise some control over their lives. They can offer and look for support from neighbours and like-minded citizens. All of these bodies promote responsibility, self-reliance, and a true community spirit.

In Ireland, the Roman Catholic Church has traditionally provided the main civic architecture for Irish society, organising a wide variety of activities under its umbrella. But a more diverse civic culture would have been stronger, and now that Catholic social infrastructure is being hollowed out at a rapid pace the weakness or absence of alternative civic networks is becoming apparent. The resulting gaps have been occupied in many cases by state organisations, but they need to be "filled in" by an extended civil society, of which the Roman Catholic Church will naturally continue to form one part.

A state sector which accounts for more than 50 per cent of the Irish economy is already large enough. Rather than taking on additional tasks, governments need to learn to share power with their citizens, and citizens need to learn to look for and take that power. Let the state provide the finance for communities to tackle their own problems rather than stepping in, pushing citizens aside, to impose its traditional answers.

Conclusion: Clients and Citizens

Ireland needs a much stronger civil society, built around a sense of power Irishness, to combat our traditional vices of negativity and defeatism, migration and mediocrity. We need fewer clients and more citizens. Merit, above all, must play a much larger role, which means showing mediocrity no mercy. While focusing carefully on improving the opportunities of the disadvantaged, we must turn a deaf ear to unjustified pleas of victimisation.

11

THE DEPENDENCY LEGACY OF IRISH HISTORY

Introduction

Professor Joe Lee has commented that in Ireland "reliance on government rather than self-reliance has become so ingrained in the public psyche that it tends to be assumed that nobody can act unless government acts."

Why is there this love affair with the Decree Economy? If the social market is superior to a Decree Economy, why has it not been adopted in Ireland?

Perhaps it is because a market economy rests on a high degree of individual endeavour whereas history has conditioned Irish people to emphasise collective over individual action.

Paraphrasing Chesterton, it can be said of Ireland not that capitalism was tried and found wanting, but that it was found hard and not tried.

Ancient Problems, Ancient Attitudes

The Irish state is rather young but our problems and attitudes are much older.

Take this comment about joblessness. "The curse of Ireland is the general want of employment for its inhabitants." This is a widely-held opinion. But it was not expressed in 1995. In fact, it was not expressed any time this century. It appeared in an Irish publication called the Quarterly Review in 1832 — more than 160 years ago.

In terms of attitudes, consider the following reference to the "grant mentality": "Everybody in Ireland instead of setting about improvement as people elsewhere do, pester the Government about Boards and public aid. Why cannot people in Ireland fish without a Board if fishing . . . be so profitable?" Once again, this quote is not from the twentieth century. The remark was made by Sir Robert Peel, when he was Ireland's Chief Secretary in 1845 — some 150 years ago.

Ireland's economic problems — and their roots — go back a very long time. It is possible to trace an attitude of state dependency — looking first to the state rather than private provision — back several hundred years in Irish history.

Politicians, British and Irish, have a long record of extending the state's role in the Irish economy. This would not necessarily have been a problem if such extensions were guided by a well-articulated statement of the precise economic roles the state and the private sector were each expected to play. But such rationales are strikingly lacking. Judging from the facts of history, we must suppose that the state was believed to be equally good at providing social welfare, hydro-electric power, air travel and advance factories.

Correspondingly, responsibility for providing these goods and services was best removed from the private sector. Irish politicians' general presumption of "private sector failure" has been widespread. But the nature and cause of these failings has rarely, if ever, been clearly stated. Irish politicians' assessment that state provision was necessary or "better" has also been widespread. But the capacity of the state to make good these gaps has been assumed rather than demonstrated. An awareness of the danger of "public sector failure" has been rare. The result has been ever-growing — but incoherent — state intervention in the Irish economy.

There is a role for the state in the economy, as described in other chapters. But in a country lacking a good understanding of a proper role for the state, the public sector will become over-extended and less effective than it could be.

Professor Mary Daly, a UCD historian, has traced Ireland's statist attitudes back some 200 years. She notes that the final two decades of the eighteenth century, which were a period of strong economic prosperity in Ireland, coincided with a short-lived national parliament in Dublin. Grattan's parliament engaged in generous public spending. For instance, a Linen Board made grants to the Irish linen industry. (Observers have since noted that most of the subsidies went to Connacht and Leinster, where the industry failed, and relatively little to Ulster, where the business thrived.) Nonetheless, a link was established between a national parliament, interventionist economic policies and prosperity.

The nineteenth century seemed to prove the reverse proposition. As the 1800s unfolded, against a background of political Union and intermittently laissez faire economics, a series of disasters struck the country. These included the demise of Irish industry (outside Ulster), the potato famine, mass emigration, a population collapse, and a shift in Irish agriculture from tillage to cattle-raising.

The most dramatic, and costly, of these changes was, of course, the famine. In several ways, its presence may still be felt today.

The Famine

At school every Irish child learns that, midway through the famine, there was a change of British government from the Tories to the Whigs. The Whig regime's approach to famine relief was even more harsh than its predecessor's. The new policy goes by the dreaded and alien name of "laissez faire". Irish schoolchildren also learn of the Marie Antoinette-like response of many Irish landlords to the mass starvation of their tenants. A failure, it seems, both of the capitalists and of the market. Inevitably, from that point on, the case for the market economy faces something of a handicap in Ireland.

The term laissez faire is often treated as a synonym for the market economy, but it only corresponds to what I have called the Degenerate Economy, in which market failures are completely neglected by the public authorities.

A failure of the Degenerate market/laissez faire should not be construed as a failure of *all* types of market. During a famine, a policy of laissez faire is a policy of laissez mourir. But famine conditions are not the norm, or there would be no human race. The general value of an economic policy, whatever its character, cannot be assessed according to whether it would be appropriate to the special circumstances of mass starvation. Laissez faire was certainly the wrong policy for Ireland in the 1840s. But that is simply irrelevant to Europe of the 1990s — a Europe, moreover, saturated with food mountains. Still, the contrary view is held by many Irish people and is receiving a good airing during the 150th anniversary of the famine.

Blaming the market economy for economic failure is not new in Ireland. One hundred years ago, contemporaries already laid the blame for the famine and for Irish economic underdevelopment at the door of market economics. An assembly of Catholic priests, meeting in Limerick in 1868, called for a repeal of the Union because "Ireland has had enough of political economy." In 1861, the nationalist leader John Mitchel wrote that "Ireland died of political economy."

Nor are such attitudes to market economics merely a quaint relic of history. Intellectually, these ideas may well be relics but they are still alive and kicking. For example, in a talk published in Cork in 1994, Professor Frederick Powell of the UCC Department of Applied Social Studies claimed that laissez faire "produced" the famine. Specifically, he noted the importance to the New Right of "laissez faire social and economic ideas that produced the Great Famine in the 1840s". There is no mention here of the potato blight, nor the dependence of most of Ireland's population on a single crop, only of laissez faire. (If laissez faire, which was practised in both Ireland and Britain in these years, "produced" a famine in Ireland, why didn't it produce a famine in Britain too?)

It would have been correct for Professor Powell to say that laissez faire thinking caused the London government's policy to be quite inadequate to famine conditions and thus had exacerbated the effects of the famine. But that might not have blackened laissez faire (treated as a synonym for the market) sufficiently for his purposes.

Killing Home Rule with Kindness
While the famine will forever be linked in the Irish mind with the idea of laissez faire, the economic policy of the British government soon underwent a considerable reversal. Despite the perception of neglect, in the later decades of the nineteenth century economic policy was — especially for its time — very interventionist. The 1845-49 famine was not the last episode of acute hunger in Ireland. During the remainder of the nineteenth century, there were repeated episodes of smaller-scale famine and serious

distress in parts of rural Ireland. Something had been learned from the mistakes of the 1840s and a gradual (and reluctant) easing took place of the terms on which the destitute were provided with public assistance. The long-term effect of lingering famine and public assistance was, as the UCD economic historian Cormac O Gráda has recently written, that "relief gradually came to permeate the rural culture." So much so, that Irish speakers were wont to refer to "bealtaí relief", "brioscaí relief", "éadach relief" and so on, as the word "relief" went into direct use in the Irish language.

Professor Daly notes that Irish citizens developed "a strong dependence on government assistance for everything from famine relief to land reform . . . Britain pandered to such dependence by doling out lollipops in the form of roads, drainage schemes, fishery development or light railways". (These are familiar lollipops. Several would not be out of place in a National Development Plan of the 1990s.)

Then came the Land War. However one might describe Gladstone's response to the Irish Land League, it could not be said to have been laissez faire. The Land Acts of the 1880s and 1890s were a form of massive government intervention. Subsidised state loans — on a scale previously unknown in Britain — allowed Irish tenants to buy out their landlords. The compulsory nature of the sales summarily overturned the property rights of landowners. (Such property rights were, of course, based on land seizures in earlier centuries, as the tenants remembered only too well. Nonetheless, laissez faire it was not.)

The Land War was, furthermore, a struggle about *possession* of land rather than its *productivity*. Horace Plunkett felt this contest had weakened Irish character and self-reliance. The very qualities which helped the political struggle — solidarity and conformity (backed up by the threat of boycotting) — were often ill-suited to economic activity. Plunkett worried about the "lack of initiative and shrinking from responsibility, the moral timidity" in the Irish character. He established his Irish Agricultural Organisation Society to promote initiative and combat dependency, remarking in 1905 on the Irish people's "extraordinary belief in political remedies for economic ills".

The American economist Barbara Solow has pointed out that the 1881 Land Act, by giving the courts the power to set "fair rents", sent "the tenants of Ireland crowding into court, [with the result that] no one was thinking about agricultural education, credit and marketing programmes, improved cropping, selective breeding" and, in general, ways of coping with the impact on European agriculture of wheat exports from the United States.

The policies of Gladstone and his successors in Ireland could never have been proposed, let alone practised, in Britain at that time. Their radicalism may be appreciated by imagining the reaction in Ireland today if the government announced that all farmers would be obliged to sell their farms to foreign forestry companies, at a price to be dictated by a government Commissioner with state subsidisation . . . of the foreigners!

Land reform was not the only large-scale government intervention during this period. The policy of "killing Home Rule with kindness" — a political, not an economic, objective — moved the state further and further away from laissez faire. As we know, kindness did not kill Home Rule, but it may have damaged other things, including Irish economic initiative. It is now well-recognised that if the state accepts responsibility for providing the population with each and every little thing, then members of the public, as well as private firms, may hold back from measures they would otherwise have taken. People may provide less for their own retirement if they believe that the state is going to. Residents may refuse to maintain local roads because they do not see it as their responsibility. And, catastrophically, if people wait for the government to provide jobs, that society's employment prospects are grim. The expectation of state action can create new gaps in private provision that are then used to justify further public action. This process has gone a long way in Ireland.

Over the course of the nineteenth century, Ireland became a social laboratory of the British government. Some of the experiments carried out were highly beneficial. For instance, Ireland was provided with large-scale elementary education. (This was partly to limit the influence of the Catholic Church.) The historian Oliver McDonagh even argues that in the second half of the nineteenth century there may have been no other country with

Ireland's living standards which could boast so low a rate of illiteracy. The authorities also established a public health system and a network of workhouses.

In addition, a plethora of government boards and bodies was created: a Local Government Board, a Land Commission, a Congested Districts Board, a Distressed Areas Board, a Board of Works and a Department of Agriculture and Technical Instruction. There is an economic rationale for some of these provisions and a social rationale for others. But two problems dogged these initiatives.

First, the public sector expanded in a purely ad hoc fashion, responding to short-term problems without any clear long-term strategy. Many commentators see this as a failing of these particular initiatives but, taking a longer and broader view, it must be considered to be a common failing of state activity.

The second problem related specifically to the attempt to stimulate economic activity in Ireland. In exasperation, Professor Joe Lee comments that the authorities "adopted the disastrous policy of creating uneconomic work which was bound to disappear the moment support was withdrawn." Public funds for lacemaking, knitting and fishing proved to be "an expensive waste of time" and a frittering away of public monies on nonviable projects. He concludes that, because of both defects, bodies like the Department of Agriculture and the Congested Districts Board did little to improve Ireland. A clear-sighted intervention, as Professor Lee argues, might have meant abandoning the western seaboard as a site for economic development and concentrating on the eastern part of the country. This would not have saved the West but might still have been better that unproductive investment which merely delayed emigration to Britain and the US. However, politically, such a hard-nosed policy would have been tremendously difficult to defend and, ultimately, political considerations drive state intervention.

Although the various public boards failed to develop the Irish economy, their considerable administrative apparatus must have added to Irish dependence on official initiatives. By 1914, there were 40 government Departments in Ireland. Although eleven were the Irish branches of British Departments, 29 had no British equivalents. These forty Departments employed some 26,000 officials.

Professor McDonagh's history of Ireland under the Union emphasises the difference between the roles of the state in Ireland and Britain. For instance, in Britain "land reform" meant the free market, demand and supply, and competition. In Ireland, it meant rent controls and fixed tenure enforced by the state against the landowner. The Chief Secretary in Ireland in the 1870s was moved to comment:

> If there is one thing which strikes Englishmen who have to deal with Irish matters, more than another, it is that, whereas in England we have something like a dread of government interference, in Ireland that interference, if not actually courted, seems at any rate to be expected.

The state in Ireland was not merely large but also quite centralised. Because of the fear of Catholic control of elected councils, local and urban government was much less decentralised than in Britain, again to the detriment of local initiative and responsibility.

What were the landowners doing all this time? The Kilkenny essayist Hubert Butler offers a scathing judgement about his own class. In his view, the aristocracy had become soft and rotten as a result of exporting all their brightest and best to England. He noted the disproportionate Anglo-Irish share in the leadership of British armies, the government of her imperial provinces and the operation of her newspapers and theatres. In contrast, they failed at home to mould Irish history according to the liberal principles of their ancestors and were wiped out as a centre of power on the island.

New public initiatives arose in 1906, following the election of the Liberal Government on a programme containing a large body of social legislation. This was adopted by the British Parliament and led to a significant rise in public spending in Ireland. Some of this spending was financed by transfers from Britain. After independence, the Irish government was unable to support social spending at the levels set by the Liberal governments. One historian described the position inherited by Ireland at independence as an impoverished government presiding over an elaborate state machine which he likened to an old banger fitted with a Rolls-Royce eight-cylinder engine. The government of Northern Ireland, paying UK-level benefits but facing Ulster-level unemployment, also found it impossible to balance its budget until finally, after World War Two, the financing of Ulster's unemployment was amalgamated with Britain's.

Irish Attitudes at Independence

Pamphleteers and politicians had linked Irish economic decline with the absence of a domestic parliament and the supposed free reign of "market forces". A long line of Irish leaders drew the conclusion that only state action, in the form of trade controls, could lay the basis for a successful Irish economy. Professor Daly notes that Jonathan Swift, George Berkeley, Daniel O Connell, Thomas Davis, Charles Stewart Parnell and Arthur Griffith all attributed economic success and failure to political forces. (Only James Connolly took a divergent view.)

Irish leaders were sympathetic to state intervention and highly ambivalent towards the market. They associated capitalism with "dark satanic mills" and urban degeneracy. Dr Daly sums up their views as a romantic rejection of "industry, modernisation, materialism and the middle class in favour of the rural, traditional and spiritual", resistance to "the cultural values of a modern industrial society" and a search for economic progress "minus the evils of capitalism, materialism and urbanisation".

In short, Ireland wanted development "but without the incursion of the modern world". By the time of independence, this viewpoint was well-established among the leaders of Sinn Fein. But the attempt to have the benefits of modernity without its costs was, to say the least, a tall order. More exactly, it was a contradiction. It led to prolonged attempts to moderate the shortcomings of the market by yet further state intervention, without much sign that thought had been given to the dangers in such a policy.

With its roots in nineteenth century history, and the teachings of Catholic social policy, the Irish approach to economics placed heavy emphasis on social and geographical income shifting with little regard to income creation. What seemed to matter were the shares into which a cake could be divided rather than the size of the cake, as though the former were independent of the latter.

In this vision, economic constraints were assumed away. There was a clear objective, but the question of how the objective was to be achieved was not addressed. No one appears to have asked whether any conceivable policy could have brought about the economic aims of Irish nationalism; it was just assumed that an independent government could deliver whatever economy it wished. James Meenan, Professor of Economics in UCD, wrote in 1970 that "in the pre-occupation with politics, other factors such as thrift, self-reliance and enterprise were disregarded."

Round One: Trade Protection

The Cumann na nGaedhael governments of the 1920s resisted trade protectionism and limited state intervention in the economy. But the arrival of Mr de Valera soon changed all that. His governments introduced a programme of generalised tariffs — taxes on imports — in the early 1930s. The level of protection offered to domestic producers was one of the highest in the western world. Research published by the ESRI in 1971 showed that as late as 1966 the average level of protection was almost 80 per cent.

Professor Daly comments that the major legacy of the 1930s was to institutionalise and considerably extend the Irish dependence on the state and on politicians which had been established in the previous century.

> Decisions on tariffs and quotas, allocations of quotas and duty-free import licences, the location of factories and numerous other matters became discretionary decisions determined by ministers and officials. In consequence, lobbying and deputations were seen as essential to attract an industry to a particular town.

Although it must have been attractive to Irish politicians to bring so many of the strings of economic power into their own hands in this way, the economic case for the state to levy tariffs was flawed. As economists like Brendan Walsh of UCD and Anthony Leddin of the University of Limerick have noted, "prolonged reliance on generalised protectionism has not proved to be an effective way of promoting economic development anywhere in the world." If the private sector is asked to choose between certain profits from a protected market or taking its chances on the open market, it will choose security. On its own, giving firms a captive market is a recipe for a sluggish, not a dynamic, economy. So another not-well-thought-out state intervention went wrong. It is possible that tariffs were politically unavoidable in the 1930s, with the collapse of international trade and the grave threat to democratic order. But even this argument would not explain why these policies were retained for more than twenty years after the last war ended.

In addition to protection, the state continued to establish new semi-state bodies in the economy. As before, the reason for the failure of the private sector to provide these services, and the way in which the public sector could overcome the obstacle which had frustrated the private sector, received little attention. Mr de Valera inherited 6 semi-state bodies on coming into office, and established 18 more. (Today, the number is close to 100. A handful of privatisations in the late 1980s reduced the figure but, on the other hand, brand-new bodies like the County Enterprise Development Boards added to them.)

The TCD economist John Bristow has commented that:

> the Irish approach to public enterprise has been pragmatic and opportunistic rather than ideological. . . . However, the obverse of [the absence of doctrine] is the absence of coherent policy-making which lies at the root of most of the difficulties [later] experienced by the state-sponsored sector.

An indication of Mr de Valera's economic thinking may be gleaned from a speech he delivered to industrialists in 1943. The Taoiseach speculated about economic arrangements after the end of the war. He maintained that:

> State control and State intervention will tend to remain and to entrench itself in many spheres where formerly private enterprise alone held the field. The State will continue to accept responsibility where before the war it accepted none. International trade will tend to become more and more directly an inter-State affair and be operated and controlled in bulk by the several States, each in the national or community interest to which private interests will be definitely subordinated.

This was not quite what Mr de Valera's own 1937 constitution had laid down. Article 45.2.3 ruled out such a concentration of economic power. It reads that the state shall direct its policy towards securing that "the operation of the free market shall not be allowed so to develop as to result in the concentration of the ownership or control of essential commodities in a few individuals to the common detriment." If this restriction does not apply to a few individual Ministers, or a few individual civil servants, as much as to a few individual private citizens, then it is ridiculous. The same clause was inconsistent with the monopolies Mr de Valera's governments had nonetheless created in the sugar, electricity, cement, tyre and other industries.

As the de Valera era drew to a close, the evidence of the failure of protection mounted. While the Taoiseach pined after crossroads-dancing and frugal living, during the 1950s some 400,000 of his citizens decided to cut their losses and emigrate to the US and Britain. Forced to choose between its policy and its population, the government slowly abandoned its aim of self-sufficiency and between the mid-1960s and mid-1970s gradually dismantled protection.

Around the same time, Dr T.K. Whitaker, in his remarkable 1958 report *Economic Development*, proposed a hard-headed economic policy of productive investment and entrepreneurialism led by the private sector. Dr Whitaker warned that to avoid economic decadence, Ireland need a massive and sustained increase in production, based on shifting resources from non-productive to productive purposes. He argued against "job creation" in favour of an expansion in productive economic activity. He argued against tax increases. He said that it would be wrong to rely on public investments alone and that one would expect "the principal source of new productive ideas, in a predominantly free enterprise economy, to be the private sector." He argued for competition and against restrictive practices. He argued that pay should rise only in line with rises in productivity. He argued against defeatism, insisting that the Irish must have a will to succeed.

Otherwise, he wrote:

the serious economic harm caused by the unproductive use of scarce capital . . . [and] the ever-higher taxation necessary to finance rapidly increasing deadweight debt charges will make further inroads on income and savings, industry and trade will be deprived of both the capital and the incentive to pursue a vigorous programme of modernisation and expansion, the gap between living standards at home and elsewhere will be widened and the attractions of emigration will be increased.

This call met with much verbal entrepreneurialism on the part of officialdom, but Dr Whitaker's strategy was not followed. Something close to the poisonous cocktail he had warned of — wasteful investments, high taxes, large debts, debilitated Irish industry, little "catch up" with European living standards and renewed emigration — duly came to pass in the 1980s.

Round Two: Export Promotion

Rather than adopt Dr Whitaker's proposals for fostering productivity and initiative, governments instead turned to a new round of state interventions centred on "industrial policy" and export promotion. Protection was replaced by a government invitation to foreign investors to set up branch plants in Ireland. Almost immediately, a brave new world seemed to dawn. But was the 1960s boom due to generous IDA grants, government tax reliefs and national planning (the Programmes for Economic Expansion)? The conventional wisdom says yes. Many economic investigators say no. Instead, they attribute the rapid growth to *free trade* which finally connected the Irish economy, via exports, to the buoyant world economy from which it had previously been cut off by de Valera's policy of self-sufficiency.

Nonetheless, the coincidence of the boom with the new policies meant that, once again, the state seemed to be the source of economic success.

It is important to realise that the nature of the switch from protection to export promotion was not so dramatic as conventionally believed. Brendan Walsh and Anthony Leddin, for instance, point out that both policies risked fostering inefficiency. Protection makes imports expensive and allows domestic firms to have high costs without being put out of business by more efficient foreign rivals. But high-cost domestic firms cannot then become exporters and find themselves trapped in their protected home market. In a similar way, grants and tax reliefs for exporting manufacturers mean that a company whose domestic costs are higher that its international competitors' can still stay in business, although only as long as the subsidies last. In both cases, public assistance risks becoming permanent, if the aid-addicted infant industries never grow up. They cannot do so if they use subsidisation merely to offset high domestic costs. They have no reason to do so if they believe that the subsidies will persist or, by recourse to political lobbying, can be made to.

Neither strategy, at least in the forms practised in Ireland, offers much prospect of long-term economic development. Long-term economic viability rests on efficiency, which neither of these policies usually promotes. Unless they are designed with exceptional sophistication, as in some South East Asian countries, protection and export promotion, though intended to be an incentive for the determined can degenerate into a cushion for the timid. A cushion, moreover, which the timid will never be able or willing to see removed.

Lemass

It is customary to revere Seán Lemass and to see him as an exceptional figure in Irish political and economic history. But the economic instruments Lemass favoured were overwhelmingly a continuation of a centuries-old statism, and ensured that businesses would continue to lobby politicians, since the political system was often more important than the market in determining business success or failure.

While Lemass's declared aims were the promotion of efficiency in Ireland, the connection between efficiency and competition seems not to have been understood. Much of Lemass's thinking was highly anti-competitive. Professor Daly comments that "Lemass . . . favoured a planned economy where . . . competition and overcapacity did not exist". At this time "official directives organising companies into non-competing specialisation were common". Decentralisation gave industrialists a ready excuse for high prices. Moreover, Lemass wished to go further and to have "mandatory licensing and control over all firms, both native and foreign, and over exports and imports". (His fellow Ministers refused to grant him such draconian powers.)

During the war, in 1942, he formulated what he called "an Aim and a Plan for the control and direction of the nation's resources of labour". As Minister for Industry, Commerce and Supplies, he already possessed the power to control wages, to restrict emigration, to refuse employment assistance to people who left employment "without due cause" and to refuse benefits to men unwilling to participate in the Construction Corps. These powers have been described (even by a highly-sympathetic historian, Dr. Brian Girvin) as "considerable, if not actually draconian", "unprecedented in democratic countries" and "closer to those of the Mediterranean dictatorships than to Ireland's liberal democratic neighbours". Nonetheless, Lemass argued that the "government has not yet provided itself with sufficient powers to enable it to apply effectively any labour policy which might be decided upon." He wished to establish a "labour pool", the members of which would receive a guaranteed wage in return for agreeing to work wherever the government sent them.

On other occasions, Lemass envisaged the state setting wages and profits and exercising control over the banks. Most astonishing of all, he did not foresee any scaling back in these powers when the war ended. Lemass failed to persuade his fellow Ministers to adopt the more coercive of these ideas.

In a speech in 1961 Lemass argued that:

> In Irish economic development the role of the government is predominant. Nobody believes that, in the circumstances of this country economic progress on the scale which is needed is likely to be realised otherwise than through the medium of a strong and sound government policy directed to that result. This does not mean reliance solely on an extension of direct state-sponsored activities . . . [but] free private enterprise cannot be fully availed of without government drive and leadership.

The implication of this passage — more state action — is clear. But the economic rationale is, as before, absent. Why does nobody believe that economic progress cannot be achieved without strong government? Why does private enterprise need government leadership? What is meant by state leadership? How will the government lead? The speech does not say. Lemass's policy was based on assumed but unexplained market failure, and assumed but unspecified state capabilities.

A state that apparently did not know the basis of the problems its initiatives were supposed to tackle should not have been surprised soon to find itself floundering in problems of its own creation.

Round Three: Public Spending

After unwinding protection and changing to export promotion, the Irish economy, like all others, was hit by the oil shocks of the 1970s. Unemployment soared. What was to be done?

A budget deficit (current government spending greater than current income) had first been introduced by George Colley in 1972, when it was hailed by the *Irish Times* as "wise . . . good psychology as well as sensible economics ... relatively radical thinking . . . more than welcome." The editorial writers sought "some form of economic regulator, which moves up and down according to immediate requirements". Well, the deficit duly moved up. But for the next 20 years, come boom or bust, it never came back into balance. Meanwhile the *Irish Times* thought the only question "is whether [Mr Colley] has gone as far as the situation demands." In 1978, this question was put to the test.

Mr Jack Lynch and Dr Martin O Donoghue, entering government in 1977, believed they had the answer to Irish unemployment. Plainly, the private sector had let the country down yet again. Now it was time to make a clean break. This time the state would finally come to the rescue. What was needed was a new government department, Economic Planning and Development. And nearly 200 years after Grattan's Parliament had first engaged in "pump-priming" — giving a supposedly initial boost to the economy after which the private sector would take over — the new Fianna Fáil government of 1977 fell back on this strategy, oblivious, it seems, to the fact that it had been tried and found wanting on numerous previous occasions.

There was a *real* increase in public expenditure, in the space of just five years (1977-82) of *one-half*. Once more, politicians were to decide where hundreds of millions of pounds of public funds were to be channelled. Further growth of the state and of political

influence in the economy was certain. The rationale for such a development was no clearer than before. If anything, it was weaker
than for previous state initiatives. On the investment side, there
was no particular reason to think that politicians, or their staff,
would have any special skill in picking successful projects. On the
racecourse, this hazardous policy of "picking winners" is called
gambling. In politics, it is called "industrial policy".

The pump-priming case for additional current spending, to the
extent that there is one, rests on the spending being directed towards productive investment. However, much of the rise in Irish
public spending between 1977 and 1982 went towards consumption spending: hiring more public servants, increasing welfare
payments, giving home-buyer grants and so on.

State *investment* spending makes perfect sense if it gets a project started and leaves a successful business in its wake whose
later tax payments will allow the government to repay its initial
loans. (The question still needs to be asked why, if the project has
good prospects, its instigators cannot just borrow the initial
funds? A project with magnificent potential for which private
funding is mysteriously unavailable probably does not have the
magnificent prospects claimed for it.)

A successful investment in a productive activity creates goods
or services which, when sold, bring a stream of income that was
not there previously. *When the subsidy stops, the new business and its
new tax payments carry on.*

But state *consumption* is quite different in its effects. With the
best will in the world, it is hard to see how hiring more public
servants, raising old-age pensions, let alone showering favours on
constituents, will subsequently increase the government's tax income enough to allow the initial borrowing to be repaid.

Take the case of higher welfare payments. They may well have
considerable social benefits. But they can never lead to enough
additional tax revenue to finance the higher benefit, since otherwise the recipient would be handing over all the increase as tax
and would be left no better off. And if, later, the increase is cancelled, the income of the recipient falls too because the welfare
spending has created no new income stream. The same will generally be true in regard to hiring extra public servants, offering

first-time home-buyer grants, and so forth. The national plans and white papers of the period have never detailed the mechanism which was supposed to allow long-term benefits to result from consumption spending.

The fact that the bulk of the 1970s rise in public spending was financed by borrowing and was not productively invested meant that it has left a huge national debt in its wake. Up until then, it could at least be said of Irish governments that they preserved the solvency of the state. But the negative effects of the failed strategy of the 1970s will be carried forward far into the future.

The Lost 1980s

The 1980s, like the 1950s, were a lost economic decade. Governments struggled to contain public borrowing and restore order to the public finances. It was not quickly or easily achieved, especially during recessionary conditions in the earlier part of the decade. However, in the late 1980s dramatic progress was finally recorded.

In the mid-1980s, the National Planning Board again proposed a market-based strategy for the Irish economy based on principles like those of T.K. Whitaker, 25 years before. The Board's report proposed two medium-term economic targets. First, public spending should be in line with the government revenue generated by tax rates which "maintain the incentives to work, save, invest, take commercial risks and innovate." Second, national economic policy should "encourage and sustain growth of output and employment in the market sector . . . by inducing private persons and agencies and public enterprises to use their time, talents and other resources more productively in Ireland."

Once again, this general philosophy was not followed. The effort to restore order to the public finances seems to have absorbed the bulk of the time and energies of the government. Other than curtailing state spending and borrowing, the status quo was maintained.

Round Four: Complacent Corporatism

In early 1992, the Culliton committee returned to the question of Irish economic development policy. Like *Economic Development* and the Planning Board's report, it proposed a change of direction. Efficiency was the keyword in the Culliton review. An efficient tax system, with fewer penalties for enterprise. An efficient infrastructure, with fewer penalties for Irish-based exporting businesses. An efficient education system, training people to acquire business-relevant skills. And an industrial development policy involving fewer subsidies and a greater focus on identifying and removing specific obstacles to the growth of efficient domestic enterprises.

It does not seem that the principles lying behind the Review Group's recommendations have been taken to heart by the political authorities and their staff. Under the umbrella of national pay bargaining, and with billions of pounds of Brussels subsidies there to be spent, difficult economic decisions have been postponed indefinitely.

Tax reform is negligible. Infrastructure is improving, but is maximising the economic return always the main criterion in selecting projects? The educational system carries on almost as before and treats the suggestion that it be "economically relevant" as an impertinence. As the leaders of education fall back on lofty generalisations about preserving culture, another generation of young Irish people bestows their cultural brilliance on foreign lands. The pace at which IDA activity is being switched towards market principles, away from the "grant mentality" and the PR stunts of Ministerial "job creation" announcements, is glacial. Although Culliton called for the grant mentality to be combated, the 1994-1999 National Development Plan involves a large increase in grants for industry. Nor is it the case that government economic interventions have been refocussed on clear goals.

Meanwhile, public spending has returned to form. According to the Department of Finance's *Economic Review* and *Outlook 1995*, total public expenditure will have reached £14.6 billion by 1995, a rise of £4.5 billion (or 45 per cent) since 1990. Three-quarters of the increase is accounted for by day-to-day (non-investment) spending. Since borrowing remains low, taxes have had to be raised to pay for this additional expenditure. Over the same five years, the government's tax revenue is budgeted to climb by £3.3 billion from £7.9 billion in 1990 to £11.2 billion in 1995 (most of the rest of the additional spending has been financed from increased Structural Funds). What has been the increase in *output* corresponding to this enormous rise in the resources being absorbed by the Irish public sector? With so little measurement of public output, it is very hard to know.

The leopard has not changed many spots. Nor has it changed its mind. The 1989-1993 National Development Plan showed the same scepticism towards the market economy and the same blindness to government failures found in Ireland since before the foundation of the state. The Plan was mainly about what the state would do to stimulate the Irish economy. Little was said about how the rest of the economy might be expected to react.

The Plan acknowledged that the efficient working of markets would help to ensure that "resources be used to best effect". However, efficient markets were to be pursued only "within accepted social conditions". What these might be was not specified.

Later in the same report, consideration was gingerly given to the idea of extending competition in the Irish economy as a way to stimulate economic growth. But this should be done only "insofar as the freer play of competitive forces offers the prospect of efficiency gains and consequent cost benefits, and is not incompatible with wider social and economic objectives". The authors did not say if they believed competition would actually improve efficiency. The possible role of markets in improving Irish economic performance remains in a very grey zone.

Similarly, the second National Development Plan (1994-1999) also focused overwhelmingly on the state, saying very little about the response of the private sector. Solving Ireland's economic problems, we are to believe, is a matter of improving government policies rather than being a question of private initiative and higher productivity.

Conclusion

Two hundred years ago, *politics* — in the form of Grattan's Parliament — appeared to deliver economic prosperity. During the nineteenth century, politics — in the form of the London government's support for free trade — seemed to have destroyed it. In mid-century, the market was blamed for the death or departure of millions of Irish people. Subsequently, political agitation during the Land War led to some improvement in the position of Irish farmers. Further political lobbying produced a host of "lollipops" from the UK government, anxious to wean Ireland away from its demand for Home Rule. Some Irish observers worried that it made the Irish feel that others owed them a living. An attitude that the state alone could resolve Irish economic problems was well established in Irish minds by the time of independence and the stage was set for more politics-driven economic policy in the new republic. For a decade, Cumann na nGaedhael resisted this tendency, but Mr de Valera's governments greatly extended ministerial control of the Irish economy using tariffs, licensing and other instruments. Mr Lemass was the prime manager of these tools, and he tried to persuade his ministerial colleagues to introduce still more extensive powers of state economic control which he believed were necessary. While policy instruments changed during the 1960s from protection to export promotion, economic development was still channelled through a host of state agencies and in a form which allowed private firms to remain inefficient. A disastrous lurch towards pump-priming in the 1970s loaded the economy with debt and took almost ten years to bring under control. Today, public spending is again increasing swiftly and, despite the appearance of documents like the Culliton report, deregulation is mostly Brussels-driven and the pronouncements of policy-makers show them to be as statist and as sceptical of the market as ever.

There is a worrying continuity from the 18th century paternalism of Grattan's Parliament to late-19th century paternalism financed by the British government, to home-grown paternalism of the protectionist, export promotion and pump priming varieties, with the Eurofunds version already in full swing.

It is ingrained in the Irish population to delegate to politicians responsibility for the economy. This is a continuation of an extremely long-standing tradition on this part of the island. Redirecting attention to the economic basis for growth — productivity — remains a daunting challenge.

At the root of this continuity is the popular view that Irish history has been a centuries-long collective struggle against an historic enemy. This struggle has put a premium on collective solidarity over individual initiative. Such an emphasis has perhaps made for successful political campaigns, but it has not been helpful to economic endeavours which rely much more on individual action.

The rationale for these continuous and massive interventions has never been clearly stated by those responsible for promoting these policies. In some cases, it simply does not exist. The interventionist strategies tried after independence — protection, export promotion and pump-priming — all delivered short-term employment and output gains but none, as implemented in Ireland, offers any long-term prospect of sustained economic development. The "temporary" expansions of the state which each policy has involved have proved to be permanent.

"Liberty" in Ireland is typically interpreted as national liberty — independence from the colonial master — rather than in the more usual sense of freedom of the individual citizen. In the modern world, the biggest single concentration of power in society is found in the state which constitutes the greatest potential threat to individual liberty. But in Ireland, because of our history, we have thought of the state as the provider of (national) liberty denied by an oppressive neighbour. This may explain why we have permitted the state to gather a set of powers which, in many other countries, would be considered at least unhealthy.

Careless state action can be self-reinforcing. Public initiatives, insofar as they shift rather than create income, and create dependent clients, weaken the link between reward and effort, undermine the legitimacy of market endeavour and bring forth demands for more intervention. To escape from this costly and wasteful maze, Ireland needs to learn from its history.

Ireland followed this path for four reasons. First, we tend to copy Britain. Second, as this chapter has shown, anti-market economics cuts with the grain of Irish opinion. Third, a larger role for the Irish state offered big benefits to the Irish political system, putting lots of spending power into the hands of politicians. State spending programmes are the bedrock on which our system of political "clinics" rests. Fourthly, we have a very anti-intellectual and uncritical culture in Ireland. Our political parties have very little stomach for "conviction" politics. But catch-all parties need to be principle-free zones. Irish political parties lack almost entirely the apparatus for serious in-house policy research and assessment. Judging by the economic performance of recent decades, the civil service may not be much better equipped. Consequently, we have tended to adopt our sense of the prevailing international economic orthodoxy without giving economic policies the detailed scrutiny they deserve.

It is time for a change of direction. Time for a shift from the Decree to the Designer Economy. This means four specific changes: (a) more competition in the marketplace; (b) a reformed electoral system in politics; (c) the state to concentrate on the core goals of promoting productivity and opportunity; and (d) public sector organisations to be made more attentive to the consumer.

For the future, we must reformulate our economic policy to ask: what specifically are the market failures that hamper the Irish private sector? How are these best remedied: can the market be made to work, or is some intervention required? If the remedy involves public action, how — specifically — can the public sector overcome the failures that defeated the private sector? What mechanism will be established to regularly measure the effectiveness of the intervention, and to compare benefits achieved with the costs of the operation?

Only by taking this approach to economic policy can the effectiveness of both the private and public sectors of the Irish economy be maximised for the future. A politician-ridden society is not much of an improvement on a priest-ridden one.

12

MEANWHILE, BACK AT THE BAR STOOL

Vorsprung durch Critique
The hostility to the market economy which has long prevailed in Ireland has led to extensive but poorly designed government involvement in the economy. Without a proper view of the economic roles of the state and the market, there is little prospect of Ireland's economic problems being successfully addressed. Striking such a balance will mean a searching reassessment of traditional attitudes. While certainly not lacking cynics, Ireland has often been short of true sceptics. For the future, we need to evaluate our economic *attitudes* much more fiercely than we have done in the past. Casual Irish anti-intellectualism has allowed, and continues to allow, sloppy economic reasoning, if not outright economic nonsense, to go unchallenged. If the Germans rely on Vorsprung durch Technik — progress through technology — in Ireland we need some Vorsprung durch Critique!

Parachutes, Pirates, Cowboys and Fat Cats
The language used in Irish life to describe business activities is indicative of our attitude to the market and to private initiative. Consider the following examples, drawn from public sector companies.

RTE and its political sympathisers delayed the establishment of independent radio services in Ireland until the late 1980s, insisting that RTE could meet any need for local radio. RTE's own news services associated the label "pirate" radio with (illegal) private radio services. In fact, local radio broadcasting was not piracy. Private business was not piracy. Competition for RTE was not piracy. Nor, outside Ireland, was radio broadcasting illegal, at least in the democratic world. But it was helpful to RTE to be able to use the national airwaves to associate its potential commercial rivals with the idea of piracy. Politicians were not in a strong position to complain since RTE has monopoly control of domestic television news and current affairs broadcasting. Soon enough, the term "pirate" radio had been absorbed into everyday usage.

Another public company, An Post, has promoted its parcel delivery service using a radio advert which portrays private delivery firms as "cowboys". Once again, we are to understand that private enterprise is unreliable and fly-by-night.

Some years ago, the trade union group in Telecom Éireann ran a glossy poster campaign which painted would-be buyers of privatised Telecom shares as "fat cats". Now, savers and investors — fat, thin or otherwise — must put their funds somewhere. Investment in shares is normal and innocuous behaviour in a market economy. It has neither good nor bad moral overtones. No doubt the employees of Telecom Éireann have been happy to draw pensions financed from investments in other companies' shares. But they do not want their governmental safety-net withdrawn so they indiscriminately picture savers as "fat cats".

RTE, An Post, and Telecom unions freely use terms like pirate, cowboy and fat cat to attempt to reduce competition in their businesses. They wish to preserve their monopolies and state ownership, which understandably they find congenial. They want to sell a simple message: private sector bad, public sector good. These monopolies and their staffs are happy with this set-up, but monopoly does not serve the public interest.

Likewise, the objections by party political insiders to the outsider "parachutist" candidates in the 1994 European elections revealed a similar resistance to the idea of open competition, in this case for political party nominations.

In Ireland, people seem instinctively to see competition as a personal threat to be resisted. Little account is taken of the social benefits that competition also offers. Precisely because it punishes slacking and a quiet life, it forces higher levels of performance from companies and individuals, and this is a gain to everyone else.

There is No Single Market

A pro-market message gets surprisingly short shrift in many Irish quarters today. There is passionate denunciation of the market in some media and Roman Catholic Church circles, and more muted rumblings in politics.

Lest it be thought that these comments are the ravings of one economist, below I quote some examples drawn from recent church and media sources. No doubt similar views are to be found in other places. The quotations selected *illustrate* certain errors and misunderstandings but they are not a full evaluation of the thinking of the writers quoted, some of whom write sensibly, even in fact brilliantly, about other topics.

Many recent statements by leading Roman Catholic Church figures, although they endorse enterprise in a cursory way, also display a quite marked hostility towards the market economy. Examples include the bishops' pastoral *Work is the key*, Cardinal Daly's controversial August 1992 sermon on the market economy and the 1995 Trocaire lecture by the Coadjutor Archbishop of Armagh, Dr Seán Brady.

In the media, what might be termed the Irish Times School of Economics — Fintan O Toole and John Waters — regularly give vent to emotional outbursts about the market system.

While politicians proclaim their support for enterprise from the rooftops, it is hard to do much of a practical nature when you are standing on the top of a roof. The journalist John Healy criticised Irish politicians for Verbal Republicanism. Today's problem is Verbal Entrepreneurialism.

Few Irish politicians take a *principled* pro-competitive-market stance. Politicians prefer pragmatism. In other words, they forego statements of principle and decide each issue opportunistically. We know where this has got us.

Detailed examination of many common criticisms of the market economy shows them to be based on a misunderstanding of the way markets operate. In particular, critics often have a very defective grasp of the fact that, in different circumstances, a private market may perform very well or very poorly. *There is no one market*. It is not as simple as being for or against the market. The issue is *when* to be for the market and *when* to be against it. But

Ireland's market-fearing intellectuals seem oblivious to this. Still, the scapegoat of the market is to hand while the truth may be far off in the bush.

Because the distinction between competitive and non-competitive markets plays little if any role in Irish discussions of economic policy, one often hears the failings of non-competitive markets — such as excessive profits — attributed quite errone-ously to the market system in general.

The worst confusion is to blame the market for things that are the result of government intervention in the economy! This is a remarkably common mistake. My colleague, Kevin O Rourke, in a 1995 talk to Irish theologians (published in *Doctrine and Life*) of-fered the following list of Irish economic failings which are not caused by the market.

> It is not the market which has taxed jobs and subsidised the use of machinery; which has created poverty traps in the social wel-fare system; which has neglected the educational requirements of our disadvantaged communities; which imposes restrictions on the number of taxi-drivers or public houses in the state; which restricts the hours during which the latter may stay open; which in the past denied local communities the right to open their own radio stations and still makes it difficult for those communities to set up private bus companies; which imposes a corporate tax rate of 38 per cent on labour-intensive services, while capital-intensive manufacturing industries pay 10 per cent; which is currently wasting the last significant allocation of EU structural funding which Ireland will receive; or which has devised a tax system so complicated that talent is diverted to the accounting and legal professions.

We cannot blame the market for any of these things. Yet commen-tators routinely do. For example, the 1992 Irish bishops' pastoral on unemployment criticised the large number of bright and tal-ented people in Ireland pursuing "handsome fees and salaries by acting as consultants in tax, legal and property matters". Now, it would be naïve not to expect people to pursue handsome re-wards. But these particular rewards are high not because of the market — which the bishops blame — but because of the gov-ernment. State legislation (our complex tax system, the restriction on entry to many professions, and land rezoning powers) is what makes this consultancy work so lucrative.

Similarly, Fintan O Toole's *Irish Times* column has variously maintained that "the great slump of the 1930s . . . had been caused by the operations of an unrestricted free market" (July 1995), that "nation states are the victims rather than the regulators of the money markets" (March 1995) and that "drug-trafficking is . . . a form of capitalism" (July 1995). He gleefully concludes from the errors in the national accounts arising from multinational profit repatriation that "the reality which has been defined by mainstream economists [is a fairytale]" (July 1994). Mr O Toole is in danger of practising One-Eyed Journalism: the right eye focused feverishly on the failings of the market and the left eye firmly shut. He ignores or, worse, is unaware of the central contribution of governments to each of these problems. Let's consider in turn each of these events that Mr O Toole blames on the market, beginning with the 1930s slump.

Two key ingredients in the Great Depression were international trade disputes and the collapse of large parts of the US banking system. But no market in history has ever created a tariff — a tax on imports. Only politicians can do that. And one of the key roles of a central bank — which is a state agency — is to lend money to financially-sound institutions suffering a panic-induced outflow of deposits in order to stop a system-wide collapse of confidence in banks. It is now generally accepted that the US Federal Reserve failed to adequately discharge its responsibilities in this area in the 1930s. During the Great Depression, governments were no innocent bystanders before the operations of an "unrestricted" free market.

Secondly, Mr O Toole described the (indeed astounding) £1 billion profits made by the currency trader George Soros when sterling withdrew in 1992 from the EU exchange rate mechanism (ERM) as an example of the stupid, nasty, anarchic and irrational workings of finance capitalism. Well, at most, that is half the story. Mr Soros was able to make his famous billion only because the Bank of England bought about £5 billion pounds sterling from him at a price which was soon revealed to be about 20 per cent above its market value. Naturally there was no shortage of sellers of sterling in these circumstances!

Markets on their own could not have produced this outcome. Had market participants bought such extravagant quantities of over-valued sterling the risk, and any losses, would have been entirely their own. In fact, Mr Soros lost $600 million just one year later trading US bonds with other private market operators. He reportedly lost the same amount on Japanese investments in 1995. But his losses are not mentioned in Mr O Toole's account of the Big Bad Money Markets.

During the lead-up to "Black Wednesday", and many other moments during the 1992-93 currency crisis, the willingness of governments to buy unlimited amounts of over-valued currencies created a risk-free bet which "finance capitalists" readily took up. The question of who was behaving stupidly and irrationally has a less clear-cut answer than Mr O Toole would wish to believe. The proof that governments were an essential ingredient of the problem is that, since the near-disbandment of the ERM in August 1993, nothing more has been heard about a currency crisis. Have all the nasty irrational finance capitalists retired? Or have European governments substantially withdrawn from currency intervention?

Thirdly, Mr O Toole blamed the market for the Black Hole of profit repatriation, yet this is primarily the result of governments competing for the jobs and factories of multinational companies. By offering low corporate taxes, the Irish government *invites* foreign companies to over-report their Irish profits in order to be able to send lightly-taxed profits home to head office. That international companies do what our tax laws reward them for doing is only to be expected. To blame the market for the state's industrial policy would be muddle-headed. As for the national accounts, it is up to the state's Central Statistics Office to address itself to the statistical errors. In principle, figures including and excluding the activities of multinationals could be published to identify the condition of the "real" indigenous sector of the Irish economy.

Finally, there is the calamity of illegal drug-dealing and illegal drug-use. Is this, as Mr O Toole alleges, a form of capitalism? If so, why does the problem affect ecstasy and heroin but not alcohol and nicotine? Do capitalists buy and sell only some kinds of drugs? No, but only some kinds are banned by governments. This makes them scarce and drives up their price. To buy the now-expensive drugs, the addict must obtain large amounts of cash, often from crime. Meanwhile, it has become worthwhile for criminal gangs to get involved in the now-lucrative "business" of drug dealing. None of this happens in the market for cigarettes or alcohol. It takes the combination of the market and state prohibition to generate drug barons, drug gangs and generalised drug crime.

For just the same reason, alcohol prohibition in the US in the 1920s drove production underground and created a wave of violent crime as gangs fought to control the supply of illegal liquor. When prohibition was lifted, all this came to an end.

The foregoing remarks do not prejudge how the authorities should tackle the problem of illegal drugs. They do not downplay the costs and the trauma of drug abuse. But without a good understanding of *all* the causes of the drugs problem, there is little hope of tackling it successfully.

In this litany of half-truths, Mr O Toole seems unaware of the way that the Great Depression, currency speculation, multinational profit repatriation and drug dealing are all the result of a malign interaction between markets and governments. None of these problems could take the form they do without both parties' involvement. Why, then, are so many opinion-makers so loathe to acknowledge this? Why the insistence on making a whipping-boy of the market while letting the state off scot-free?

Disentangling the role of different social institutions — markets and governments — is the first step towards lessening the above problems. That requires intellectual even-handedness and some grasp of economics. These are not always on offer.

When all else fails, the attack shifts from the message to the messengers. Not infrequently when discussing economic policy, columnists in the *Irish Times* resort to low-level mud-slinging and name-calling. John Waters dismisses economics as "the sanctified telling of lies" (August 1993). He describes economists as "so-called "economic experts", who are themselves comfortable as a result of poncing off the economics of contentment" (May 1992). Mr Waters' *Irish Times* colleague, Fintan O Toole, penned the following picture of economists at work in September 1992:

> In the graveyard of economic analysis, the glimmer of midnight lamps has been spotted again, as the Resurrection Men go about their dirty work, digging through the layers of rotted newsprint to open the creaking coffin of clapped-out "solutions" [to unemployment]. Meanwhile, back in their dusty labs, the mad scientists await the delivery of freshly-exhumed organs which they will soon sew together to make new monsters.

In a later piece he claimed that morality was "an element hitherto undreamed of in [economists'] philosophy" (January 1993).

These are desperate but telling tactics. To kill a hated message, against which one can present no rational objections, one must attempt to kill the messenger. You must say: pay no attention to economics because it is the wicked work of liars, pimps, graverobbers and nutters. This barrage of abuse may have some initial novelty and distraction value. But the conjuring-up of a conspiratorial priesthood and high-octane character assassination are required only by those who need to hide their intellectual destitution behind emotional denunciations.

John Waters criticises Ireland's "thought deficit". Quite so.

Opinions of the "Academics": Four Myths about Economics

Many commentators who are dismissive of the assumptions of economic theory proceed to make a multitude of their own *assumptions* about economic behaviour. Such assumptions are often more "academic" — partial, simplified, out-of-date — than the assumptions of academic economists.

Assumption 1: Economics is About Theory, Not the Real World.

Reflecting Ireland's deep anti-intellectualism, many dismiss economic theory precisely for being theory. For instance, Dr Brady, in his 1995 Trocaire lecture, criticises economic commentators and international bodies like the World Bank for "dealing with abstractions" rather than with the real world. Their métier, or business, he says sniffily, is theory. John Waters argues that the free market would be fine "in a world inhabited by stainless steel robots" but that it does not work in "the real world" (August 1993). We previously encountered Fintan O Toole consigning economics to a graveyard for clapped-out theories.

But no one can think without some kind of abstract framework. There is no theory-free observation; if you urge a roomful of people to "Observe!", they will soon respond "Observe what?" You cannot make a "real world" observation independently of the ideas in your mind about the things you are observing.

There is a role for theorists, who study a subject, as well as practitioners, who work at an applied level. Both groups deserve a hearing. If I suffered from life-threatening cancer, I would certainly want to talk to an "academic" medical specialist, even if they had never directly experienced the disease. I might also want to talk to a fellow-sufferer to get some first-hand information about the experience of the disease. I would want the doctor's *knowledge* as well as the cancer-victim's *experience*. I would not dismiss the doctor's "theories" just because the doctor was not at death's door.

A theory of the economy is unavoidable because its workings are so complicated. Even in a highly-simplified Dream Economy, the roles played by prices, profits and competition are not self-evident. Just because we all "live" in an economy does not guarantee that we will automatically understand how it works.

The (implicit) theories of commentators, as shown by the assumptions discussed below, are not one iota less theoretical — just different — from those of economists.

Assumption 2: Economics is Just Ideological Propaganda.
In John Waters' words, economics is "obscurantist mumbo-jumbo spouted by paid propagandists called economists" (February 1994). It is a "quasi-religious belief in the power of the marketplace to decide everything for the best" (May 1992). Fintan O Toole maintains that the ethic of the market "justifies itself in terms yet more mystical and irrationally religious than any old morality". It needs "some magic [by which] the pursuit of private greed . . . will creat[e] wealth, creat[e] jobs, creat[e] a better society for all" (autumn 1991).

Well, readers may feel that earlier chapters of this book offered arguments for the market that did not — at least as far as I noticed

— depend on mysticism, religion, black magic, witch-doctoring or voodoo. As for ideology, Irish economists can be found in all political parties and in none. Colleagues who have worked in the US report that as many, if not more, economists are supporters of the Democratic as of the Republican party. Economics does not predispose one to any particular political viewpoint.

For those who insist that any pro-market economic policy must be the economic programme of the "New Right", here are some of the main differences between the two.

The New Right seeks "free" markets, which need not be the same thing as competitive markets. The New Right favours private over public ownership. The New Right broadly considers the distribution of rewards that occurs in a private economy to reflect the relative efforts of private individuals, and consequently frowns on income redistribution. The New Right, generally sceptical about government regulation, is suspicious of the need for public agencies charged with maintaining competition. The New Right sees a market system as sufficiently close to competitive conditions to need very little intervention, if any, to deal with spillovers or other problems. Finally (although properly speaking it is an entirely separate issue), the New Right advances a moral agenda of very conservative social values which have come to be closely associated with its economic policies.

The social market programme is free of all this baggage. A policy more different to that of the New Right would be hard to imagine. The *only* overlap between the two approaches is that they rely on markets. But, to repeat, there is not just a single market. The social market programme uses markets as an instrument to social democratic ends. For the New Right, the market is practically an end in itself.

Critics of the market insist on the equivalence of all markets, whether competitive or not. These muddy waters lead them to denounce all market-based systems as small variations on a Thatcherite theme. This is confusion. The charge of Thatcherism is a large blue herring.

Assumption 3: Economics is Slavishly Pro-market.
Economists do not claim that markets always work any more than doctors claim the human body always works. If markets never

failed, there would be no need for economics in the same way that, without ill-health, there would be no need for medicine. But a doctor cannot treat a failure of the body without knowing what a well-functioning body would be. Likewise, economists cannot treat market failure without a good understanding of market success.

Economists do not claim that markets are always the most appropriate way of organising an economy. Whole chapters of this book have been taken up with explanations of when markets can be expected to perform well and when they need to be supplemented. A glance at a university economics textbook would also show the considerable space devoted to treatments of various kinds of market failure.

Economists study the circumstances when markets will work and when they will fail. When they fail, economists believe that it is up to governments to create incentives for people to behave differently. Economists are not slaves to the market. It is the assumption that they are which has about it the real air of dogmatism.

Assumption 4: Economics is Indifferent to Poverty and Unemployment.

Unemployment and poverty are great evils. No economist possessed of both a head and a heart would disagree. In fact, there are strong grounds for believing that economists — because they know unemployment can be tackled — are the least complacent people in regard to joblessness.

Nor are economists indifferent to poverty and other social problems. Economists are well aware that the record of private markets in reaching social goals has often fallen dramatically short of many people's ideals. It is certain that there are many social goals which an unaided private market cannot deliver and are only attainable by collective public provision.

But economists refuse to indulge in naïve delusions about governments. Economists insist that market failures on their own do not establish a carte blanche for public intervention because the capacity of governments too is limited. The record of indiscriminate state intervention has been a terrible, and often a very costly, disappointment. To justify state intervention, one must show how a particular government programme will meet its targets. Also, the costs of public intervention need to be compared with the benefits to establish whether the initiative will do harm or good.

Irish public programmes often fail to meet these requirements for a rational system of state intervention in the economy. It is for this reason, not callousness, that economists so often, and quite correctly, challenge public initiatives.

Opinions of the "Academics": Six Myths about the Market
Just as false assumptions are routinely made about economists, there is a closely-related set of myths concerning the market itself. Some of the most important, and fallacious, are the following.

Assumption 5: The Market Harms the Environment.
In recent years, environmentalism has swelled the ranks of the anti-marketeers.

But it is not always well-informed environmentalism. In 1994, a Columban priest, Fr Seán McDonagh, wrote in the *Irish Times* that only *one* book had ever been published on the economics of the environment (by A.C. Pigou in the 1920s). A UCD colleague of mine, on reading this letter, used the Internet to log into the catalogue of the library of Harvard University. He searched the catalogue to find the number of books with the words economics and environment in their title. There was a pause while the computer software worked away. Then the following answer flashed up on the screen: *too many books to list.* In fact, there are thousands of books on the economics of the environment, which is one of the most active areas of current economic research.

Like Fr McDonagh, many Greens see the market system as always and everywhere the source of pollution and environmental degradation. Some demand that economic growth be stopped completely to "protect the environment". This is a highly debatable position.

Because the physical environment is owned collectively rather than by anybody in particular, an unregulated private economy can seriously damage the environment. People treat their own property with care but treat collective property as though it were free. We are all sparing in the use of costly things but extravagant about using "free" public parks, "free" clean air, "free" water and so on. The problem here is less the market than the absence of the market! No one owns assets like clean air, so no one charges for their use and therefore they are neglected. An earlier chapter explained how charging for pollution could be used to mimic the market and correct the failure.

Stopping economic growth is neither necessary nor helpful. Environmental protection is very costly. In countries with low incomes and slow growth, problems with poor water and sanitation, air pollution and loss of soil cover go untreated. Better-off countries are generally the ones with stiffer environmental regulations. Lack of growth can be as much a cause of pollution as unregulated growth.

Nor should it be assumed that governments are not also to blame for pollution. Developing countries spend billions of dollars every year on subsidies for energy use — the same energy whose waste products cause pollution. In some countries, logging fees represent only a small part of the cost of tree replacement, encouraging deforestation. At home, EU sheep headage payments have lead to sheep numbers which risk transforming the uplands of the West of Ireland into naked rock. Some municipal authorities continue to pour waste into our rivers and bays. Without government behaviour of these kinds, there would be less environmental damage.

The most telling rejoinder to the view that markets damage the environment is the pollution caused during the Communist regimes of Eastern Europe and the USSR. This was far more severe than anything found in the industrial West.

In 1990 the British Royal Institute of International Affairs reported that in the former East Germany the male mortality rate attributable to lung diseases was double the European average. In some industrial regions of the former East Germany, more than 90 per cent of children suffer respiratory diseases. In England and Wales, 90 per cent of the length of rivers and canals was classed in 1985 as of "good" or "fair" quality, but only 17 per cent of Czechoslovak river water was of Class 1 quality and the figure was just 4 per cent for Poland.

Whatever caused the horrifying pollution in the former Communist states, it was certainly not the market. Market failure can lead to the neglect of collective assets. So can misguided government policies. Charges for the use of collective assets would tackle environmental problems at the least cost to community. The sometimes legitimate concerns of Greens certainly do not imply a repudiation of the market itself.

Assumption 6: The Market Causes Ireland's Economic Problems.
Ireland's unemployment (and its other economic problems) are often blamed on "the market". Fintan O Toole writes about "the high unemployment and marginalisation that the free market creates" (January 1990). The bishops' pastoral *Work is the Key* argues (in an admittedly convoluted passage) that one of the things which "the market cannot produce but which, alas, it can significantly erode . . . [is] of particular importance in Ireland's case — the opportunity to work" (page 41). Cardinal Daly's sermon states that today "whatever the market dictates must be accepted, even if this means mass unemployment".

But does the market "dictate" developments in Ireland? Well, not in agriculture, planned by politicians in Brussels. Not in housing, heavily subsidised by the state. Not in education and health services, publicly-financed and part-controlled. Not in most forms of transport other than the private car. Not in most postal and telecommunications services. Not in electricity supply.

In those parts of the economy outside state ownership, the effect of the state is still pervasive. Extensive networks of rules, taxes and subsidies mean that governments influence, often heavily, the decisions of the private sector. Industrial grants draw factories into certain locations; taxes cause firms to use more machinery and less labour; corporation tax rewards manufacturing over service businesses. The treatment of savings affects the amount and cost of finance available to firms. The type and quality of FÁS trainees, and of school and college graduates, influence the rate and kind of business set-ups.

One measure of the global impact of the state on the "market" is the share of public spending in the economy. Irish government spending, as a percentage of the size of the economy, has risen almost without a break since the establishment of the state. In the early 1920s the state's share of spending was below 25 per cent of GNP. According to ESRI Director, Dr Kieran Kennedy, by the mid-

1980s (if all central and local public spending is included) it reached 67 per cent of GNP. Insofar as Ireland's economic misfortunes of the 1970s and early 1980s coincided with a shrinking market sector and a rapidly expanding public sector, those who want exclusively to blame the market for Ireland's economic problems would seem to have their work cut out for them.

During the MacSharry era, the state's day-to-day spending stabilised at about £8.5 billion. But since 1990, current spending has jumped to a budgeted £11.9 billion for 1995. Since the public and private sectors each now accounts for about half of the spending in the Irish economy, each must bear some of the responsibility for Ireland's economic problems. The *particular kind* of mixed economy we have in Ireland must account for our economic problems. It cannot be due to market "dictation".

Assumption 7: The Critics of Irish Market "Orthodoxy" are the Radical Voices in Ireland Today.

In the minds of many anti-marketeers, market economics and economists represent the status quo. "For about the last 15 years or so", writes Fintan O Toole, "political discussion in Ireland has been utterly dominated by conservative economics" (July 1994). The ethic of Adam Smith's invisible hand "is now the official one, held to with a dogmatism unaffected by its patent failure to create the jobs" (autumn 1991). John Waters sees the "only philosophy or vision on offer is the law of the naked market" (August 1993). In his 1992 sermon, Cardinal Daly claimed that the collapse of communism has left free market capitalism "virtually without economic critique". The bishops' pastoral *Work is the Key* criticised the present "abject worship of the market". And so forth.

But, as just noted, the assumption on which this thinking rests is false: at least half of the Irish economy is not a market economy and the behaviour of the remainder is heavily swayed by state regulations, taxes and subsidies.

Can Ireland's supposedly "free market" economy really be the same place where the government, in its 1995 budget *alone*, introduced 100 per cent subsidies for college education, subsidies on the rental payments made by tenants, a £1,000 subsidy to buyers of certain cars, subsidies for certain seaside resorts, adjusted the preferential tax rate on certain savings accounts, granted flood

relief to farmers, extended Dublin's Financial Services Centre incentives and offered tax relief on paintings donated to public col-
lections? All these policies encourage people to invest in certain
seaside resorts, consume certain kinds of education, buy certain
kinds of car and open certain kinds of bank deposit. Which kinds?
The government-preferred kind.

If these tinkerings, whatever their individual merits, were the
"free market", I would be a KGB Colonel.

Mistakenly thinking the market to be the status quo, radicals
argue for more state action. John Waters calls for a repudiation of
repayments on the national debt to allow a diversion of spending
towards "a radical programme of national reconstruction, building hospitals, schools, railways and other socially useful infrastructure, and providing work and prospects for the hordes of
young people" (June 1993). Is this radical? Or just rehashing a
tired and ancient Irish theme of state interventionism?

The bishops' 1994 *Developing the West* report, despite acknowl-
edging the failure of existing institutions and despite much
rhetoric about "bottom-up" development, proposed a plethora of
new state interventions: a Western Development Board, a state
five-year development plan, a Forbairt plan for western industry,
a Green Paper on the West, a Minister for the West, soft government loans for the West, preferential grants for firms in the West.
(According to the *Irish Times* western correspondent, at the report's launch one of the Bishops present stated that government
money must be used to save the west and he didn't want to hear
any "nonsense" about market forces in such a crisis.) Radicalism?
Or more of the same?

The Irish status quo has undoubtedly failed — everyone agrees
on that. *But what is the status quo?* Does it lie, as John Waters argues, "with the market-driven [ideology] which gave [the preferred model of development] its impetus and reach" (November
1993)? Or should the failure of government-driven protectionism
(followed by mass 1950s emigration) and the later failure of government-driven public spending and grantsmanship (followed by
mass 1980s emigration) be seen as failures of *traditionalist* state
intervention in the economy? If the latter, then true radicalism today means putting the drug of *inappropriate* state dependency

behind us and turning to a market-*based* strategy such as that of the Designer Economy.

Many on the Irish left-of-centre remain wedded to an old-style, traditionalist, market-fearing politics. Time has overtaken them. The world, and our understanding of it, has moved a long way since the 1960s. Regrettably, they have not.

Happy the Establishment whose radical critics unwittingly prop up reactionary policies.

Assumption 8: The Private Realm is Sinful, the Public Saintly.

Many commentators believe the market to be unethical; in the words of an *Irish Times* editorial marking Dr Brady's 1995 Trocaire lecture: "individualism and greed . . . underlie market policies." Fintan O Toole believes that "the forward march of the nation is driven by one force and one force only — greed" (autumn 1991) and, as we have seen, that all economics is immoral. John Waters writes that "much of what is acceptable in what is now called 'business' would in the real world be indistinguishable from theft" (May 1993). We previously encountered epithets like pirate, cowboy and fat cat used to describe private economic activity.

The state, on the other hand, is assumed to be the embodiment of virtue. When the state blatantly deviates from the path laid down for it, some commentators are startled. In his excellent account of the Beef Tribunal, *Meanwhile Back at the Ranch*, Fintan O Toole discusses the Attorney-General's decision to distinguish the public interest from the interests of the state. Mr O Toole says that if such a divorce is permissible "then the state becomes a kind of free-floating entity, an apparatus whose interests no longer derive directly from the people but exist independently from it". Mr O Toole writes in a shocked tone, as thought realising for the first time the possibility of this divorce of interests. Yet, for many people, grimly acquainted with the divorce, the real issue is how to *marry* the public interest with that of the state. Many whom the *Irish Times* characterises as "ideological" critics of the state are acutely conscious of just how free-floating the state is, and they wish to see public policies designed accordingly rather than on the basis of some idealistic assumption about the state's motives.

Surely only an assumption of superior state virtue can explain the statement in the bishops' pastoral that "Irish people expect the

State to play the leading role" in job-creation, for which no supporting reasoning or justification whatever is offered?

In earlier chapters of this book, it was argued that citizens who work in the market and those who work for the state are morally indistinguishable. Markets are a social institution. Governments are another. All economic systems, whatever their moral character or that of their citizens, need to co-ordinate the decisions of their members. An economy may be populated by saints, who may even by growing more saintly every day, but if the system functions inefficiently they will be poor or even unemployed saints.

It is a mistake to claim, as in Dr Brady's Trocaire Lecture that "the proponents of [neo-liberal economic theory] are attempting to raise individualism and its corollary, greed, to the level of a value". Economists do not seek to justify greed or selfishness. What they assume is *self-interested behaviour*: the pursuit by a person of their own interests. The latter could mean eating endless Haagen-Dazs ice creams or mindlessly accumulating an ever-larger bank balance. It could mean improving the environment, helping the Third World, or saving for old age. Economics seeks to work out the consequences of self-interested behaviour for economic life. Because a larger income allows a person to better pursue their interests, whatever these may be, we should expect people in general, both saints and sinners, to seek to maximise their income.

What a person does with their lawful gains is what defines their morality, not whether they earn a high salary or make a large profit. Would the world really be a better place to require Mother Teresa to strive to minimise her income while Donald Trump is busy maximising his?

Much discussion of the morality of the market centres around the issue of profit. Anti-marketeers say markets place profits before people. But in discussing the Dream Economy, it was shown how the profit motive cannot be chucked aside without losing the behaviour that profits reward. An economy without profits is less responsive to consumers. But are consumers not people too?

Profits are just a way of making producers meet consumer demand while using the fewest resources to do so. They are neither good nor evil. Since competition acts to keep profit to a minimum, in an economy with competitive markets and adequate mechanisms to promote social equity, profits should be judged in an ethically neutral light. Besides, state mechanisms do not invariably place people first. The CAP shows little regard for those Irish *people* who eat food, or for the desperately-poor farming *people* of developing countries who are excluded from rich western export markets.

Only in one sense does suppressing the profit motive "put people first". It puts *some people* first, but at the expense of others. When uneconomic rural post offices are kept open, this has to be paid for by taxpayers elsewhere. When assistance is given to the West, this must be paid for by non-Western taxpayers. Yet are those taxpayers not people too?

Undoubtedly, profits can be excessive. This is most likely to occur in a market with weak competition between producers. There is a straightforward answer to this problem. Adopt strict competition laws, outlaw anti-competitive practices, and, where necessary, charge a public agency with monitoring and enforcing those laws. Profits can also be criticised when they arise from economically-unproductive activities such as land rezoning, tax sheltering and, in general, restrictions on the normal operations of a competitive market. Such profits are earned through establishing or exploiting administrative rules, not by meeting consumer needs. But they usually have nothing to do with the market, and everything to do with state regulations.

If none of the above is convincing, recall that a large fraction of corporate profits is paid out in dividends to shareholders. But who are the shareholders? Today, they are mostly pension funds. So a significant part of the capitalists' profit goes towards paying pensions to the likes of you and me. It is not all spent on fat cigars, fur coats and Ferraris.

Assumption 9: The Market Favours the Rich and Powerful.
Cardinal Daly's August 1992 sermon states that "left to themselves, market forces favour the wealthy, the strong and the powerful, and hurt or even crush the poor, the weak and the powerless." The bishops' pastoral writes of "uncontrolled and blind market forces" favouring the powerful and neglecting the weak. John Waters writes that "the free market fantasy . . . result[s] in

the perpetuation of inequality and the supremacy of the strong" (August 1993).

All of these observations are applicable to the Degenerate Economy: its cartels suppress competition and dish out the spoils to favoured insiders. Equal opportunity has no place in an economy devoted to preserving the privileges of the commercial and political establishment.

But this is not the only possible form of market. A Designer Economy is also an available option which, in addition to being founded on the market, firmly polices competition, judiciously corrects market failures and vigorously promotes equality of opportunity. All these latter tasks can only be organised collectively.

Nor are Decree Economies slow to help their powerful élites at the expense of the weak and the powerless. Big business benefits most from trade restrictions and barriers flung in the path of possible rivals. Medical consultancy posts make millionaires of some medical consultants. Sloppy public spending procedures make millionaires of beef tribunal barristers. State monopolisation of transport and telecommunications services protects powerful insiders but hampers job creation in the wider Irish economy.

Degenerate and Decree Economies favour the rich and the powerful. Competitive market economics, with its insistence on competition, tears down undeserved commercial privilege in favour of the outsider, the new-entrant and the person with a new idea.

Why should "good" markets be jettisoned because some markets are "bad"?

Assumption 10: The Market Causes Third World Poverty.
Two distinct issues arise here: famine and poverty.

In the case of famine, Dr Seán Brady's Trocaire Lecture argues that "today, neo-liberal economic theory marches under the banner of "market forces", but it is the same doctrine as that which dominated Ireland during the Famine." He is absolutely right that laissez faire would be a cruel and absurdly ineffective response to famine conditions. But laissez faire should not be equated to *any and all* market-based policies. A sophisticated, humane study of famines, *Hunger and Public Action* (1989) by two renowned economists (Drèze and Sen), argues that famine is often due to a decline in income rather than to a decline in the availability of food. It recommends that where food imports are possible, the hungry need *government* cash so that they can buy food in the *marketplace*. This minimises the danger of bureaucratic inefficiency from exclusively-government food distribution. It also minimises the unreliability of the food supply if markets are used exclusively. Tackling famine means avoiding an all-market policy as well as a no-market policy and relying on a some-market policy.

As regards underdevelopment, Third World poverty is sometimes too casually blamed on the market. This is decidedly odd when so many newly-independent Third World countries explicitly banished the market from within their borders, opting instead for a Soviet-style command economy. It seems perverse to blame the economic model which was not adopted for the economic results which obtained.

In an August 1992 column in the *Irish Times*, Trocaire argued that it had experienced "the net results of unfettered market forces when they impinge on the weak and the defenceless [in the third world]." The three *specific ways* in which the developed world was said to gain at the expense of underdeveloped countries were: debt repayments from South to North, restrictions on third world exports, and the arms trade. Even if the industrial world does gain from each of these mechanisms, what has any of them to do with market forces? Trade restrictions are imposed by governments. Africa's public debts — just like Ireland's — were incurred by politicians. And the arms trade would dry up without the extravagant militarism of third world dictatorships.

Hunger and underdevelopment are appalling features of the modern world. With the correct policies, they can be tackled. The framework needed to tackle them is, in fact, no different to that needed in the first world: Designer Economics. Liberalised but competitive markets and enlightened governments promoting efficiency and equity: providing butter before guns and public investments instead of public liabilities.

Markets, if well-designed, are less a cause of third world poverty than an essential component of its solution.

But the mistakes of the past cannot be wished away. Nor should their awful consequences be dumped on the innocent victims of undemocratic and criminal politicians. So the burden of third world debt *does* need to be lessened. It will be easier to persuade Northern governments to do this when the policy regime of the South has been reformed to reduce the likelihood that yesterday's bad debts, once forgiven, would quickly be replaced by new debts. Southern countries *should* be allowed to export to the North — these markets need *un*fettering. And both Southern governments and the Northern arms industry should get out of the weapons trade.

Conclusion

Economic policy is much too important to be left to economists. All Irish citizens have an inalienable right to participate in public policy discussions. All viewpoints are welcome, this chapter's title notwithstanding. The present contribution has the same right to be heard and may, in turn, prompt further responses. Severe criticism of the Irish Times School of Economics, and of some economic pronouncements by the Roman Catholic Church, is not therefore a slapping-down of "non-economists" by an "expert". It is a debate between citizens.

What is regrettable is that so many well-intentioned contributions to economic debate should rest on fallacies, asserted with little attempt at substantiation. Public discussion would be more conclusive if critics of the market were prepared to reveal more of the reasoning and evidence that lead them to the beliefs they hold. From its perspective, that is what this book has tried to do.

Perhaps, from time to time, anti-market commentators might consider re-examining their own assumptions?

13

CURING THE IRISH DISEASE: CIVIC CULTURE, MERITOCRACY AND POWER IRISHNESS

Irish economic policy has long been overly sceptical about the market and overly optimistic about the state. As a result, our economy embodies key shortcomings both of the private market (weak competition and unequal opportunities) and of crude state intervention (waste, unaccountable bureaucracy, political constraints) without managing to capture enough of either system's advantages.

Some rebalancing is therefore needed. But the key word is balance. Failings in the public sector do not justify an uncritical lurch towards the private sector, where other risks continue to apply. The overall aim of reform should be to build a meritocracy in Ireland. Productive economic activity should be better rewarded whereas unproductive economic conduct should attract fewer rewards. Each citizen should be left to make their own decisions, but as a society we need to indicate what we want to encourage and what we consider less desirable.

Clear thinking and recent history show that a system of competitive markets is the most effective way to achieve high productivity. But efficiency is not the only objective that social democrats pursue. They also want more equal opportunities, so that each Irish child can enter adult life in a position to make the most of their abilities. What is required is not just a competitive market but a social market: the Designer Economy.

The solution to the Irish Disease will require four specific changes.

First, a redrawing of the border between the state and the market. Privatising those commercial semi-state bodies which would be better run as private firms, and rededicating the public sector to its core roles of public administration, resolution of serious market failures and the promotion of opportunity and social equity throughout Irish society.

Second, revamping the Irish competition laws and establishing modern regulatory bodies and procedures.

Third, redesigning the structures of public bodies so that they would have clear objectives, professional management, measurement of performance, effective outside inspection, a separation of purchasing from providing, and a strong voice for the customer, preferably by giving them the option of switching to an alternative supplier.

Fourth, reform of the present multi-seat PR electoral system to create a proper balance between local and national interests. This would help the formulation of a coherent national response to the Irish Disease.

Apart from these institutional reforms, curing the Irish Disease will require a greater commitment to meritocratic principles while turning a deaf ear to unjustified pleas for state intervention. Ireland needs a cultural shift away from victim Irishness, dependent and clientilist, towards power Irishness, civic and meritocratic.

There is a further reason to embrace competition and the market system. It's coming anyway. The Irish status quo is unsustainable. If the GATT agreement and the Single Market could be summarised in a single sentence it would read: sharply intensified competition in domestic and foreign markets. A more brutal statement would be: firms will be left to slog it out with each other and the dole queues will take the hindmost. We have been down this road before in 1973; we know that very many domestic companies did not survive and that a whole swathe of Irish employment crumbled and disappeared. We can do without any more total eclipses of the home-owned economy, but for that we will need serious economic reform.

There are plenty of rival explanations to "institutional failure" to account for Ireland's economic performance. Factors such as Ireland's smallness, peripherality, lack of natural resources or colonial history are popularly cited. But all these are outside our control, so no amount of time spent worrying about them can contribute to improving our economic circumstances. Sensibly, two ESRI researchers, Patrick Honohan and Philip O Connell, have recently argued that Ireland should stop trying to compensate for factors which we can cannot change and concentrate on correcting things that can be changed.

Even if commentators are right to place some of the blame for Irish underdevelopment outside Ireland, the key issue now is what we make of our present situation. Fate may create a problem but it is foolishness to give up in the face of it.

Ireland's citizens must decide whether they wish to have a society that offers reasonably certain shares of a slow-growing pie, or to have an expanding pie whose shares depend on economic performance. Historically, Ireland has chosen the first, leaving hundreds of thousands of our citizens to emigrate to faster-growing economies. This suggests that, from a wider community viewpoint, the wrong choice has been made.

Notwithstanding the examples of impoverished emigrants given in Chapter 1, the Irish outside Ireland seem on the whole to have been remarkably successful. If the Irish worldwide do better than the Irish-in-Ireland, the problem can only lie in Ireland.

If we truly want growth and catching-up, a steady decrease in poverty and in emigration, then we are going to have to embrace capitalism — a competitive and social capitalism — in a much more wholehearted way than we have ever done to date.

Of course, the future is unknowable. To act is to gamble. But it should be a gamble based on the best decisions we can make. And, however unsatisfactory are some aspects of today's Ireland, it is essential and justifiable to take a positive attitude towards our prospects in the 1990s and beyond.

In 1970, the economist James Meenan closed one chapter of his study of the Irish economy with the words: "Ireland can never be more than its people and . . . only their labour, their thought and their spirit can make it better." The question, then as now, is how to design an economy that turns a people's labour, thought and spirit in the direction of productive economic activity.

EPILOGUE:
OF EGGHEADS AND THE MERELY BALD

In the late 1980s, a Professor of Economics in Trinity College, Dublin, became embroiled in public controversy. He had written a research paper which pointed out that during the MacSharry years, welfare payments had not only been exempt from the spending cuts but had in fact been increased in real terms.

The Professor's statement of fact was not welcomed by many groups. They proceeded to heap abuse on his head, sometimes in stinging terms. One particular riposte rang across the airwaves: "This is just the opinion of one economist!".

Well, suppose you were on a aircraft taxiing into position for take-off. Over the intercom, the pilot is making some small talk about the weather and the flight's expected arrival time. In concluding, he mentions that the engineer has just stated that one of the plane's engines is about to fall off. But, with a loud snort, this warning is dismissed: "Ladies and gentlemen, that's just the opinion of one engineer!"

The time for odium is past. Assessing an argument according to a headcount of its supporters or a classification of their jobs is kindergarten commentary. We must demand a more serious level of public economic debate in Ireland. The present book is indeed the work of one person. But that does not invalidate the case it makes, which rests or falls on the strength of its arguments.

But the time for gurus is also past. In rejecting a childish approach to debate, we must not fall into the opposite trap of deferring unquestioningly to the claims of "experts". It's much too easy to confuse eggheads with the merely bald. The present book is certainly the work of an economist. But that is no guarantee of its validity. The reader must assess the plausibility of its arguments, something which the general public is perfectly well able to do.

Finally, the time for idleness is past. The impact of this book depends on the reader's response. There are no magicians who will lift the burden of Ireland's problems from the shoulders of mortals. Irish citizens must act or resign themselves to more of the same.

Arise — and follow yourself.

INDEX

Index

255